Freedom in Christ

Understanding
Paul's Epistle to the

Galatians

Meno Kalisher

Dedicated to

m y   w i f e   A n a t

Faithful and beloved wife,
my helpmeet who shows by her life that

*"He is a Jew who is one inwardly; and circumcision is that of the heart,
in the Spirit, not in the letter;
whose praise is not from men but from God."*

(as is written in Romans 2:29)

Freedom in Christ
Understanding Paul's Epistle to the Galatians
by Meno Kalisher
Copyright © 2013

Jerusalem Assembly — House of Redemption
P. O. Box 10608
91105 Jerusalem / Israel
www.jerusalemassembly.com

All rights reserved. No part of this book may be reproduced, stored in a retrieval system, or transmitted in any form or by any means, electronic, mechanical, photocopying, recording, or otherwise, without prior written permission from the publisher.

Translated from the Hebrew
חירות במשיח

Translation:
Language Services, Rivkah Nessim
languageservice4u@gmail.com
Editing, graphics and layout:
Jerusalem Assembly — House of Redemption

Published in the United States of America by
The Friends of Israel Gospel Ministry Inc.,
P.O. Box 908, Bellmawr, NJ 08099
www.foi.org

Unless noted otherwise, all English-language Scripture is taken from the New King James Version, Copyright © 1982 by Thomas Nelson, Inc. Used by permission. All rights reserved.

Library of Congress Catalog Card Number: 2013945369
ISBN-9780915540532
Printed in the United States of America

Table of Contents

Part One   *Introduction to Paul's Epistle to the Galatians*

    1. Background to the Epistle to the Galatians 9

    2. The Author of the Epistle 15

    3. The Addressees — Who Are the Galatians? 17

    4. The Date of the Epistle 19

    5. Who Were the False Teachers (False Brethren)? 19

Part Two   *Studying the Epistle to the Galatians*

    Chapter **1**   A True Apostle of the True Gospel 24

    Chapter **2**   Many Apostles — One Gospel
                Jews and Gentiles — One Church 63

    Chapter **3**   The Tutor, the Promise, and the Faith
                of Abraham 105

    Chapter **4**   The Adoption as Sons 157

    Chapter **5**   Freedom in Christ 188

    Chapter **6**   The Law of Christ and the New Creation 229

Appendices   247

    A. The Original Plan
    Why Did God Choose the People of Israel,
    and For What Purpose? 247

    B. When a Jew Says "Torah" (Law), What Does He Mean?
    The Oral Law (Rabbinical Judaism) 256

    C. Frequently Asked Questions 283

Abbreviations of Bible Book Names

The Hebrew Scriptures (Old Testament)

Abbreviation	Book
Gen.	Genesis
Ex.	Exodus
Lev.	Leviticus
Num.	Numbers
Dt.	Deuteronomy
Josh.	Joshua
Jud.	Judges
Ruth	Ruth
1 Sam.	1 Samuel
2 Sam.	2 Samuel
1 Ki.	1 Kings
2 Ki.	2 Kings
1 Chr.	1 Chronicles
2 Chr.	2 Chronicles
Ezra	Ezra
Neh.	Nehemiah
Est.	Est.
Job	Job
Ps.	Psalms
Prov.	Proverbs
Eccl.	Ecclesiastes
Song	Song of Solomon
Isa.	Isaiah
Jer.	Jeremiah
Lam.	Lamentations
Ezek.	Ezekiel
Dan.	Daniel
Hos.	Hos.
Joel	Joel
Amos	Amos
Obad.	Obadiah
Jon.	Jonah
Mic.	Micah
Nah.	Nahum
Hab.	Habakkuk

Abbreviation	Book
Zeph.	Zephaniah
Hag.	Haggai
Zech.	Zechariah
Mal.	Malachi

The New Testament

Abbreviation	Book
Mt.	Matthew
Mk.	Mk.
Lk.	Lk.
Jn.	John
Acts	Acts of the Apostles
Rom.	Romans
1 Cor.	1 Corinthians
2 Cor.	2 Corinthians
Gal.	Galatians
Eph.	Ephesians
Phil.	Philippians
Col.	Colossians
1 Th.	1 Thessalonians
2 Th.	2 Thessalonians
1 Tim.	1 Timothy
2 Tim.	2 Timothy
Ti.	Titus
Phile.	Philemon
Heb.	Hebrews
Jas.	James
1 Pet.	1 Peter
2 Pet.	2 Peter
1 Jn.	1 John (Epistle)
2 Jn.	2 John (Epistle)
3 Jn.	3 John (Epistle)
Jude	Jude
Rev.	Revelation

Clarifications to the Reader

The words "Law" or "the Mosaic Law" when used in this book refer only to the written law in the first five books of the Bible, and not to the Oral Law that continues to be written by the rabbis throughout history.

The terms "Scriptures," "Word of God," and "Bible" in this book are synonyms for God's truth as we have it in the Old and New Testaments.

Quotations from the Scriptures make up a large part of this book. I hope that this method will remind you, the reader, of a very important truth: the centrality of God's Word in the life of the believer in Christ. In order to get the greatest benefit from the study, we recommend you read the verses referred to in parentheses.

PART ONE

Introduction to Paul's Epistle to the Galatians

1. Background to the Epistle to the Galatians

A. The Birth of the Christian Church

Acts chapter 2 describes the birth of the first Christian church. Before Jesus ascended to heaven, He commanded His disciples to stay in Jerusalem, until the Holy Spirit would fall on them, and they would thus be empowered to serve Him (**Acts 1:8**):

> *But you shall receive power when the Holy Spirit has come upon you; and you shall be witnesses to Me in Jerusalem, and in all Judea and Samaria, and to the end of the earth.*

At the Feast of Pentecost, 10 days after receiving Jesus' final commission (**Acts 1:3**), the believers (all of them Jewish) were gathered together in

Jerusalem. Since Pentecost (Hebrew *Shavu'ot*) is one of the three biblical pilgrimage festivals, the city was full of visitors (**Dt. 16:16-17**), Jews who had made their way up to the Temple from all over Israel and the Diaspora.

Suddenly the Holy Spirit fell on the group of believers in Jesus, and they began to speak in the languages of all the pilgrims from around the world. The crowds who heard them *"were all amazed and marveled, saying to one another, 'Look, are not all these who speak Galileans? And how is it that we hear, each in our own language in which we were born? Parthians and Medes and Elamites, those dwelling in Mesopotamia, Judea and Cappadocia, Pontus and Asia, Phrygia and Pamphylia, Egypt and the parts of Libya adjoining Cyrene, visitors from Rome, both Jews and proselytes, Cretans and Arabs'"* (**Acts 2:7-11**).

This supernatural event gave an opportunity to Simon Peter to declare the gospel of Christ to the crowd who had witnessed the miracle. The preaching of the gospel by the apostle did not fall on deaf ears. The hearts were ready, and on that same day 3,000 people were saved and baptized. In the days following many more Jews were saved (**Acts 4:4; 5:14; 6:7**).

Note:

There were scores of *mikvahs* (ritual baths) near the Temple next to Dung Gate and the Huldah Gates, so that it was possible to baptize a large number of people in a short time.

B. From Jerusalem...to Galatia

At the end of the holiday the pilgrims returned to their countries, with many new believers among them. These Jews proclaimed the gospel of Jesus Christ among their families and in their synagogues. God-fearing Gentiles who heard the gospel of salvation also joined the congregations of believers in Jesus.

At the outset the church was made up of a majority of Jews who observed the Law, i.e. the commandments contained in the five books of Moses. They understood that Jesus was the Messiah promised in the Hebrew Bible (the Old Testament), who had come to atone for their sins. They did not think of themselves as changing their religion or deserting their people, but as Jews who kept the Law and wholeheartedly obeyed the Word of God.

At this early stage they had not yet internalized one crucial fact: In the death of Christ all those commandments in the Law that are symbols and types foreshadowing the Messiah's character and work had been fulfilled. Although they were no longer subject to the authority of these commandments, those early churches kept their religious Jewish character and continued to observe all the ordinances of the Mosaic Law **(Acts 21:20; Gal. 3:23-25; 4:10-11; Col. 2:16-17)**.

As the numbers of Jesus' disciples increased significantly, the Jewish establishment began to persecute them in an attempt to stop the spread of the gospel **(Acts 9)**. What in effect happened was the complete opposite to the intent of the persecutors: Many believers fled from Jerusalem to other countries in the Middle East and the Mediterranean region, and through their witness the gospel spread even further among both Jews and Gentiles. These new believers either joined existing congregations or established new ones.

Because of the demographics in countries distant from the land of Israel, the new churches were filled with a majority of saved Gentiles. Those had no Jewish background whatsoever and even introduced foreign traditions and customs into the church. Thus the Jewish-religious character of the church was diluted. The saved Gentiles did not immediately shake off their idolatrous past and its improper practices. We must bear in mind that they were often the only believers in their families and continued to live under the influence of an idolatrous environment. Inevitably, ways of life and customs that were offensive to the Jewish believers began to seep into the churches.

In light of the new reality threatening the Jewish character of the church, the following questions arose:

1. What could be done to preserve the Jewish nature of the church?
2. Is a Gentile who believes in Jesus subject to the authority of the

entire Mosaic Law, even after the New Covenant has become a reality? Does he have to convert to Judaism, be circumcised, and observe all of the Mosaic Law in order to be saved?

C. Salvation Is by Grace Alone

The apostle Paul travelled widely throughout Asia Minor and Greece. Everywhere he went he taught the gospel of salvation and established churches. **(See the travels of Paul in the book of Acts, chapter 13 and onwards.)** By the inspiration of the Holy Spirit, he taught the truth regarding

1. the messiahship and divinity of Jesus Christ.
2. the atonement obtained by the sacrificial death of Christ for us and in our place.

Paul taught that the salvation of both Jew and Gentile is — and always has been — based on faith in God as Savior, and it is not dependent on the perfect observance of commandments, since no man is able to keep all the commandments of God's Law perfectly **(Eph. 2:8-10)**:

> *⁸ For by grace you have been saved through faith, and that not of yourselves; it is the gift of God, ⁹ not of works, lest anyone should boast. ¹⁰ For we are His workmanship, created in Christ Jesus for good works, which God prepared beforehand that we should walk in them.*

Paul was not attacking the commandments of the Law, God forbid! He explained what their purpose was — that they were never intended to save, but to:

1. define what is sin.
2. point to the Savior and Redeemer who atones for sin **(Gal. 3:23-25; 4)**.

This is confirmed by two facts:

1. People like Noah and Abraham were called righteous in the sight of God many years before the Law was given, while they were still uncircumcised.

2. Even **after** the giving of the Mosaic Law, the prophet Habakkuk said: *"The just shall live by his faith"* (Hab. 2:4).

D. False Teachers

In the epistle to the Galatians Paul confronts the phenomenon of false teachers. These were Jews who posed as believers in Jesus Christ but held to the belief that all the commandments of Moses were still binding. Since they understood the church to be nothing more than a new branch of Judaism, they taught that every Gentile who believed in Jesus must be circumcised and become a Jew in order to be saved. They did not believe in Jesus as God and failed to understand the significance of the New Covenant sealed in His blood on the cross.

These same false teachers tried to "correct" the understanding and lifestyle of the Gentile believers in a way that detracted from the truth of God as taught in the Scriptures. Their priority was keeping the Jewish character of the church through adherence to time-honored traditions and customs, instead of striving in prayer and in submission to Christ towards bringing all believers to greater maturity and Christlikeness.

The apostle Paul does not relate to these false teachers as erring brethren but as enemies of God (Gal. 1:8).

The false teachers filtered into the churches in Galatia with the intention of correcting the misleading teachings of Paul. To their mind, those teachings threatened to destroy the Jewish nature of the church.

In order to sway the hearts of the believers, they claimed that:

1. Paul was not qualified to be called an apostle, therefore he was not teaching with God's authority.

2. Contrary to Paul's teaching that the Mosaic Law is no longer binding, it is forbidden to **not** observe the Law! According to them, failure to keep the Law would deprive Jewish believers of the only means to preserve their Jewish character and national identity. If

they failed to keep the Law they would become more and more like the Gentiles. They would gradually drift into the depraved lifestyle of idol worshipers, and the final outcome would be their complete assimilation.

The apostle knew what the false teachers were doing, since the deadly poison of their influence was already becoming apparent in the churches of Galatia. Paul was amazed how fast the Galatian believers had adopted these wrong ideas **(1:6)**, even though he himself had taught them the truth faithfully and thoroughly, and they had witnessed the miracles and signs of God's power that had accompanied his teaching **(3:1-5)**:

> *¹ O foolish Galatians! Who has bewitched you that you should not obey the truth, before whose eyes Jesus Christ was clearly portrayed among you as crucified?*
>
> *² This only I want to learn from you: Did you receive the Spirit by the works of the law, or by the hearing of faith? ³ Are you so foolish? Having begun in the Spirit, are you now being made perfect by the flesh? ⁴ Have you suffered so many things in vain — if indeed it was in vain?*
>
> *⁵ Therefore He who supplies the Spirit to you and works miracles among you, does He do it by the works of the law, or by the hearing of faith?*

The message of the false teachers was destructive. Paul called it ***"a different gospel"*** (1:6-9), and he warned the believers that whoever adopted it would be cut off from the grace of Christ. **(For a detailed explanation see commentary on Galatians 5:4.)** ***A different gospel*** — means a gospel that cannot save. Whoever follows it is destined to be lost. Paul knew he could not sit idle in the face of such danger.

2. The Author of the Epistle

The epistle opens naming Paul as its author (**1:1**): *"Paul, an apostle (not from men nor through man, but through Jesus Christ and God the Father who raised Him from the dead)."* In chapter 2 Paul adds his autobiography and details his service for the Lord Jesus. In chapter 5:2 he writes again, *"I, Paul, say to you,"* so that there is no doubt whatsoever regarding the identity of the author of the epistle. The style is unique to the apostle Paul (and is especially similar to the epistle to the Romans, which has much the same content as Galatians). Furthermore, the early fathers of the church (Clement of Rome, Polycarpus, Barnabas, Hermas, and Ignatius) who lived in the first centuries A.D., also indicate Paul to be the author of the epistle to the Galatians.

Paul, whose Hebrew name was Saul, was a Jew of the tribe of Benjamin. He was born in Tarsus (in modern Turkey), a city in the region of Cilicia and close to Galatia, which made him a Roman citizen by birth (**Acts 22:27-28; Phil. 3:4-6**). He was educated in Jerusalem at the feet of Gamaliel in all the minutiae of the Law, including tradition and the Oral Law. He belonged to the Pharisees and was zealous for God (**Acts 22:3**). Paul tells about himself: *"And I advanced in Judaism beyond many of my contemporaries in my own nation, being more exceedingly zealous for the traditions of my fathers"* (**Gal. 1:14**).

Paul persecuted the believers in Jesus and wreaked havoc on the church. To him, belief in Jesus was heresy, and he considered it his religious duty to silence, imprison and even kill anyone who claimed Jesus was the Messiah. He confesses: *"This I also did in Jerusalem, and many of the saints I shut up in prison, having received authority from the chief priests; and when they were put to death, I cast my vote against them. [11]And I punished them often in every synagogue and compelled them to blaspheme; and being exceedingly enraged against them, I persecuted them even to foreign cities"* (**Acts 26:10-11**).

Motivated by deep religious conviction, Paul gave himself up completely to God's service, with the intention of "cleansing" his people from the heretics who believed Jesus to be the promised Messiah, their Lord and only Savior. He went from house to house, dragging men and women from their homes to send them to prison. Because of his zeal in persecuting the believers, many of them fled the country **(Acts 8:1-4)**.

Paul received authorization from the High Priest to imprison Jewish believers in Jesus even beyond the borders of the land of Israel and to bring them to trial in Jerusalem. In Galatians 1:13 he writes: *"For you have heard of my former conduct in Judaism, how I persecuted the church of God beyond measure and tried to destroy it."*

On his way to Damascus, Syria, with this intent, his life was turned around: Jesus Christ — in all His divine glory — revealed Himself to the persecutor of the believers. Paul was temporarily blinded, and a disciple by the name of Ananias was sent to heal him. The Messiah revealed to Ananias in a vision the purpose for which He had chosen Paul: *"He is a chosen vessel of Mine to bear My name before Gentiles, kings, and the children of Israel"* **(Acts 9:15)**.

This personal encounter with the Messiah started Paul on his way as a messenger of Christ and the gospel, and in time he became the most famous of the apostles.

Paul's apostleship was conferred upon him directly by the Lord Jesus. All the other apostles recognized him as one of their number and his teachings as the Word of the Lord. In Galatians 2:6-10 he describes the reception he received from the apostles and the heads of the church in Jerusalem: *"But from those who seemed to be something — whatever they were, it makes no difference to me; God shows personal favoritism to no man — for those who seemed to be something added nothing to me. ⁷But on the contrary, when they saw that the gospel for the uncircumcised had been committed to me, as the gospel for the circumcised was to Peter ⁸(for He who worked effectively in Peter for the apostleship to the circumcised also worked effectively in me toward the Gentiles), ⁹and when James, Cephas, and John, who seemed to be pillars, perceived the grace that had been given to me, they gave me and Barnabas the right hand of fellowship, that we should go to the Gentiles and they to* the circumcised. ¹⁰ They desired only that we should remember the poor, the very thing which I also was eager to do." (See also 1 Timothy 1:12.)

Paul experienced a face-to-face encounter with Jesus, like all the other apostles. He did not just hear about Him from others. This fact motivated him to dedicate his life as *"a living sacrifice, holy, acceptable to God"* (**Rom. 12:1**), and he even said: *"I have been crucified with Christ; it is no longer I who live, but Christ lives in me; and the life which I now live in the flesh I live by faith in the Son of God, who loved me and gave Himself for me"* (**Gal. 2:20; Phil. 3:7-11**).

3. The Addressees — Who Are the Galatians?

In the opening verses of the epistle, the apostle states that he is writing *"to the churches of Galatia"* (**1:2**). Where is this place and who are the Galatians who made up those churches?

In the third century B.C. a large region stretching from the north to the center of modern-day Turkey, was known as Galatia. It was settled by Gauls, who had migrated there from the area of modern-day France. Its principal cities were Ancyra (now Ankara, capital city of Turkey), Pessinus (today a small village called Balihisar), and Tavium (today a village called Büyüknefes). In the year 25 B.C. Galatia became a Roman province. Additional territory was added in the south, which included the cities of Antioch (south central Turkey — today's town of Yalvaç), Ikonium (the Turkish city of Konya), Lystra, and Derbe (both of which are no longer inhabited).

As the descriptions of Paul's missionary journeys mention only the southern cities of Galatia, not the cities of the north, we can assume that he was now writing to the churches he had established in the course of his first journey, in Pisidian Antioch, Iconium, Lystra, and Derbe. (**See the first journey of Paul in Acts 13—14; map p. 59.**) The main route west passed from Tarsus (Paul's birthplace) through the above cities in the south of Galatia.

In contrast to the north, the south was heavily populated and therefore had

The Cities of Southern [▢] and Northern [▪] Galatia

a larger Jewish population. The farther north one goes, the fewer indications there are of Jewish settlement during this period. Thus, the churches seem to have been in the south of Galatia, and these are the ones the false teachers chose to infiltrate. Their destructive teachings were directed first and foremost at mixed congregations of Jewish and Gentile believers, and none of those were to be found in the north.

4. The Date of the Epistle

No date of writing is included in the epistle, but the events Paul mentions can help us determine an approximate time frame.

In chapter 2 he writes about his visit to Jerusalem together with Barnabas and Titus. Is Paul referring to the council of the elders and apostles in Jerusalem described in Acts 15? Apparently not, as he does not cite the conclusions and decisions arrived at during that meeting — something that would have immediately shut the mouths of his opponents. He must be referring to his earlier visit to Jerusalem, mentioned in Acts 11:30.

The purpose of this visit was to bring a financial donation to the needy, which was collected between the years A.D. 45-46. We can conclude from this that the letter to the Galatians was written shortly afterwards.

5. Who Were the False Teachers (False Brethren)?

The Purpose for Writing the Epistle

The false teachers, also called Judaizers or legalizers, were Jews who:

- **on the one hand** claimed to believe in the atoning work of Jesus the Messiah;
- **on the other hand** believed and taught that salvation can only be attained by also keeping the Mosaic Law.

In other words:

- They did not hold to salvation by faith alone.

- They did not believe the death of Jesus the Messiah to be the beginning of a New Covenant that would bring the Sinai Covenant to an end (**Jer. 31:31-33**).

- They opposed the belief that all those ordinances of the Mosaic Law which were types and symbols foreshadowing the character and work of the Messiah had been fulfilled by the coming of Jesus, His death and resurrection — that they are now obsolete and have no authority over believers.

In light of the above they taught that:

- In order to be saved, a Gentile who believes in Christ must convert to Judaism, undergo circumcision and take on himself the authority of the Mosaic Law;

- A Jew who is saved must continue to observe all the Mosaic Law, just as he did before he believed in Jesus (that is, place himself under the dominion of commandments that are no longer in effect).

These false teachers infiltrated churches throughout the Roman empire with the intention of opposing the gospel of Christ as Paul taught it, and of stealing the hearts of the believers. (**See also Acts 15:1-2.**)

In order to achieve their goals, the false teachers:

- tried to undermine Paul's authority as an apostle.

- taught *"a different gospel"* that glorified their Jewishness (**Gal. 1:6**).

- taught that Paul's doctrine leads to a decadent way of life.

Paul, on the other hand, proves in his epistle that:

- He was appointed to be an apostle by Jesus Christ Himself.

- The ordinances of the Mosaic Law were never intended for

salvation, but rather to identify sin, to teach man about his absolute dependence on the grace of God and to point him to his Savior. People have always been saved by grace through faith. Noah and Abraham were justified before the giving of the Law **(Gen. 6:9; 15:6)**, and many years after the Law was given, the prophet Habakkuk still upheld that same principle by saying: *"The just shall live by his faith"* **(Hab. 2:4)**.

- Faith in Jesus as our Lord and only Savior will never lead the believer to a life of decadence. On the contrary, by the Holy Spirit the saved person is reborn. He becomes a *"new creation"* **(Gal. 6:15)**. The Holy Spirit gives him the characteristics of Christ **(5:22-23)**, and by these he uses the gifts of the Spirit (qualifications and abilities that are given to man by God and with which he serves the church).

- In all that has to do with salvation there is no difference between Jew and Gentile, or between man and woman **(3:26-29)**. The redeemed are all equal in the sight of God, but they differ in their service in the body of Christ, the church.*

The purpose of the epistle to the Galatians: to warn the believers in the Galatian church, firmly and uncompromisingly, not to submit to the teachings of the false teachers who taught *"a different gospel."* Whoever was drawn after them risked losing his freedom in Christ. The false gospel of these teachers was lifeless and completely dependent on the success of man's deeds. Paul told the believers in Galatia to regard them in a manner befitting false teachers and to excommunicate them, in accordance with Matthew 18:15-20 **(Gal. 1:6-9)**.

The general theme of the epistle: Salvation is by God's grace alone, through faith in Jesus Christ as Lord and Savior.

---

* The fact that there is equality in the church among the redeemed does in no way minimize the special place of the people of Israel in the plan of God. Paul expounds this subject further in his epistle to the Romans, chapters 9—11.

Key verses of the epistle are:

Chap. 3:10-11: *For as many as are of the works of the law are under the curse; for it is written, "Cursed is everyone who does not continue in all things which are written in the book of the law, to do them." But that no one is justified by the law in the sight of God is evident, for "the just shall live by faith."*

Chap. 5:1: *Stand fast therefore in the liberty by which Christ has made us free, and do not be entangled again with a yoke of bondage.*

Subdivisions of the epistle by main subjects:

Chapters 1—2 Personal matters

Chapters 3—4 Teaching the fundamentals of the faith

Chapters 5—6 Application

PART TWO

Studying the Epistle to the Galatians

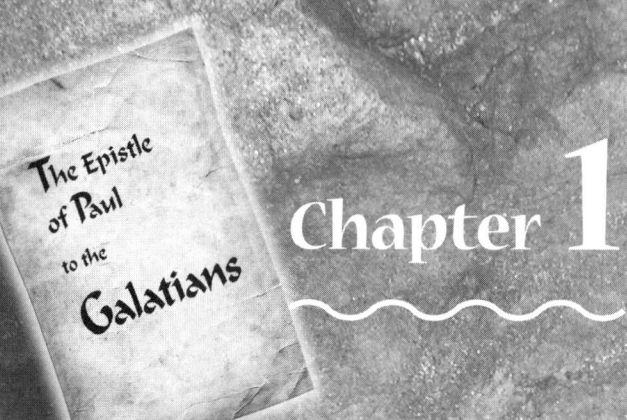

Chapter 1

A True Apostle of the True Gospel

Galatians 1:1-2:

> ¹*Paul, an apostle (not from men nor through man, but through Jesus Christ and God the Father who raised Him from the dead), ²and all the brethren who are with me, to the churches of Galatia.*

In his letters to other churches (Romans, 2 Corinthians, Ephesians, Philippians, Colossians, and Thessalonians), Paul opens with praise for his readers because of their works and their endurance in the faith. But he has no words of praise for the Galatians.

The central problem he is coping with becomes apparent already in the very first verses.

The false teachers had undermined Paul's authority as an apostle in the eyes of the believers. Thus they succeeded to divert them from the instructions they had received from Paul in the past. He is now forced to open his letter with almost intimidating firmness: "I am an apostle appointed directly by the Lord!"

"An apostle ... through Jesus Christ"

From Paul's choice of words we learn what he believes to be the correct way of appointing an apostle in the service of the Messiah. He says he was not chosen by men, but by the Lord Himself.

 How exactly did that work in practice?

Jesus personally chose His 12 disciples, who were later called apostles, including Judas Iscariot. After Jesus was arrested and sentenced to death by the leadership of the people, Judas took his own life by hanging himself **(Mt. 27:5)**.

When Jesus appeared to the disciples after His resurrection, He commanded them to remain in Jerusalem **until they would receive the Holy Spirit (Acts 1:4-8)**.

But then, while they are still waiting for the promise of the Holy Spirit to be fulfilled, Peter proposes to elect a new apostle to replace Judas. A group of believers numbering about 120 — and among them all the other apostles — agrees to his proposal and then follows a three–step election process:

1. The group agrees upon some logical criteria which determine who is eligible in principle **(Acts 1:21-22)**.

2. Two candidates who fit those criteria are chosen (**"Joseph called Barsabas, who was surnamed Justus, and Matthias"** — **Acts 1:23**).

3. Lots are cast for the final choice between the two **(Acts 1:26)**.

As far as the apostles and the 120 believers were concerned, casting lots was a safe way of arriving at the right choice since, after all, **"The lot is cast into the lap, but its every decision is from the LORD" (Prov. 16:33; Acts 1:24-25)**. But did this procedure leave God the option to say, "I have chosen neither of the two"? That we do not know.

Even though there may have been no fault whatsoever in the two candidates, it was the point in time that was unfit for such an election. The believers decided to choose an apostle before the promised Holy Spirit had come.

While their choice may look perfectly sensible, it was the initiative of mere men and not necessarily an act of God.

Had this choice been from God, Jesus would not have personally added Paul — who is now, as it were, apostle number 13.

The ruling of Jesus that His apostles would be 12 in number is valid for eternity. This we learn from Revelation 21:14 where the new Jerusalem, God's eternal city, is described with the words: *"And the wall of the city had twelve foundation stones, and on them were the twelve names of the twelve apostles of the Lamb"* (NASB / see NKJV footnote to v. 14).

It is no coincidence that this verse emphasizes the number 12 three times.

If Paul was in fact chosen as an apostle *"through Jesus Christ and God the Father,"* then there will be no foundation stone in the new Jerusalem bearing the name of Matthias.

Therefore, when Paul introduces himself as *"an apostle not from men nor through man, but through Jesus Christ and God the Father,"* his words constitute criticism of the process in which Judas Iscariot was replaced, at a time when the power of the Holy Spirit had not yet indwelled the 11 apostles. Paul, on the other hand, had been personally chosen by the Lord, in precisely the same manner as the 11 original apostles.

Who can confirm Paul's testimony?

- **Ananias of Damascus** (Acts 9:7-22):

In Acts 22:12-16 Ananias testifies that Paul had in fact seen Jesus, heard His voice and was commissioned by Him to be a "witness to all men": *"The God of our fathers has chosen you* [Paul] *that you should know His will, and see the Just One, and hear the voice of His mouth. For you will be His witness to all men of what you have seen and heard"* (vv. 14-15).

- **The people who accompanied Paul on his journey to Damascus** (Acts 9:7-22; 26:12-15).

- **The other apostles** (Acts 15; Gal. 2:8-9):

    All other apostles were in agreement with him.

    a. Barnabas, Simon Peter, and the elders of the Jerusalem church — some of them apostles themselves — encouraged Paul in his ministry and accepted his authority as an apostle chosen by Christ (**Gal. 2:8-9**).

    b. Even after the apostle Peter had been sternly rebuked by Paul (**Galatians 2:14**), he accepted his words and encouraged other believers to obey what was written in Paul's epistles. Peter placed those epistles on one level with *"the rest of the Scriptures,"* which was just another way of saying, "Paul's writings are the Word of God" (**2 Pet. 3:14-16**).

The title *apostle* (ἀπόστολος / *apostolos* = "sent one") was first given to a man who was sent to represent the interests of the empire. He was authorized to speak on behalf of those who sent him and to declare their will.

The apostles of Jesus were so called because they were sent to proclaim the gospel. For this purpose Jesus bestowed His full authority on them. In other words: The teaching of the apostles is the Word of God that must be obeyed by all people. The apostles even received supernatural abilities and powers as a confirmation that the message they preached came in fact from God (**Acts 2:42-43; 2 Cor. 12:12; Eph. 2:20; Heb. 2:1-4**).

The false teachers who came to Galatia rejected Paul's apostolic authority.

Where do we find the accounts of Jesus personally commissioning Paul as an apostle?

1. In Acts 9 Luke relates the encounter between the Messiah and Saul of Tarsus:

What awaited Saul on his way to Damascus was the surprise of his life. He met Jesus the Messiah face-to-face, and this encounter shook him to the depth of his being (**Acts 9:27; 22:14; 26:16; 1 Cor. 15:8**). Saul learned firsthand that Jesus is alive and that He truly is the promised Messiah. At that very instant Saul became a new man. He stopped persecuting the believers in Jesus; he no longer imprisoned men and women, trying to force them to blaspheme the name of their Lord. From now on he himself was a part of the body of Christ, the church, and as such he proclaimed to the world the message of salvation from sin and death — the gospel of Jesus Christ.

There at Damascus Jesus made it perfectly clear to Saul: Though hitherto a persecutor of the believers, he was now chosen to become the Messiah's messenger to the nations of the world. Jesus Himself commissioned him by saying: *"I have appeared to you for this purpose, to make you a minister and a witness both of the things which you have seen and of the things which I will yet reveal to you. I will deliver you from the Jewish people, as well as from the Gentiles, to whom I now send you"* (**Acts 26:16-17**).

During this supernatural encounter, Saul realized that the power of Jesus is in fact the power of Almighty God (**Acts 9:3-6; Gal. 1:11-12**). He understood that all those testimonies he had heard from Jews who came to faith were not imaginations but solid truth. The intellectual knowledge he had acquired by hearing and learning about the Messiah in the past was instantly translated into a living, active faith. He gives witness to that in **Acts 26:19-20**: *"I was not disobedient to the heavenly vision, but declared first to those in Damascus and in Jerusalem, and throughout all the region of Judea, and then to the Gentiles, that they should repent, turn to God, and do works befitting repentance."*

2. **In Acts 22:17-21** we find the account of Jesus confirming to Paul that he was to be His messenger — His apostle — to the Gentiles: *"Now it happened, when I returned to Jerusalem and was praying in the temple, that I was in a trance and saw Him [Jesus] saying to me, 'Make haste and get out of Jerusalem quickly, for they will not receive your testimony concerning Me. Depart, for I will send you far from here to the Gentiles.'"*

Conclusions:

1. Since all the other apostles of Jesus recognized Paul as an apostle, we must do likewise (Jn. 13:20). Whoever rejects his teachings acts contrary to the will of God.

   The apostle Paul wrote several epistles that are part of the Holy Scriptures. Therefore, it is critical to determine how we stand in regard to him.

2. As far as Paul was concerned, the revelation of Jesus to him was sufficient proof of his apostleship. Paul decided that he would give account to God alone, not to men (Gal. 1:10).

3. We have compared two facts in the New Testament account:

   a. Simon Peter and the other apostles chose Matthias as the 12th apostle at their own discretion, before the Holy Spirit had fallen on the believers.

   b. The new (eternal) Jerusalem is described in Revelation 21:14 as having 12 foundation stones, adorned by the 12 names of the 12 apostles of Christ.

      This proves that Paul — not Matthias — must be the 12th apostle, since he was chosen *"through Jesus Christ and God the Father."*

"I completely agree with all that Jesus taught, but I have a problem with Paul!"

This is a sentiment often expressed in Christian circles. When listening to the speakers closely, one notices that they also have a tendency to filter through what Jesus taught — generally on the basis of theories "proving" that this or that verse are not authentic quotes from Christ.

The reason behind this is their unwillingness to submit completely to the will of God in every area of life. Since they call themselves Christians, they will not, of course, express this unwillingness in so many words. Instead, they will find ways to undermine the authority of certain Scriptures and to define them as Paul's personal opinion.

The methods used by the false teachers of our generation are identical to those used in the days of the apostles. This is why I am enlarging on the authority of Paul as an apostle of Christ.

If Paul was indeed an apostle, then his epistles are the Word of God, and every word in them was written by the inspiration of the Holy Spirit.

The Term *Apostle* and the Number 12

If we take Revelation 21:14 (see p. 26) as conclusive proof that there are no more than 12 apostles, then why does the New Testament bestow that title on several others in addition to the 12?

For example in

Acts. 14:14: *"But when the apostles Barnabas and Paul heard this, they tore their clothes."*

Romans 16:7: *"Greet Andronicus and Junia, my kinsmen and my fellow prisoners, who are outstanding among the apostles, who also were in Christ before me"* (NASB).

This is because the word **apostolos** *(ἀπόστολος) simply meant "messenger" to the Greek-speaking people in Paul's day. Today, when we hear apostle, we immediately think of the 12 disciples of Jesus, but in New Testament days that could also denote an emissary sent out by the imperial government.*

Barnabas was not one of the 12, and therefore not an apostle in the narrow sense of the word. Just like Paul, however, he was a messenger (Greek *apostolos*) sent out by the church at Antioch for the purpose of preaching the gospel. We could therefore render Acts 14:14, "But when the missionaries Barnabas and Paul heard this."

Also Andronicus and Junia had probably been sent out to proclaim the gospel. That is how they ended up being sentenced to the same punishment as Paul —Incarceration.

In other instances where the Greek N.T. has *"apostolos,"* translations do not even render it as "apostle." Philippians 2:25, for example, reads: **"I considered it necessary to send to you Epaphroditus, my brother, fellow worker, and fellow soldier, but your messenger** [apostolos] **and the one who ministered to my need."**

Even Jesus Himself is called an "Apostle" in Hebrews 3:1. That is a fitting title, since He emphasizes many times (especially in the Gospel of John) that He was **sent** by the Father.

❶ *An apostle...through Jesus Christ and God the Father."* — Here Paul states that God the Father is also involved in his appointment as apostle. The mention of God the Father in the same breath as Jesus, God the Son, emphasizes their equality. God the Father and God the Son have different roles, but there is no difference in their status in the one God. Both are called "Lord" (YHWH) in the Bible.* Moreover, the mention of God the Father and God the Son supports the authority of Paul's words. The apostle is God's mouthpiece, just as the prophets of the Old Testament were.

❷ *"And all the brothers with me."* — The false teachers were trying to portray Paul as a lone wolf in order to undermine his position and authority. This is why the apostle mentions the many brethren who worked with him: "I am not a lone wolf who makes up principles foreign to the Scriptures. I am teaching the Word of God, and faithful, notable brethren testify to that."

What is the central theme of the epistle to the Galatians? —
The pure gospel!

❸ — ❺ The first two verses have served as a preface to the subjects taught in the epistle, establishing Paul's apostolic authority. Let us now turn to verses 3-5, which define the purpose of the pure gospel.

---

* For an in-depth study on this subject, see the book *Jesus in the Hebrew Scriptures,* by Meno Kalisher, available at www.foi.org

Grace and Peace

Galatians 1:3-5:

> ³ *Grace to you and peace from God the Father and our Lord Jesus Christ,* ⁴ *who gave Himself for our sins, that He might deliver us from this present evil age, according to the will of our God and Father,* ⁵ *to whom be glory forever and ever. Amen.*

❸ *"Grace...and peace from God"* come to us because of Christ's atoning sacrifice. This sacrifice was according to the will of God the Father for the salvation of men from sin. Since Jesus' sacrifice was divine — perfect — it is sufficient to bring every believer from death to eternal life with God.

The grace and peace of God are not received by anyone because of circumcision or conversion to Judaism. They are the fruit of genuine faith in Jesus as Lord and Savior, our Redeemer from sin **(Mt. 26:42; Jn. 6:38-40; 14:6; Acts 2:22-23; 4:12; Rom. 8:3, 31-32; 10:9-10; Eph. 1:7, 11; Heb. 10:4-10).**

Grace and *peace* are two of the more prominent words in the Bible. Let us have a look at what they mean:

Grace — a gift of God's self-sacrificial and unconditional love to men, who are unworthy of it and will never be able to pay its full price. The essence of God's grace is salvation from the penalty of sin **(Isa. 53:5-6; Eph. 2:8-10).**

Peace — the absence of hostility between God and the saved person. The peace of God is also part of the fruit of the Spirit **(Gal. 5:22-23)**, the result of the work of grace in the saved person **(Rom. 5:1).**

❹ *"Who gave Himself for our sins, that He might deliver us from this present evil age, according to the will of our God and Father."* — In the epistle to the Romans, Paul teaches that the Messiah gave Himself as a sacrifice to atone for our sins while we were still sinners and even "enemies" of God **(Rom. 5:8-10).** So verse 4 stresses the power of God's grace in contrast to the unworthiness of man. Our salvation depends from beginning to end on God's goodness — on His grace alone, not on the quality of our works or our perfection. **(See also 1 Timothy 2:3-7; Titus 2:14; 1 Peter 3:18.)**

Thanks be to God for His great love! He chose to come to Earth as a man and die for us as a sacrifice for sin in order to grant us His peace (**Isa. 53:5**). (See also **Acts 20:28**, a verse that speaks of *"God who purchases [the believers] with His own blood"*; and **Titus 2:13-14** that praises *"our great God and Savior Jesus Christ [in the original Greek "God and Savior" both refer to Christ], **who gave Himself for us, that He might redeem us from every lawless deed."*)

There is a purpose in the sacrifice of Jesus. We call it salvation, but many have failed to fully understand what that means:

- Our salvation ensures that we will be saved from the wrath of God, from the heaviest punishment that can fall on man — eternal separation from God in the Lake of Fire (**1 Th. 5:9; Rev. 20:11-15**).

- Our salvation promises the presence of God in our bodies by the Holy Spirit, already here and now (**1 Cor. 3:16; Eph. 1:13-14**).

- Only through the presence of the Holy Spirit do we receive the ability to serve God (**Rom. 12; 1 Cor. 12; Eph. 4**).

- Our salvation promises us eternal life with God in the new, sinless world He will create (**2 Pet. 3:13; Rev. 21—22**).

Paul names the age in which we live with the unflattering term *this evil world*. In our age, Satan is called:

- *"the god of this age"* (**2 Cor. 4:4; 1 Jn. 5:19**).

- *"the prince of the power of the air, the spirit who now works in the sons of disobedience"* (**Eph. 2:2**).

- *"your adversary the devil* [who] *walks about like a roaring lion, seeking whom he may devour"* (**1 Pet. 5:8**).

This enemy and his power are so mighty that we find ourselves battling *"against principalities, against powers, against the rulers of the darkness of this age, against spiritual hosts of wickedness in the heavenly places"* (**Eph. 6:12**). Since this is so, man has no chance to contend on his own with the powers of this world, with the results of sin and with the real enemy — Satan. There is no way we can save ourselves. Salvation has to be an act of the grace of God — an act that is initiated by Him.

"This present evil age." — Our age is evil because it gives false teachers the freedom to attack the church of Jesus Christ in an effort to destroy it. Whoever teaches that we need to add our own works to God's act of grace in order to be saved, is saying that the atonement by Jesus Christ is not sufficient. Anyone thinking this way proves that he has failed to understand

- who the Messiah is;
- what was the purpose of His coming;
- what He accomplished on Earth.

Such a person remains with a twisted gospel that has no power to defend him from the results of sin or from his enemy, Satan.

Since our salvation is entirely dependent on the grace of Christ, He, His Word, and His will must be at the center of our lives. This teaching is markedly different from the understanding of the false teachers with whom the apostle Paul debates throughout the epistle. Their main emphasis was on their Jewish identity.

Please pay attention to the following statement:

> In any society or group that places more emphasis on their national identity and the traditions of men than God intended, the belief in the divinity of Christ will inevitably be eroded.

"[Our God and Father,] to whom be glory forever and ever." — At first glance this simply seems to be praise to the Creator. Read the sentence again and place the emphasis on the One to whom glory is due: **"GOD..., to whom be glory."** Now the verse exposes the wicked purpose of the false teachers: Today, just as then, they clothe themselves with an imposing aura of religion, all the while seeking glory for themselves. They are trying to hide God from those who listen to them, and their aim is to make disciples who focus on **THEM** — not on the Messiah **(Gal. 1:10; 4:17; 6:13)**.

To God, and only to God, be the glory! Whoever tries to detract even the slightest bit from the glory that belongs to God, is doing the same as the "father of lies" — Satan.

- Now that we have established that Paul was a true apostle of Christ and his teaching is the Word of God;

● and after we have made it clear that salvation relies entirely on the work of grace of Jesus Christ, let us look at what God tells us through His servant.

No Other Gospel

 Why did the Galatians need a letter?

The following verses answer this question:

Galatians 1:6-10:

> ⁶*I marvel that you are turning away so soon from Him who called you in the grace of Christ, to a different gospel, ⁷which is not another; but there are some who trouble you and want to pervert the gospel of Christ. ⁸But even if we, or an angel from heaven, preach any other gospel to you than what we have preached to you, let him be accursed.*
>
> ⁹*As we have said before, so now I say again, if anyone preaches any other gospel to you than what you have received, let him be accursed.*
>
> ¹⁰*For do I now persuade men, or God? Or do I seek to please men? For if I still pleased men, I would not be a bondservant of Christ.*

"I marvel." — Paul is amazed at the ease with which the believers in Galatia have abandoned the truth for false teaching (**2 Cor. 11:4**).

The phrase *you are turning away ... from Him who called you* can be understood in two ways:

1. The apostle is grieved and distressed that the Galatians have left **God** who called them. Instead of being faithful to His calling,

they have been led astray by charlatans who offer them a life of no peace and without God's grace.

2. Another possibility is that Paul describes **himself** as the one who called the Galatians. (NKJV translators opted against this possibility by capitalizing "Him.") The apostle is amazed that the Galatians have now strayed from his clear teaching in favor of false doctrines that oppose the truth of God's Word **(4:14-16)**.

When Paul and Barnabas were first with them, these believers witnessed the work of the Holy Spirit through the apostles, who did miracles and wonders by the power of Christ. There had been no doubt that their teaching was the truth from God **(3:1-6)**.

Why did they nevertheless turn to "a different gospel"?

It becomes apparent that the message of the false teachers was designed to flatter Jewish believers. This is why they had so much success so quickly. What a shame! People tend to be quick to adopt a message that flatters them, that is comfortable and does not require any major changes, and they oppose the message of God's truth that gives life but requires thorough change and daily correction — in short: needs lots of effort.

Let us look at the background of the false doctrine Paul is dealing with.

At the Beginning There Was — the Truth

When the first church was established after the outpouring of the Holy Spirit at the Feast of Pentecost **(Acts 2)** most of the believers were Jewish. After the feast, the Jewish pilgrims returned to the countries they had come from and spread the gospel among their families and neighbors. Shortly afterwards the believers in Jerusalem began to suffer persecution. Many of them were forced to leave Jerusalem and migrated to other cities and countries **(Acts 11)**. Some arrived in places where there was already a small nucleus of Jewish Christians, others settled in Jewish communities that did not persecute them for their faith.

But it was not only the outbreak of persecution that furthered the spread of the gospel: the Roman Empire invested heavily in the construction and maintenance of an extensive road network. This enabled the preachers of the gospel to reach even the farthest regions of the empire in a short time.

Before long, many Gentiles believed God's message as taught in the churches. Since all of these new believers came from a background of idolatry, pagan influence in the churches increased, which created tension between Jewish and Gentile believers.

Remember: Gentiles who began to believe in Jesus

- had for the most part never read the Bible before joining the church;
- did not come from a background where basic biblical values of morality were self-evident;
- did not necessarily exhibit rapid spiritual growth.

They brought their Gentile customs and traditions with them into the church. Time, forbearance, and teaching was needed until they would put these wrong and impure practices completely behind them. Of the Jewish believers, on the other hand, great spiritual maturity was required before they even agreed to gather with the Gentiles under the same roof!

False Teaching in the Making

As time went by, the number of Gentile believers in the churches grew at a much higher ratio than the Jewish believers. Jewish influence decreased as Gentile influence grew. Right at this point the false teachers came in, trying to preserve the Jewish nature of the church by using corrupt means and for selfish purposes:

1. They taught *a different gospel*, which was: Gentiles who come to faith must be circumcised and keep the Mosaic Law in order to be saved (**Acts 15:1; Gal. 2:3-5, 11-14; 3:3-5; 4:8-11, 21-31; 5:1-4; 6:12-13**). In this way they thought to curb Gentile influence within the church and set themselves up as examples to be followed.

2. The false teachers had a second motive: they were unwilling to suffer and be persecuted *"for the cross of Christ"* (**6:12**).

- They wanted to continue to enjoy the religious freedom the Roman Empire granted to Judaism under the status of *religio licita* ("permitted religion").

- They were not prepared to suffer as Christians who were persecuted by the authorities as adherents of a new religion, forbidden by Roman law **(6:12; 2 Tim. 3:12)**.

- They were looking to avoid the religious ostracism imposed on believers in Jesus by the non-believing Jewish majority.

Since the false teachers had already started to cause harm, the apostle Paul wrote this letter with great urgency, hoping to stem the tide of misleading teaching and of confused people being swept into the folds of the legalists.

The false teachers claimed that salvation depends on two things:

1. observance of all the laws and commandments as prescribed by Jewish tradition;
2. belief in Jesus as Messiah.

They were basically saying: "Be first of all an observant Jew, just like us, and then a disciple of Jesus."

In addition they found fault with Paul, rejecting his authority as an apostle and teacher appointed by Christ. On what basis?

1. The apostle Paul taught that:

    "A man is justified by faith" **(Rom. 3:28)**. — Atonement for sin and salvation are granted by genuine faith in Jesus Christ as Lord and Savior, who came to Earth as a man and gave His life an atoning sacrifice for sin.

    "A man is justified... apart from the deeds of the law" **(Rom. 3:28)**. — Salvation is granted by the grace of God, not as a reward for keeping the commandments. **(See also Romans 10:8-10.)**

    "Israel, pursuing after righteousness, has not attained to the law of righteousness" **(Rom. 9:31)**. — If even the most godly men of Israel were unable to keep all the commandments perfectly, then

there is no one who is able to keep them. According to **Deuteronomy 27:26** we are all under the curse and in need of the grace of God.

In his doctrine, Paul left no room for the works of man — but those were precisely what the false teachers emphasized.

2. Paul emphasized that the conditions for salvation are the same for Jew and Gentile. His assertion that in the Messiah there is no difference between the two **(Rom. 3:26-29)** took away the high ground the false teachers thought they stood on. Paul taught that they also fell short and needed the grace of God, just like the Gentiles who had never even heard of the Law.

   Paul's doctrine allowed for no superiority on the basis of nationality — but this was precisely what the false teachers were trying to preserve.

3. The false teachers accused Paul of lowering the standard of holiness required of man, in order to depict God's salvation as something easy to obtain and thus to draw in the Gentiles. They were afraid that Paul's gospel would encourage loose living and water down the high moral standards the Law required of the Jews.

   Paul rejects that accusation and points out that the believer is preserved from a depraved life because **the Holy Spirit** dwells in him. Proof of this are Noah, Abraham, and all the righteous men of the Old Testament until Moses: They all lived holy lives long before the Law was given.

   The apostle also actively fought against all expressions of sin and did not allow pagan customs introduced by believing Gentiles to gain a foothold in the church **(1 Cor. 5)**.

Unlike the false teachers, Paul was not ready to use inappropriate means (misleading teaching, traditions, and commandments originating with man and not with God) in order to achieve the desired result.

The saying "the end justifies the means" is not part of the Christian's terminology.

We can only achieve a holy outcome by using holy tools:

- complete submission to the written Word of God alone;
- complete dependence on the power of the Holy Spirit who works in the believer and enables him to obey the will of God **(Eph. 5:18-19)**.

"Jesus Plus"

The false teachers taught that Jesus is not the one determining factor for salvation. They emphasized the advantages they had over the Gentiles: Jewish heritage, extensive knowledge in the Law and rich experience. Thus they enhanced their importance in the eyes of the believing Gentiles. At the same time, they emptied the gospel of all value, because they took Jesus out of its heart.

Instead of teaching the believers to become more like Christ, they presented **themselves** as an example to follow **(Gal. 4:17)**.

The false teachers, and in fact many other Jewish believers at that time, failed to understand that the death of Jesus Christ is the starting point of the New Covenant promised by Jeremiah **(Jer. 31:31-34)**. They did not understand that the sacrifice of Christ fulfilled all the types and symbols in the commandments that pointed forward to the Messiah and His work, and that these commandments are now no longer in effect **(Gal. 3:23-25; 4:8-11; 2 Cor. 3; Col. 2:16-17; Heb. 7—10)**.

They refused to accept the fact that belief in Jesus transforms us, whether Jew or Gentile, into a new creation — into a person who is born again — into one who has received a new identity by belonging to Jesus Christ and submitting to Him **(Acts 11:26; Gal. 6:15)**.

Every saved person, Jew or Gentile, serves the Lord in the church of Christ by means of the spiritual gifts God has given him, with no regard to his national identity **(1 Cor. 12)**. Nothing that belongs to the believer's past, to the time before he was saved, can serve to boost his value, and it certainly did nothing to help him obtain salvation in the first place (**Phil. 3:1-11**).

 Note: Paul does not by any means minimize the status of the people of Israel in the eyes of God and does not detract from the nation's importance. He knows and teaches that the promises of God to Israel will be fulfilled. (See more about this in Romans 9—11.)

As to the spiritual state of false teachers we can say: Whoever does not understand the significance of the death and resurrection of Christ and does not submit to the authority of the Scriptures reveals that he is not a true disciple of Christ and has not been saved.

A Different Gospel

❼ *"Which is not another."* — The false teaching contradicting Paul's doctrine cannot really be a "gospel." After all, it cannot give life, because Jesus is not its center as the only means of salvation. If it is necessary to add anything to our salvation, beyond what Christ has done to obtain it, then Christ is not enough.

Whoever adopts the teachings of the false teachers must know that he will not find salvation there. Paul gives an explanation and a chilling warning to those who hold to "a different gospel" in **Galatians 3:10-14**.

Even so, there are people today who claim that there is one gospel for the Jew and a different one for the Gentile. This contradicts what we read in **John 14:6; Acts 4:12; and Romans 10:9-10** — that God has **one** gospel of salvation for both Jew and Gentile.

"Some who trouble you and want to pervert the gospel of Christ." — There is a basic difference between a false teacher and a teacher who makes an honest mistake. Here we are speaking of those who **"want to pervert"** — **want** to lead astray. They know very well what the true gospel is, and they battle against it and against the servants of Christ who teach it.

The gospel of Christ is clearly defined in other epistles by Paul:

1 Corinthians 15:1-4:

> ¹*Moreover, brethren, I declare to you the gospel which I preached to you, which also you received and in which you stand,* ²*by which also you are saved, if you hold fast that word which I preached to you — unless you believed in vain.*
>
> ³*For I delivered to you first of all that which I also received: that Christ died for our sins according to the Scriptures,* ⁴*and that He was buried, and that He rose again the third day according to the Scriptures.*

Romans 10:8-9:

> *The word of faith which we preach:* ⁹*that if you confess with your mouth the Lord Jesus and believe in your heart that God has raised Him from the dead, you will be saved.*

Now the apostle tells us exactly what the false teachers do. They

- *"pervert the gospel."*
- *"trouble"* the people of the church (NIV: "are throwing you into confusion").

Note!

The greatest harm to the church of Christ is never caused by unbelievers who mock or oppose us. Real damage is always inflicted by people **within** the church (**1 Jn. 2:18-19**). This is why Paul entreats Timothy to *"hold fast"* the gospel he has received (**2 Tim. 1:13-14**). Only the pure gospel gives life. Whoever twists it endangers the church — and since the church is the body of Christ, he finds himself fighting against God.

What about us, today?

What kind of teachers do we like to listen to — those who support our own opinions and our way of life, the kind who will compromise the truth of the gospel in order to avoid suffering for Christ — or those who will tell us the truth in love, no matter the cost?

"Let Him be Accursed!"

8–9 *"But even if we, or an angel from heaven, preach any other gospel to you than what we have preached to you, let him be accursed. ⁹ As we have said before, so now I say again, if anyone preaches any other gospel to you than what you have received, let him be accursed."*

The apostle employs repetition to emphasize his words: Whoever twists the gospel of Christ that was preached by Paul during the early days of the Galatian church — and even if that teacher is the apostle himself — must be excluded from the fellowship of believers. ***Accursed*** means that the person is excommunicated — completely cut off.

In Old Testament usage the word ***accursed*** described a person, a group of people or things that were destined for destruction (**Josh. 6:17-18; 7:1, 25-26**).

"Let him be accursed!" — why does Paul use such extreme language?

Because the teaching of the false teachers leads people to hell!

On the one hand it promises salvation, and on the other it prevents them from trusting in the only One who can grant that salvation. Paul describes the false teachers as worthy of eternal punishment, because they draw many other souls after them to hell (**Mt. 24:24; Jn. 8:44; 1 Tim. 1:20; Ti. 1:16**).

What must we do to prevent false teaching or the infiltration of our churches by false teachers today?

1. Learn and know the Word of God.

2. Compare what we are taught in church to the Scriptures, as the new believers in Berea did (**Acts 17:11**): *"They received the word with all readiness, and searched the Scriptures daily to find out whether these things were so."*

3. Point out to a teacher humbly and lovingly where his words did not line up with Scripture.

4. If our criticism is examined and found to be justified, the teacher must adopt the correction with humility.

5. Should he try to justify himself and insist on teaching what has been proven wrong, the church must exclude him from the fellowship or avoid listening to his teaching. While this process has no place for violence of any sort, it must nevertheless be followed through to the point of total disassociation from the false teacher, so he will be prevented from further influencing those who come to worship in the house of God **(Mt. 18:15-20)**.

A True Apostle and Servant of Christ

10 *"For do I now persuade men, or God? Or do I seek to please men? For if I still pleased men, I would not be a bondservant of Christ."* — Paul points out the difference between him and the false teachers. They came with their own message, not a message from God. Their message was intended to justify their way of life and free them from the necessity to change.

This kind of message is in great demand, which is why false teachers have many friends in the world. However, they are not friends of God. They are His enemies and can only expect His judgment and punishment. If they choose to remain cut off from the salvation of Christ until the day they die — despite all they learn from studying the principles of God's Word — they will not enjoy eternal life with Christ in His Kingdom.

"For if I still pleased men." — If Paul at this point had sought the favor of men and an easy life at the cost of distorting the gospel, he would never have dared to declare someone accursed. Standing for the truth and making such a declaration was bound to draw fire and to bring much suffering upon him. He knew he would suffer at the hands of men but would receive courage and strength from God to continue to preach the truth. He desired God's glory alone and did not seek his own. **(See also Matthew 10:26-31; 2 Corinthians 10; Galatians 6:12.)**

Paul knew firsthand the compulsion to be a people-pleaser. He himself had persecuted believers in Jesus in order to find favor in the eyes of his spiritual leaders. Now his ultimate aim was to please God and to live according to His leading only. Paul knew that in the service of Christ he would not have many friends. Instead, his life would be characterized by suffering (**2 Tim. 3:12**).

He was not the first to feel that! Most of the prophets in the Bible stood alone, because their message exposed the sins of those around them and required drastic change.

"A bondservant of Christ." — The apostle teaches us that there is a price to pay in walking with Jesus and proclaiming the gospel. He was ready to pay even with his life so he could be called *"a bondservant of Christ"* (**Rom. 12:1; Gal. 2:20**).

If only all of us were willing to give up some pleasures and privileges in order to gain a few more minutes in which to tell the gospel to every soul (**1 Cor. 9:19-22**).

What characterizes the behavior and way of life of servants of Christ?

1. **A life focused on Jesus alone**

    Hebrews 12:1-2: *"Let us run with endurance the race that is set before us, looking unto Jesus, the author and finisher of our faith."*

2. **Humility**

    John 3:30: *"He must increase, but I must decrease."*

3. **Putting others first**

    Philippians 2:3: *"Let nothing be done through selfish ambition or conceit, but in lowliness of mind let each esteem others better than himself"*; **Romans 12:10:** *"Be kindly affectionate to one another with brotherly love, in honor giving preference to one another."*

4. **Submitting to the will of God**

    Matthew 26:39: *"O My Father, if it is possible, let this cup pass from*

Me; nevertheless, not as I will, but as You will"; 1 Peter 5:6: "Humble yourselves under the mighty hand of God, that He may exalt you in due time"; Matthew 6:33: "Seek first the kingdom of God and His righteousness, and all these things shall be added to you."

Before and After

Jesus Changes Our Priorities

Galatians 1:11-24:

> ¹¹But I make known to you, brethren, that the gospel which was preached by me is not according to man. ¹²For I neither received it from man, nor was I taught it, but it came through the revelation of Jesus Christ.
>
> ¹³For you have heard of my former conduct in Judaism, how I persecuted the church of God beyond measure and tried to destroy it. ¹⁴And I advanced in Judaism beyond many of my contemporaries in my own nation, being more exceedingly zealous for the traditions of my fathers.
>
> ¹⁵But when it pleased God, who separated me from my mother's womb and called me through His grace, ¹⁶to reveal His Son in me, that I might preach Him among the Gentiles, I did not immediately confer with flesh and blood, ¹⁷nor did I go up to Jerusalem to those who were apostles before me; but I went to Arabia, and returned again to Damascus.
>
> ¹⁸Then after three years I went up to Jerusalem to see Peter, and remained with him fifteen days. ¹⁹But I saw none of the other apostles except James, the Lord's brother. ²⁰(Now concerning the things which I write to you, indeed, before God, I do not lie.)
>
> ²¹Afterward I went into the regions of Syria and Cilicia. ²²And I was unknown by face to the churches of Judea which were

> in Christ. **²³ But they were hearing only, "He who formerly persecuted us now preaches the faith which he once tried to destroy." ²⁴ And they glorified God in me.**

These verses allow us to compare between:

1. what was most important to Paul **before** he believed in Jesus (his priorities were similar to those of the false teachers);
2. what was most important to him **after** his encounter with Jesus.

11 — 12 "**The gospel ... not according to man.**" — On the one hand, Paul's gospel was not a figment of his mind or his religious fervor. On the other hand, he had not had much opportunity to learn from the other apostles. The story of his life since he met Jesus shows that he did not spend a long time with them and did not stay long in Jerusalem.

"**But it came through the revelation of Jesus Christ.**" — The apostle's knowledge was based on the revelation of Jesus to him on the way to Damascus (**Acts 9**). Since then, he had remained faithful to the gospel of truth and had no intention of adapting it to suit his hearers, even if such faithfulness to his Messiah would cost him his life (**Rom. 1:16**).

By stressing this point Paul makes clear that the "gospel" of the false teachers is a fruit of their own thoughts and does not come from God.

What is the gospel? ● ● ● ● ● ● ●

Jesus Christ, God the Son, came to Earth as a man in order to pay the price of atonement for man's sin with His life. If you believe that God sent His Son, Jesus Christ, in order to die for the atonement of your sins, and if you believe that Jesus rose from the dead on the third day, then you are saved. — That is the gospel in a nutshell (Isa. 7:14; 53; Ps. 2:2, 7, 12; Prov. 30:1-4; Lk. 16:30-31; 24:27; Jn. 3:16-21; 14:6; Acts 4:12; 26:6-7; 28:23-24; Rom. 10:9-10; 1 Cor. 15:1-4).

Whoever rejects the atonement for sin that God gave by the atoning death of Jesus, remains in sin and is destined to spend eternity in the Lake of Fire, eternally cut off from God.

The vast majority of Jews grow up thinking that Jesus "belongs" exclusively to the Christian Gentiles. This understanding and the teaching that results from it label the one and only way to salvation from the curse of sin as something that is foreign to the Jewish people.

The truth is that one meets Jesus throughout the entire Hebrew Scriptures, the Old Testament. He is God the Son, the divine entity humans have been allowed to see "face-to-face" — and to remain alive (Gen. 32:30; Ex. 33:11). God the Son is the One who appeared to Abraham as a man, introducing Himself by the name **El-Shaddai**, Almighty God (Gen. 17:1; 18:1-33).*

The gospel is considered foolishness to many, but it is the truth of God. For the sake of this gospel Paul was prepared to suffer rejection by people and ostracism from his own nation (**1 Cor. 1:18-31**).

13—**17** *"You have heard of my former conduct in Judaism."* — "You know yourselves that in the past I fought with all my strength against this faith and against those who follow it, but when God opened my eyes I understood the difference between truth and error."

"And I advanced in Judaism beyond many of my contemporaries in my own nation." — Paul was an observant Jew and a very gifted man. If judged by standards of religious observance he would have received top marks (**Acts 22:3-5**). Had he rejected the truth he heard from Jesus and continued in the rabbinical traditions, he would most likely have attained a place of honor among the religious leaders, while at the same time remaining cut off from God.

The apostle is saying in effect: "The false teachers want you to be Jews that observe all the commandments and traditions God no longer expects you to keep. But know that I, Paul, have been there! While I was (in the eyes of my people) perfect in observance, I knew nothing of the grace and peace of God through Jesus Christ. Outwardly I wore an impressive guise of religiosity, but my life was void of God's presence. Those who looked at me would see a devout Jew, a worthy representative of God's Chosen People, but in

---

* For a more in-depth study of this subject, see the book *Jesus in the Hebrew Scriptures*, available at www.foi.org

my heart I was an enemy of God. That is why I persecuted the followers of Christ and pursued the wisdom of man. Do not follow the false teachers, they are leading you away from the truth!"

What Is More Important?

In the epistle to the Philippians Paul compares his national identity with his identity in Christ.

Philippians 3:1-11:

> ¹*Finally, my brethren, rejoice in the Lord. For me to write the same things to you is not tedious, but for you it is safe.*
>
> ²*Beware of dogs, beware of evil workers, beware of the mutilation!* ³*For we are the circumcision, who worship God in the Spirit, rejoice in Christ Jesus, and have no confidence in the flesh,* ⁴*though I also might have confidence in the flesh. If anyone else thinks he may have confidence in the flesh, I more so:* ⁵*circumcised the eighth day, of the stock of Israel, of the tribe of Benjamin, a Hebrew of the Hebrews; concerning the law, a Pharisee;* ⁶*concerning zeal, persecuting the church; concerning the righteousness which is in the law, blameless.*
>
> ⁷*But what things were gain to me, these I have counted loss for Christ.* ⁸*Yet indeed I also count all things loss for the excellence of the knowledge of Christ Jesus my Lord, for whom I have suffered the loss of all things, and count them as rubbish, that I may gain Christ* ⁹*and be found in Him, not having my own righteousness, which is from the law, but that which is through faith in Christ, the righteousness which is from God by faith;* ¹⁰*that I may know Him and the power of His resurrection, and the fellowship of His sufferings, being conformed to His death,* ¹¹*if, by any means, I may attain to the resurrection from the dead.*

Paul is not minimizing or belittling his status as a Jew, a member of the people of Israel. What he does is compare his origins and his national identity on the one hand with salvation and fellowship with Christ on the other. In such a comparison, even the most exalted lineage on Earth is like rubbish. Our identity in Christ, which gives us citizenship in heaven, is more valuable than all the temporary things of this earth: *"For our citizenship is in heaven, from which we also eagerly wait for the Savior, the Lord Jesus Christ"* **(Phil. 3:20)**.

To put it simply, Paul is pointing out that everything on this earth is of no value compared to heavenly, eternal things. Any parent who is made to choose between a photograph of his child or the child himself will without hesitation opt for the latter. In the same way, we must prefer Jesus over any shadow or symbol **(Gal. 3:23-25; 4:8-11; Col. 2:16-17)**.

14 *"Being more exceedingly zealous for the traditions of my fathers."* — After Jesus Christ was revealed to Paul on the way to Damascus, Paul understood what was the main thing in life. At this point he understood that all the man-made commandments and traditions he had observed until then had not enabled him to recognize and receive his Savior. They only hid the true way. The traditions of the sages, which he had followed as if they were the Law of God, had taught him to be an enemy of God and a stranger to the Messiah of Israel.

Note!

Paul is not attacking the Torah, the Law. The Law of God is pure and holy, and the apostle emphasizes this himself in **Romans 7:12:** *"Therefore the law is holy, and the commandment holy and just and good."* The centuries-old traditions of the sages were what led Saul astray. They turned the people aside from God's Word and hid the face of their only Redeemer from them **(Isa. 29:13-14; Mt. 23 "the leaven of the Pharisees"; Mt. 5:20; Rom. 9:30-10:4)**.

The false teachers had not yet met Jesus. Their behavior proves that beyond all doubt. They were still embracing what was unnecessary.

"I did not ... confer with flesh and blood" (v. 16). — "Since it was God who corrected my understanding in person, face-to-face, there was no need to go back

to Jerusalem to receive confirmation of the truth of the gospel. I had seen the heart of the gospel — Jesus Himself — alive with my own eyes."

Remember:

Paul was well-versed in the Bible. Before his salvation he had lacked only one puzzle piece to complete the general picture of God's purpose: the most important piece — Jesus Christ. After Jesus opened his eyes, Paul did not need anyone to add to his knowledge. His proficiency in the Old Testament Scriptures and his understanding were in no way inferior to that of the other apostles, and it could be that in some points he knew more than them.

Preelection

15 *"God, who separated me from my mother's womb."* — The apostle touches here on a very significant subject: preelection (Isa. 49:1; Jer.1:5; Ps. 139; Rom. 8:28-29).

This subject raises questions such as:

- If God sovereignly chooses His children — why does He punish those He has **not** chosen?

- If God chooses His children — why do we have to preach the gospel? In any case, everyone He has chosen will inevitably be saved.

- If God is the One who chooses us — how can man have a free will?

… and many other important questions.

I will not attempt to answer those, but will note a few facts and principles from the Bible which show that God has chosen His children from before time. Knowing these facts and principles will help us to better understand the helplessness of man, his absolute dependence on the grace and love of God and the eternal, irrevocable nature of our salvation.

Even if, after going through these points, we still do not completely understand the subject of preelection, we will hopefully have gained a fuller trust in God, who is righteous, holy, pure, and all-knowing.

1. God has chosen His children from before time. This is an expression of His sovereignty (Jer. 1:5; Lk. 1:13-17; Rom. 9:11-13; Eph. 1:4; 2 Th. 2:13-14; 2 Tim. 1:8-9; 1 Pet. 1:15).

2. God chose the people of Israel of His own free will and for His own special purpose, even before they had become a nation (Ex. 19:5-6; Dt. 7:7-8; 1 Sam. 12:22; Isa. 43:7, 21; 44:23).

3. All men are sinners in need of atonement for their sins (Ps. 51:5; Eccl. 7:20; Rom. 3:23).

4. King David understood that he was chosen to be king by the grace of God and not because of anything he had done (1 Chr. 28:4-5).

5. Paul was saved while on the way to Damascus to kill God's children. He had no intention to surrender to Christ of his own free will (Rom. 5:10; 1 Cor. 1:1; Gal. 1:15-16; Phil. 3:1-10).

6. God is a God of justice, truth, grace, and mercy (Ex. 20:6; 34:6; Num. 14:18; Dt. 5:10; Neh.1:5-10; Ps. 25:10; 103:4; 145:17; Isa. 45:21; Jer. 9:23-24; Dan. 9). If man has any complaints, they derive from his own failings and shortcomings, not from God's (Isa. 55:7-11).

7. There is no God other than the God we read of in the Old and New Testaments (Isa. 43:10-11; 44:6-8; 45:5-7, 14, 21-22).

8. God will judge every person who rejects His salvation (Dan. 12:2; Rev. 20:11-15).

9. God created man with a conscience that enables him to distinguish between good and evil (Rom. 1: 20).

10. God has proven His existence in creation, the wonder of which every man can see for himself (Ps. 19).

11. God is man's only Savior and Redeemer from sin (Isa. 43:25; 53:6; John 3:16).

12. God desires that all should be saved. His salvation is for all mankind (Isa. 2; Mt. 28:18-20; Acts 1:8-9; 1 Tim. 2:3-5).

13. Man is given the intellectual ability and the responsibility to understand that there is a Creator (Ps. 19; Rom. 2).

14. Whoever truly seeks the Creator will find Him (Ps. 51:17).

15. Man can never compare to God and is incapable of comprehending the extent of God's wisdom and His motives. For this reason man is in no position to complain against God (Isa. 55:8-9; Job 40:1-5).

16. The saved person, through the Holy Spirit that dwells in him, can see and understand the things God does. The unsaved person is blind to the work of God (Jn. 3:5-8; 1 Cor. 2:10-16).

17. God expresses His love to mankind in that He gave His only Son, Jesus Christ, as a sacrifice for their sins, so that *"whoever believes in Him should not perish but have everlasting life"* (Jn. 3:16).

18. Nothing can separate us from the love of Christ (Rom. 8:31-39).

19. God, who chose us and began His work in us, has promised to complete that which He began (Phil. 1:6).

20. After man "finds" the Creator, he discovers that God chose him from the beginning, even before the foundation of the world.

21. *"Faith comes by hearing, and hearing by the Word of God"* (Rom. 10:17).

22. God commands all His children to proclaim the gospel, so that people will hear and be saved (Mt. 28:18-20; Acts 1:8).

23. The saved children of God preach the gospel because the love of Christ burns within them (Ezek. 3; 2 Cor. 5:11-21).

24. God is sovereign, righteous, and holy. It is His right to do what He wills with His creation, and we are all sinners who deserve punishment (Jer. 18).

25. Man is unworthy to confront God, to argue with Him, and to claim that God is in the wrong (Job 40:1-5).

In light of the above facts and principles we can establish that:

a. God sovereignly chooses His children.

b. God reveals the truth to everyone and requires us to respond to it.

c. Whoever does not seek the Creator will stand before His judgment seat.

d. God is righteous, holy, and pure. All His works and ways are right and full of wisdom. He chooses His children, but in His grace He also allows us to participate in the labor of preaching the gospel (Acts 1; Rom. 10:17).

God says in Isaiah 55:7-9:

> **⁷ Let the wicked forsake his way, and the unrighteous man his thoughts; let him return to the LORD, and He will have mercy on him; and to our God, for He will abundantly pardon.**
>
> **⁸ "For My thoughts are not your thoughts, nor are your ways My ways," says the LORD. ⁹ "For as the heavens are higher than the earth, so are My ways higher than your ways, and My thoughts than your thoughts."** (See also to the end of verse 13.)

Even if you do not completely understand the sovereignty of God in choosing His children and in judging those who reject Him, the above facts and principles (which are only a small sample of what is found in Scripture) should be sufficient to move you to ask the Creator to work in your life and to open the eyes of your heart to recognize Him as your Redeemer, the Lord of your life and your Savior from sin.

From a Persecutor of Christ to an Apostle of Christ

Do You Want to Prove You Are for Real? — Be Consistent!

Galatians 1:15-17:

> ¹⁵ But when it pleased God, who separated me from my mother's womb and called me through His grace, ¹⁶ to reveal His Son in me, that I might preach Him among the Gentiles, I did not immediately confer with flesh and blood, ¹⁷ nor did I go up to Jerusalem to those who were apostles before me; but I went to Arabia, and returned again to Damascus.

15 — 17 "But when it pleased God...to reveal His Son in me, that I might preach Him among the Gentiles...I went to Arabia." — Paul now gives us a few details of his life, after he was born again, that expand on what we are told in Acts 9.

After his encounter with Jesus Christ he went "to Arabia" (east of Damascus). There, in a desert region, far from any influence of traditions of men, Paul spent time alone with God and searched his soul. In an environment similar to the one in which God first gave His Law to His people, Paul went through a time of preparation for the service that awaited him.

"And returned again to Damascus." — At the end of his time in the desert he returned to his point of departure, to Damascus in Syria:

Galatians 1:18-24:

> ¹⁸ Then after three years I went up to Jerusalem to see Peter, and remained with him fifteen days. ¹⁹ But I saw none of the other apostles except James, the Lord's brother. ²⁰ (Now concerning the things which I write to you, indeed, before God, I do not lie.)
>
> ²¹ Afterward I went into the regions of Syria and Cilicia. ²² And

> *I was unknown by face to the churches of Judea which were in Christ.* ²³ *But they were hearing only, "He who formerly persecuted us now preaches the faith which he once tried to destroy."* ²⁴ *And they glorified God in me.*

18—**24** *"Then after three years I went up to Jerusalem."* — Paul's visit with Simon Peter was not in order to learn from the Scriptures, since he was already well-versed in them. After he met Jesus, his understanding was in no way inferior to that of the other apostles. Remember, Paul was a student of the Law, while the other apostles had grown up in Galilee, and most of them were fishermen. The purpose of the 15-day visit was to strengthen the relationship between himself and Simon Peter and enable him to become acquainted with the local church of Christ.

Paul mentions the two leaders he met: Peter and James, the brother of our Lord.

- **Peter** was Simon Peter, one of the apostles **(Mt. 10:2; Acts 1-12)**.

- ***"James the Lord's brother"*** was the half-brother of Jesus. Jesus was born to Mary by the supernatural conception of the Holy Spirit. Her other sons and daughters were fathered by her husband Joseph **(Mt. 12:46-50; Mk. 6:1-3; Acts 15:13; Gal. 2:9, 12; Jas. 1—5)**.

Why did Paul not settle in Jerusalem immediately following his conversion? — There are two reasons:

1. The first one is in verses

    15—**16** Paul himself says here: *"It pleased God…to reveal His Son in me that I might preach Him among the **Gentiles**."* — He was chosen to preach the gospel primarily to non-Jews, and they lived for the most part outside the borders of Israel **(Acts 9:15; 22:15; Gal. 2:8)**.

2. **22** *"And I was unknown by face to the churches of Judea which were in Christ."* — Here is the second reason: Because Paul had in the past violently persecuted the believers in the land of Israel, they were

all afraid of him and kept their distance from him. The believers in Jerusalem did not immediately take in the fact that their enemy had become a brother in the faith. Had he stayed in Jerusalem, he would have most likely been a source of problems and mistrust and thus unable to freely serve the Lord **(Acts 9:26; Gal. 1:22-24)**.

"Afterward I went into the regions of Syria and Cilicia" (v. 21). — This sentence marks the end of Paul's short visit to Jerusalem. From there he returned to his place of birth.

Let us combine the facts from the epistle to the Galatians with what we know from the book of Acts, to get a clear picture of Paul's movements.

Chronological Order

Here is a timeline of central events in Paul's life since his name first appears in the New Testament:

1. **Acts 7:58:** Paul is called *"a young man"* at the time he participates in the stoning of Stephen. He is apparently in his 20s.

2. **Acts 9:1-25:** Paul leaves for Damascus with a document from the high priest authorizing him to arrest Jews who believe in Jesus. While he is still on the way, Jesus reveals Himself to him in all His glory. Jesus appoints him to be an apostle to bring the gospel of salvation to both Gentiles and Jews. From the moment of his conversion, Paul lives in order to serve the Messiah. He stays in Damascus and preaches the gospel of Christ for *"many days"* **(v. 23)**. When he learns that the local Jews are plotting to kill him, he flees.

3. **Galatians 1:17:** Paul leaves for *"Arabia"* (where he apparently stays for three years). He does not state the name of a country or an exact place, but most likely "Arabia" stands for a desert region. We assume that there the Lord Jesus gives him time for prayer, meditation, and study. In this way He prepares Paul for service as an apostle. At the end of this time Paul returns to Damascus.

4. **Galatians 1:18-19:** Paul goes up to Jerusalem to see Peter. After 15 days he is forced to flee because of persecution **(Acts 9:26-30)**.

5. **Galatians 1:21:** The apostle travels through *"the regions of Syria and Cilicia"* **(Acts 9:30)**, i.e. he returns to the place of his birth and there preaches the gospel.

6. **Acts 11:25-26:** Barnabas finds Paul in Tarsus (the capital of the Roman province of Cilicia) and brings him to Antioch in Syria. The two teach in the church of Antioch for a year: *"Then Barnabas departed for Tarsus to seek Saul. And when he had found him, he brought him to Antioch. So it was that for a whole year they assembled with the church and taught a great many people."*

7. **Galatians 2:1:** Fourteen years after he was saved, Paul goes up to Jerusalem with Barnabas and Titus. This trip is decided upon following the prophecy of Agabus, foretelling *"a great famine throughout all the world."* Paul and his companions bring a financial contribution for the needy in Judah **(Acts 11:27-30)**. Paul is given the opportunity to present his ministry of the gospel before the important men of the church in Jerusalem. At the end of the visit Paul and Barnabas return to Antioch.

8. **Galatians 2:11:** During Peter's stay in Antioch, Paul rebukes him for his improper behavior.

9. **Acts 13:2—14:28:** The first of Paul's journeys to preach the gospel.

10. **Acts 15:1-29:** Paul comes to Jerusalem to a conference of elders and apostles.

11. **Acts 15:36—18:22:** The second missionary journey.

12. **Acts 18:23—21:16:** The third missionary journey.

13. **Acts 21:27—28:31:** Paul's arrest and journey to Rome.

Paul's Missionary Journeys (A)

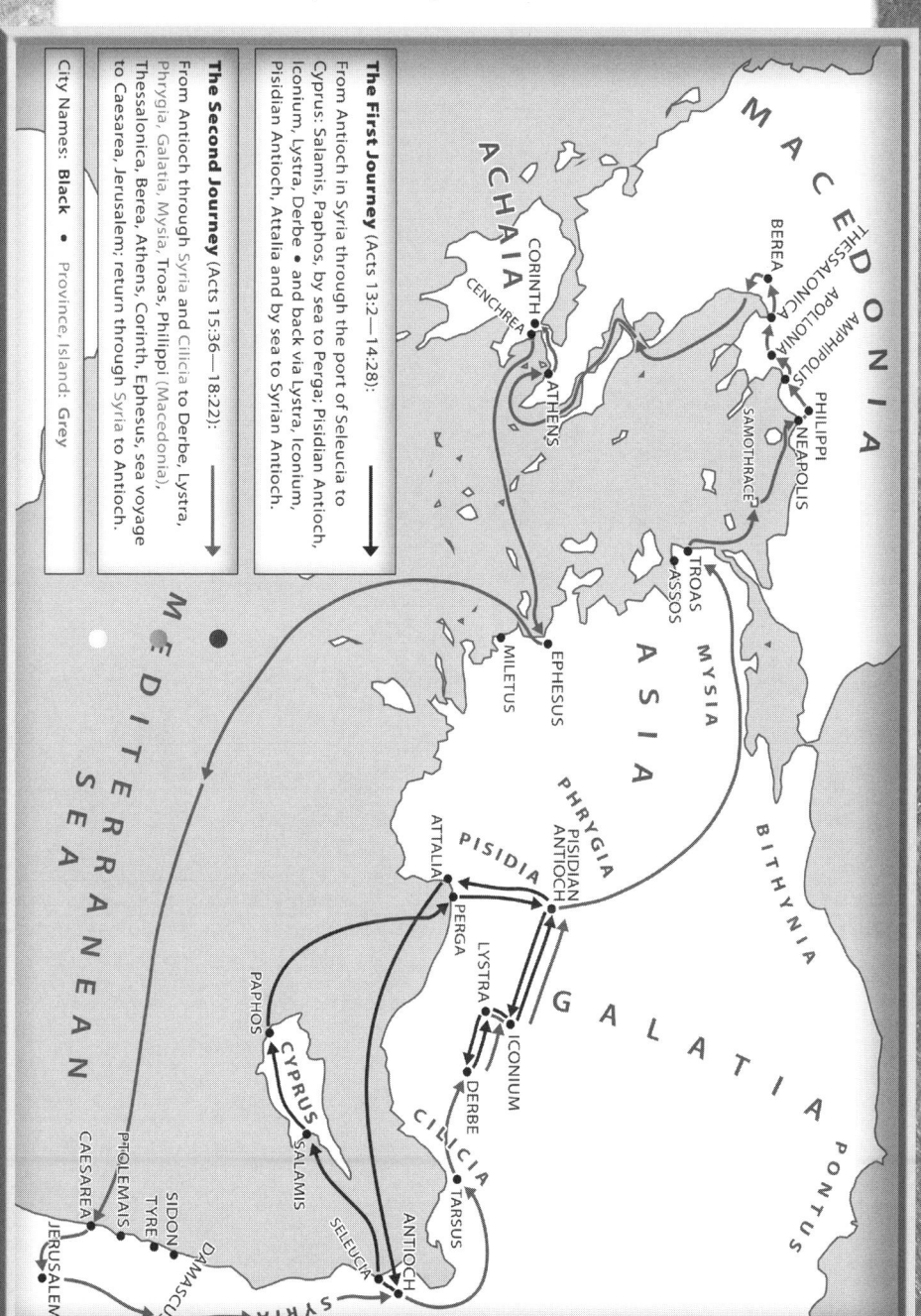

Paul's Missionary Journeys (B)

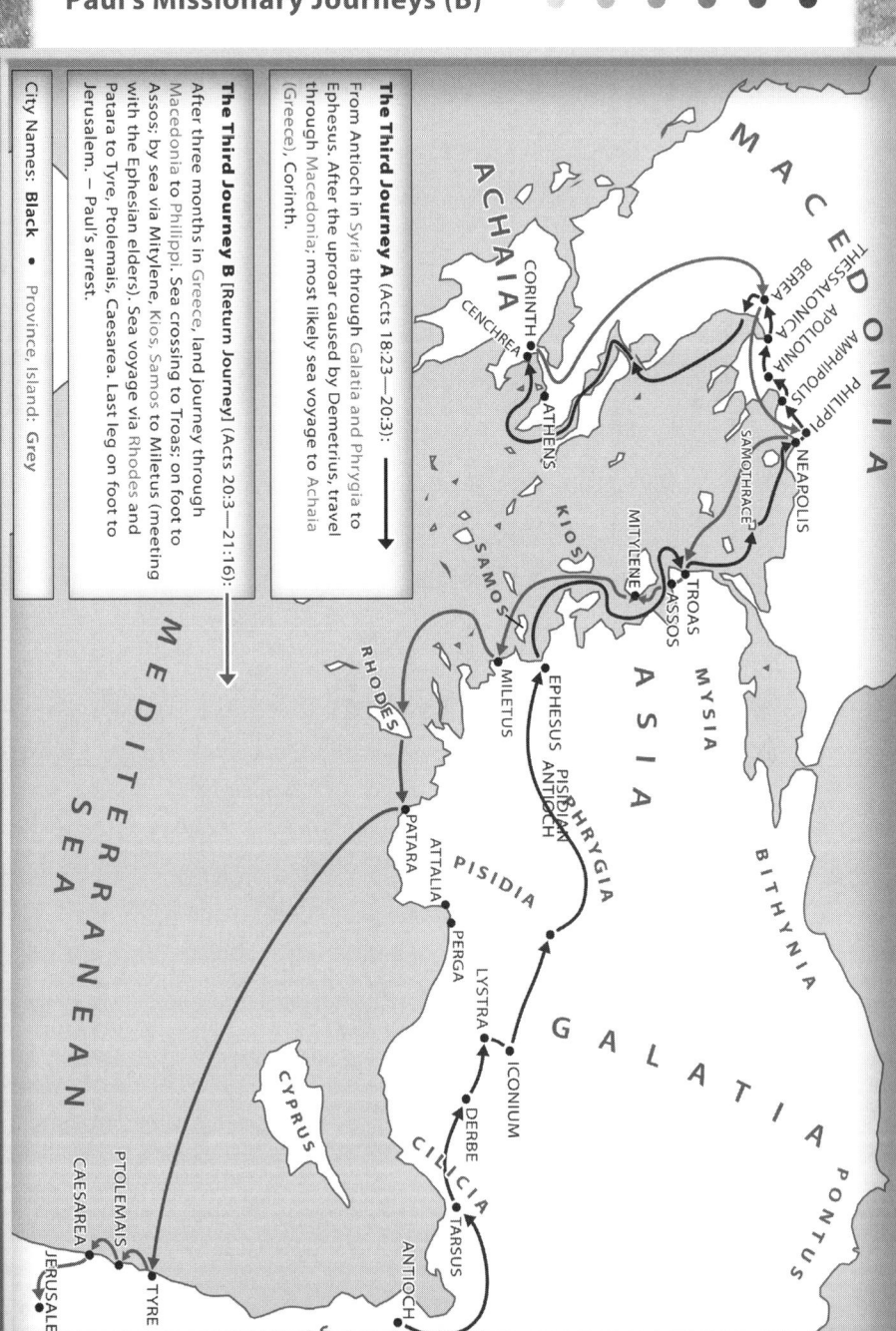

The Third Journey A (Acts 18:23—20:3): From Antioch in Syria through Galatia and Phrygia to Ephesus. After the uproar caused by Demetrius, travel through Macedonia; most likely sea voyage to Achaia (Greece), Corinth.

The Third Journey B [Return Journey] (Acts 20:3—21:16): After three months in Greece, land journey through Macedonia to Philippi. Sea crossing to Troas; on foot to Assos; by sea via Mitylene, Kios, Samos to Miletus (meeting with the Ephesian elders). Sea voyage via Rhodes and Patara to Tyre, Ptolemais, Caesarea. Last leg on foot to Jerusalem. — Paul's arrest.

City Names: **Black** • Province, Island: Grey

Appendix to Chapter 1

The principles of faith discussed in the epistle to the Galatians are similar to those in the epistle to the Romans. What distinguishes **this** epistle is its emphasis on the Jewish perspective.

Comparisons:

Gal. 2:16	Rom. 3:20
Gal. 2:19	Rom. 7:4
Gal. 3:6	Rom. 4:3
Gal. 2:20	Rom. 6:6
Gal. 3:7	Rom. 4:10-11
Gal. 3:11	Rom. 1:17
Gal. 3:22	Rom. 11:32
Gal. 3:27	Rom. 6:3
Gal. 4:5-7	Rom. 8:14-17
Gal. 5:14	Rom. 13:8-10
Gal. 5:16	Rom. 8:4
Gal. 5:17	Rom. 7:23, 25
Gal. 6:2	Rom. 15:1

Names and expressions used by Paul in the epistle to describe the false teachers and their influence

People who trouble you	1:7; 5:10; 5:12
People who pervert the gospel of Christ	1:7
Pleasers of men	1:10
Not bondservants of Christ	1:10
False brethren	2:4

Those who come in by stealth to spy out our liberty which we have in Christ Jesus	2:4
Wanting to bring us into bondage to their opinion	2:4
Bewitchers	3:1
Zealous for you but for no good	4:17
Wanting to turn you from God to them	4:17
Estranged from Christ and fallen from grace	5:4
Let them be cut off!	5:12
Conceited	5:26
Provoking one another, envying one another	5:26
Sow to their flesh	6:8
Wish to make a good showing in the flesh	6:12
Pervert the gospel in order to avoid persecution	6:12
Boast in your flesh	6:13

Pay No Attention to the Chapter Division!

We know that the Scriptures were not originally written with divisions into chapters and verses. This division was added later. Without it we would find it very difficult to locate specific passages when studying. But there are some places where the division seems to be very arbitrary, as for instance the break between the first and second chapters of Galatians. Paul has not yet finished telling his life story when we are abruptly moved on to the next chapter.

Chapter 2

- **Many Apostles — One Gospel**
- **Jews and Gentiles — One Church**

**Paul's Teaching
Is Affirmed by the Other Apostles**

Galatians 2:1-2:

> ¹*Then after fourteen years I went up again to Jerusalem with Barnabas, and also took Titus with me.* ²*And I went up by revelation, and communicated to them that gospel which I preach among the Gentiles, but privately to those who were of reputation, lest by any means I might run, or had run, in vain.*

1 *"I went up again to Jerusalem."* — Paul mentions his trip to Jerusalem to prove to the readers that his doctrine, which he received from Jesus, had the full affirmation of the other apostles.

"Again" — means that this was a different visit from the one during which he stayed for 15 days and met Simon Peter **(1:18)**.

"And I went up by revelation." — The apostle went up to Jerusalem by God's leading, not because of pressure from any earthly factors.

"Privately." — Paul is not referring to the meeting described in Acts 15. If he were, he would have cited the decisions made by the elders and apostles and thus shut the mouths of the false teachers. This is apparently the visit during which he brought financial aid to the church in Jerusalem, following the prophecy of Agabus (**Acts 11**).

"That gospel which I preach among the Gentiles." — **What were the main ingredients of Paul's gospel?**

- Both Gentile and Jew are saved through faith in Jesus Christ as their Lord and Savior.
- Circumcision or observance of commandments of the Mosaic Law which are no longer in effect are not prerequisites to salvation.
- Christ's atonement fulfilled all the ordinances of the Mosaic Law which foreshadowed the Messiah and His work.

Learning From Titus

"And also took Titus with me." — Paul mentions the two companions who joined him at his meeting with the apostles. Pay attention to the wording! He does not simply write "I went up to Jerusalem with Barnabas and Titus," but places a certain emphasis on the presence of Titus (this is found also in the original Greek).

Why Titus?

In order to prove the justness of his stand against the false teachers (i.e. that it is not necessary to be circumcised or to keep the Law in order to be saved), Paul describes how the apostles and elders in Jerusalem accepted Titus, who was a Gentile believer:

Galatians 2:3:

"Yet not even Titus who was with me, being a Greek, was compelled to be circumcised." — Titus was Paul's spiritual son and a co-worker in the service of the gospel. (**See also 2 Corinthians 2:13; 7:6, 13-16; 8:6, 16-17, 23; 12:18; Titus 1:4-5.**)

The leaders of the church in Jerusalem recognized that a Gentile was saved on the basis of his faith in Christ, without having to be circumcised. In other words: The gospel of Paul was also their gospel. If it were otherwise, they would have thrown Titus out and made corrections to the gospel Paul preached.

"Was [not] **compelled to be circumcised."** — That is an important declaration, as the Judaism of those days considered circumcision to be a binding commitment to take on the burden of the Mosaic Law and the commandments. Circumcision was not a cosmetic matter. It was a physical expression of the decision to observe the Law and a commitment to an orthodox Jewish lifestyle. By receiving Titus the elders declared that circumcision or conversion to Judaism are not necessary for salvation.

This means that Paul brought Titus to Jerusalem so he would, later on, have **legal evidence** proving that God's salvation is by grace alone — to both Jew and Gentile.

The affirmation of this principle by the elders in the Jerusalem church should not come as a surprise. Even Abraham was still uncircumcised when he was justified by faith. His circumcision occurred only later:

- Genesis 15: **Abraham is declared righteous**
- Genesis 17: **Abraham obeys God and performs circumcision**

"Lest by any means I might run, or had run, in vain." — The confirmation Paul received from the apostles in Jerusalem did not add anything to him (**Gal. 1:12**). He did not go there for his own sake. Paul's purpose was to make it clear to **the Galatians** that he was in fact speaking for the Lord. This was to cause them to receive Paul's words unhesitatingly and to be firm in ridding themselves of the false teachers.

The leaders of the church in Jerusalem received Titus as a brother in Christ. — What does that say about Paul's opponents?

"False Brethren!"

Galatians 2:4-5:

> ⁴ *And this occurred because of false brethren secretly brought in (who came in by stealth to spy out our liberty which we have in Christ Jesus, that they might bring us into bondage),* ⁵ *to whom we did not yield submission even for an hour, that the truth of the gospel might continue with you.*

❹ *"Because of false brethren."* — Whoever teaches that you must be circumcised in order to be saved is not a brother. He teaches things that are contrary to the Word of God, and believers must disassociate themselves from him **(1:8-9)**.

"Who came in by stealth." — Just as in those days, in our day also false teachers enter our churches like wolves in sheep's clothing. They do not come to learn in order to change or to conform to the righteousness and truth on which the church is founded. They come with the purpose of manipulating the church to suit their own destructive ideologies.

When they first turned up in Galatia, they probably presented themselves as believers who wished to fellowship with their brothers in Christ. Then they covertly began to spread ideas that were contrary to the Word of God, to shake the faith of the believers in the churches and to divert them from the truth.

"To spy out our liberty which we have in Christ Jesus." — *To spy out!* The false teachers are not with us in order to learn and to apply correctly what they have learned. They are collecting information in order to know what to attack.

In the first century, at the time this letter was written to the Galatians, false teachers were bothered by the fact that there were Gentiles in the church who had been saved by faith alone and enjoyed the freedom that is in Christ. In the eyes of the false teachers, this same freedom made salvation too cheap. They decided it should be harder to obtain. **(See also Galatians 5:1-4** on Freedom in Christ.)

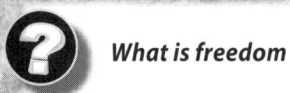 **What is freedom in Christ?**

With salvation, the believer in Jesus gains several liberties:

1. His sins are forgiven and the peace of God fills his heart (**Isa. 53; Rom. 5; 1 Jn. 1:9**).
2. He is released from bondage to sin (**Ti. 2:14**).
3. He is saved from the wrath of God (**1 Th. 1:10; 5:9; Rev. 3:10**).
4. He is considered a son of God and by grace may call his Creator "Abba, Father" (**Rom. 8:15; Gal. 4:6**).
5. The sting of death is taken away and he looks forward with confidence to eternal life with God (**Rom. 5:1-5; 8:1; 1 Cor. 15:54-57; Col. 1:13**).
6. God promises that His Holy Spirit will dwell within him, will give him wisdom, power, and faith and will enable him to discern the will of God and to obey His Word (**Jn. 8:36; Rom. 6:18; 7:6; 2 Cor. 3:17; Gal. 5:13, 16; 1 Pet. 2:16**).
7. He is no longer under the dominion of the Law (**Gal. 3:25**). That is, the saved person is not expected to keep those commandments that foreshadowed the Messiah and His ministry, because Jesus Christ has fulfilled all those. On the other hand, the saved person does keep the commandments of God through the indwelling of the Holy Spirit, not because he is obligated by the written Word (**Rom. 7:6; 2 Cor. 3:1-6; Gal. 4:8-10; Col. 2:16-17**).

The believer's freedom is expressed by the voluntary submission of his will to the Word of God alone. He is free from man's traditions and from commandments that are no longer relevant. At the same time, the believer has the freedom to choose to observe symbolic commandments, keeping in mind that they are just that: a symbol, not an end in and of themselves.

Paul expands on the subject of freedom in Galatians 4 and 5.

"That they might bring us into bondage." — That is to say: "The false teachers oblige you to keep commandments that are no longer in effect and additional commandments that they have invented. They try to convince you that a life of holiness in the ways of God means a life like theirs. They want you to copy **them!** If you walk in this way, you will come into bondage to the false teachers and their errors, instead of obeying God and His Law." **(See 4:17.)** While Paul was striving to establish Christ in the hearts of the believers, the false teachers were trying to establish themselves in those same hearts **(4:19)**.

How should we relate to false teachers?

"To whom we did not yield submission even for an hour." — Paul's behavior toward the false teachers should be our example to follow, even if the process is painful and causes separation between friends or family. We can fellowship with all believers in Christ who live according to what is written in the Bible — the Old and the New Testaments. Within that circle there are bound to be people with different opinions, and that is normal! We discuss and argue respectfully and in this way hone the study of the truth. Dialogue and brotherly kindness, peace, and respect should be the rule even when we disagree.

The problem begins when teachers pop up in the church whose message contradicts the Word of God, and they are unwilling to learn in humility and to correct their mistake. Such teachers must not be submitted to, so that the purity of the Word of God is preserved.

Why is Paul so uncompromising regarding the purity of God's Word?

"That the truth of the gospel might continue with you." — The Word of God alone leads to salvation and to eternal life! Any digression from the teaching of the pure Word of God could

1. prevent people from learning the way of salvation.

2. pervert the spiritual understanding of the disciples of Jesus, hamper their growth, and damage their Christian testimony, ultimately destroying the church.

Circumcision of Believers —
When Is It Acceptable ... When Is It Not? ● ● ● ●

Although Paul was uncompromising in the matter of purity in teaching, he well knew how far the freedom of a believer in Christ could be stretched.

Let us have a look at his actions regarding circumcision in the case of two believers: Titus and Timothy. That is how we will discover exactly what role circumcision has in the life of a believer — Jew or Gentile.

In Acts 16:1-5 we are told that Paul met Timothy during his missionary journey to Derbe and Lystra. Timothy was a young disciple of good reputation among the believers. His mother was a believing Jewess and his father a Greek:

> ¹*Then he [the apostle Paul] came to Derbe and Lystra. And behold, a certain disciple was there, named Timothy, the son of a certain Jewish woman who believed, but his father was Greek.* ²*He was well spoken of by the brethren who were at Lystra and Iconium.* ³*Paul wanted to have him go on with him. And he took him and circumcised him because of the Jews who were in that region, for they all knew that his father was Greek.*
>
> ⁴*And as they went through the cities, they delivered to them the decrees to keep, which were determined by the apostles and elders at Jerusalem.* ⁵*So the churches were strengthened in the faith, and increased in number daily.*

The apostle circumcised Timothy and took him along while he preached the gospel of salvation to Jews and Gentiles in Asia Minor and Greece.

 Why did Paul circumcise Timothy and not Titus? After all both were his coworkers in the same type of ministry.

Paul **did** circumcise **Timothy** because:

1. His mother was Jewish.
2. Timothy served with Paul among Jews and Gentiles. His circumcision allowed him a wider sphere of service at a time when contact between Jews and Gentiles was considered an abomination by most Jews and contrary to the (religious) Law.

The apostle did **not** circumcise **Titus** for two reasons:

1. Titus was a Gentile (Gal. 2:3).
2. The circumcision of a believing Gentile would have meant giving in to the demands of the false teachers — that is, it would have given the impression that a Gentile must be circumcised in order to be saved.

Conclusion:

The apostle Paul considered circumcision to be something a Jewish believer could **choose** to perform, but not as necessary for salvation.

Note!

In Galatians 5:3, Paul says: *"I testify again to every man who becomes circumcised that he is a debtor to keep the whole law."* This is directed at those who believe that circumcision is a condition of salvation. Whoever thinks this way must keep **all** the commandments perfectly — to the very last one!

What is the purpose of circumcision?

Genesis 17 teaches that circumcision is an outward sign of Abraham's descendants — the people of Israel — who are in covenant with God. (For more information on this, see Philippians 3:1-3; Colossians 2:10-11.)

Summary — A Different Gospel

1. Paul's immediate, decisive response to the false teachers and the manner of his rebuke teach us how to respond to false teaching that appears in the church. Distortion of the gospel of Christ is extremely dangerous, because an impure gospel loses its power to save and to instruct us in the way of Life (Acts 4:12; Rom. 10:9-10).

   In such instances, there is no room for compromise or concessions.

2. *Circumcision has never saved anyone!*

   Paul did not abolish circumcision, but he taught that it is not a requirement for the salvation of a Gentile, or indeed of anyone. Anyone circumcising his sons, or being circumcised himself with the idea that this will contribute to his salvation or that it is a prerequisite for being saved, is mistaken.

   The circumcision that saves is the one originating in the heart — in faith. Abraham was saved (justified by faith) while still uncircumcised. Let us examine the circumcision of our heart, because that is what determines our closeness to and our relationship with God (Dt. 10:12-21; Ezek. 36:25-31).

Distribution of Tasks

Galatians 2:6-10:

> ⁶*But from those who seemed to be something — whatever they were, it makes no difference to me; God shows personal favoritism to no man — for those who seemed to be something added nothing to me.* ⁷*But on the contrary, when they saw that the gospel for the uncircumcised had been committed to me,*

as the gospel for the circumcised was to Peter ⁸*(for He who worked effectively in Peter for the apostleship to the circumcised also worked effectively in me toward the Gentiles),* ⁹*and when James, Cephas, and John, who seemed to be pillars, perceived the grace that had been given to me, they gave me and Barnabas the right hand of fellowship, that we should go to the Gentiles and they to the circumcised.* ¹⁰*They desired only that we should remember the poor, the very thing which I also was eager to do.*

❝ **"For those who seemed to be something added nothing to me."** — Paul reinforces what he said in verse 2:

- **On the one hand,** his teaching of the gospel did not need man's affirmation, because he was commissioned by the Messiah Himself.

Remember!

Paul had studied the Law and the rabbinical commentaries all his life. He was thoroughly learned in the Bible, more than any of Jesus' disciples, most of whom had originally been fishermen! Until his encounter with the Lord, on the way to Damascus, all Paul had lacked was the understanding that Jesus was the Savior promised in the Law. Once this piece of the puzzle had been given to him, his understanding of the Bible and the full counsel of God was exceptionally comprehensive **(2 Cor. 12:1-15; Gal. 1:14; Phil. 3:1-11)**.

- **On the other hand,** the evident agreement of all the other apostles with Paul did confirm to his readers that he was speaking the truth. Now he was sure that he had not "run in vain" — that is to say, his labor among the Gentiles had not been wasted **(Gal. 2:2)**.

7—**8** **"The gospel for the uncircumcised had been committed to me."** — We know that Paul was called the apostle to the Gentiles. Here he explains that this was not his choice but the choice of Him **"who worked effectively in Peter for the apostleship to the circumcised,"** that is, the Spirit of God. In **Acts 22:17-21** Paul describes how Jesus appeared to him while he was praying in the Temple and commanded him: **"Make haste and get out**

of Jerusalem quickly. Depart, for I will send you far from here to the Gentiles."

In addition to this main mission, Paul was told to proclaim the gospel of Christ in the synagogues of the Diaspora Jews, in every place he came to in his travels **(Acts 9:15; 13:5; Rom. 1:16)**.

Can verse 7 be understood to imply that there is one gospel for the Jews and another gospel for the Gentiles? God forbid! There is **one** gospel: the same one Paul and Peter preached to both Jew and Gentile. In fact, the Galatians could corroborate the faithfulness of Paul's teaching by the fact that it was identical to what Peter preached **(Jn. 14:6; Acts 4:12)**.

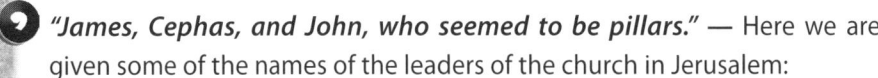 *"James, Cephas, and John, who seemed to be pillars."* — Here we are given some of the names of the leaders of the church in Jerusalem:

James — the half-brother of Jesus Christ **(Gal. 1:19)** and author of the epistle of James. He should not be confused with the disciple of Jesus, James son of Zebedee, the brother of the apostle John, who was murdered by Herod Agrippa because of his faith in Jesus **(Acts 12:2)**.

Cephas — the well-known disciple of Jesus, also called Simon or Peter.

John — the son of Zebedee. He is the apostle who wrote the Gospel of John, the epistles of John, and the book of Revelation.

These men were considered pillars of the church. They were faithful to the Lord and mature in their faith. The other believers recognized their authority as apostles of Jesus Christ, as well as the special standing of James as elder of the Jerusalem congregation. The doctrine they taught was accepted as the Word of God **(1 Cor. 12:27-28; Eph. 2:20)**.

 Note:

The book of Revelation decribes the heavenly Jerusalem. The city has 12 gates, and each gate is named after one of the tribes of Israel. The wall of the city has 12 foundations, named after the 12 apostles of Christ **(Rev. 21:14)**. This description brings to mind what Paul said when he called the apostles "pillars."

"They gave me and Barnabas the right hand of fellowship." — Giving the "right hand" here is a promise of full cooperation and support. The complete agreement between the apostles and recognized leaders of the church and Paul was the necessary confirmation of the authority and gospel of the "apostle to the Gentiles." According to this, the gospel that teaches that Jew and Gentile alike are saved by faith in Jesus Christ as Lord and Redeemer from sin, is the true gospel.

Help the Needy

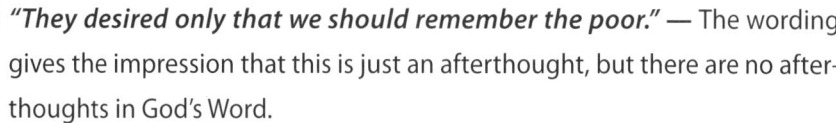

10 *"They desired only that we should remember the poor."* — The wording gives the impression that this is just an afterthought, but there are no afterthoughts in God's Word.

When the church was established, many of the believers were poor and needy. This verse is intended to remind all of us: "Teach the Word of God, but never forget to practice what Jesus taught about caring for the poor and needy!"

This lesson is taught throughout the Scriptures. God's gospel has always been expressed in the care for the needy, and it calls us to be sensitive to their needs. The Old Testament prophets told the Israelites that all their sacrifices and religious observance were not acceptable if they did not treat the foreigner well and if they did not care for the widow and the orphan.

The principle is the same in the New Testament: ***"Thus also faith by itself, if it does not have works, is dead"*** **(Jas. 2:14-26; see also Dt. 10:12-22; Isa. 1:10-20; Hos. 6:6; Mic. 6:6-8)**. The strength of a society is measured by how it treats its weakest members.

The elders of the church and the apostles in Jerusalem agreed not only with the content of the gospel Paul and Barnabas were preaching, but also with how they treated the poor. After all, Paul had come to Jerusalem with a contribution to help the needy in the church (**Acts 11:29-30**).

Constructive Criticism

What God has Joined Together, Let Not Man Separate. • • • • • • • • •

Galatians 2:11-14:

> ¹¹ *Now when Peter had come to Antioch, I withstood him to his face, because he was to be blamed;* ¹² *for before certain men came from James, he would eat with the Gentiles; but when they came, he withdrew and separated himself, fearing those who were of the circumcision.* ¹³ *And the rest of the Jews also played the hypocrite with him, so that even Barnabas was carried away with their hypocrisy.*
>
> ¹⁴ *But when I saw that they were not straightforward about the truth of the gospel, I said to Peter before them all, "If you, being a Jew, live in the manner of Gentiles and not as the Jews, why do you compel Gentiles to live as Jews?"*

Before we discuss these verses, let us remember that it was Simon Peter who preached about Jesus to the Gentile Cornelius and his household, after God had told him clearly: "Go to them to preach My gospel" (**Acts 10—11**).

God had proved to Peter that salvation is the same for both Jew and Gentile and is received through faith in Jesus alone. With his own eyes Peter saw the gifts of the Holy Spirit given practical expression in the lives of the believing Gentiles, in exactly the same way as with the believing Jews.

With this personal experience of Simon Peter in mind, let us now study verses 11-14:

⑪ *"Now when Peter had come to Antioch."* — Our attention is drawn to the church of believers in Antioch (today Antakia, Turkey). The unity and brotherhood between the Jewish and Gentile believers in this community caused their unbelieving neighbors to call them by a new name: Christians. That is to say, the most obvious characteristic of the church was their unity in Christ, that bridged all differences of background or nationality **(Acts 11:26)**.

12 *"He would eat with the Gentiles."* — After arriving in Antioch, Peter fellowshiped freely with his believing Gentile brothers, sharing their meals. He knew there was nothing wrong with that, because God had demonstrated and proven this truth to him **(Acts 10—11)**.

He understood his freedom in Christ and knew that Christ's death marked the beginning of a New Covenant — the same covenant Jeremiah had prophesied about **(Jer. 31:31-34)**. Simon Peter had heard Jesus say at the Last Supper that the cup He drank with them was "the New Covenant," sealed in His blood **(Mt. 26:26-29; Lk. 22:20)**. As a believer in Jesus, he was no longer subject to the Mosaic Law. Its commandments belonged to the previous covenant that had been fulfilled and was no longer binding upon him.

"Certain men came from James." — After some time, several Jewish believers in Christ arrived from the church in Jerusalem. From that moment, Peter began to avoid sitting around the same table as his Gentile brothers. He was afraid the visitors from Jerusalem would see him eating with the Gentiles and would disassociate themselves from him. He did not want to be considered as one who had abandoned the Law.

We must remember that in those early days of the church not all Jewish believers had fully understood that the New Covenant made the Old obsolete. For many of them, fellowship with believing Gentiles, in particular eating with them, was a gross transgression of the ordinances of the Law. They still viewed such behavior as spiritual lawlessness, as shaking off all that was most sacred to the Jew. Most of them had not yet seen with their own eyes that believing Gentiles received the same gifts of the Spirit as their Jewish brothers.

13 *"And the rest of the Jews also played the hypocrite with him."* — Peter's fear caused him to act wrongly, with dire results. Everyone respected him as a mature leader and an example in all things. When he distanced himself from his Gentile brothers, the rest of the Jewish believers in the church followed his example. Peter's guilt **(Gal. 2:11)** had now affected others.

There is no need to point out how the Gentiles felt! Here is the apostle Peter, behaving in a manner diametrically opposed to what he had taught them. After all, up to this point he had declared to the church:

- We all have **one** Messiah, and His blood atones for the sins of all men, whether they be Jew or Gentile.
- Christ's atonement has destroyed the wall of partition between Jew and Gentile. Together they now form **one** body.

In his personal testimony Peter had said:

"I saw with my own eyes how Gentiles were saved, and we rejoiced to see the power of God at work in them!"

"If therefore God gave them the same gift as He gave us when we believed on the Lord Jesus Christ, who was I that I could withstand God?"

And how had the Jewish believers in Jerusalem reacted to Peter's report?

When they heard these things they became silent; and they glorified God, saying: "Then God has also granted to the Gentiles repentance to life" (Acts 11:17-18).

This apostle, who had received one of the highest offices the Lord bestows on Earth, now rejected those believing Gentiles he had recently fellowshiped with and called brothers.

It is sad to see that in the same place where people began to call Gentile and Jewish believers by one name — Christians (**Acts 11:26**) — and regarded them as one united body, a respected apostle like Peter became guilty of discrimination and came near to causing serious division in the body of Christ.

What Will the Neighbors Say?

*The fear of man brings a snare, but whoever trusts in the L*ORD *shall be safe* (Prov. 29:25).

Peter's behavior is a reminder to us that we all need the grace of God and His power day by day and in every area of our lives, so that we will not fear the reactions of other people. Simon Peter wanted to please people at the expense of the purity of the gospel and with devastating consequences: discrimination against believers from a non-Jewish background, within the body of Christ.

> *Simon Peter had learned personally, several years earlier, that when he took his eyes off Jesus and allowed physical reality to influence him, he failed ("drowned" — Mt. 14:22-33). Here he falls once again into the same trap.*

Even Barnabas!

Paul writes in amazement that "even Barnabas" was negatively influenced by the bad example of Simon Peter.

Below is a list of the times Barnabas is mentioned in the New Testament. From these we get a picture of a faithful brother, stable in his faith, who stood up boldly for what he knew was right:

Portrait of Barnabas: Acts 4:36; 9:27; 11:22, 30; 12:25; 13:1, 2, 7, 42, 43, 46, 50; 14:12, 14, 20; 15:2, 12, 22, 25, 35, 37, 39; 1 Corinthians 9:6; Galatians 2:1, 9, 13; Colossians 4:10.

> *If fear of the reactions of others could cause such a mature believer as Barnabas to stumble, then how much more should **we** stand on guard and pray for strength to stand against similar pressures felt every day (Mt. 26:41; Mk. 14:38).*

14 A Painful Rebuke

When Paul saw what was happening, he knew he could not remain silent and acted decisively. It is not easy to criticize a friend and colleague, but Paul's example teaches us that faithfulness to God and His Word must come first.

It is certainly worth pointing out our friends' mistakes and reproving them, because in this way we can encourage them to stay in the way of God. But at the same time we must ask God for love and for wisdom to know what to say and **how** to say it (Gal. 6:1).

The wrong behavior of Simon Peter, Barnabas, and the other Jewish believers was no less destructive than the twisted teaching of the false teachers. The Gentile disciples observing them began to feel that they themselves were different and detached from the Jewish believers in Jesus, and somehow inferior. The message they received threatened to re-establish the wall of partition between Jew and Gentile — a partition that Jesus Christ had paid with His life to remove (Eph. 2).

The apostle Paul challenges Peter: *"If you, being a Jew, live in the manner of Gentiles and not as the Jews, why do you compel Gentiles to live as Jews?"*

In other words:

- "You, Peter the Jew, sat with Gentiles and shared their meals with them with no dietary restrictions. Why would you now force them to become as Jews and observe the commandments (which have become obsolete, since their purpose has been fulfilled) as a condition for fellowship with you?"

It is likely that the visitors from Jerusalem felt embarrassed by Paul's words, but he was right.

- "You yourself once gave an example of how Jews and Gentiles, after becoming a new creation in Christ, should fellowship together! Why do you now prevent that same fellowship?"

- "How is it possible that in the past you openly demonstrated the freedom you have as a believer in Christ, but now you are shackling Gentile believers by imposing commandments on them that are unnecessary to their salvation?"

Peter was indeed being a hypocrite and the consequences of his behavior threatened the unity of the body of Christ. It is no wonder that Paul was so vigorous in his criticism!

How to Accept Justified Criticism

1. Scripture does not record an immediate reaction of Simon Peter to Paul's rebuke.

2. When Peter wrote his epistles years later, he praised Paul and urged his readers to receive Paul's words as the doctrine of God **(2 Pet. 3:14-16)**. From this we infer that Simon Peter received the justified words of his colleague with submission and humility.

Note!

Paul did not bring this up with the Galatians in order to blacken Peter's reputation. We must remember that it was all written by the inspiration of the Holy Spirit. He handed down this truth to us, so that we might learn the principles of God's Word. The tests and trials our brothers in the faith went through are recorded, so that we can learn to behave in a worthy manner and to glorify the name of our Messiah even 2,000 years later.

We are all human, and we all experience the same fears Peter and the other apostles faced. Just as Peter failed in his testimony, we also could fail.

How can I as a Christian avoid that kind of failure in my life?

1. It is very important to acknowledge my personal weakness and my total, daily dependence on God's grace in order to keep my testimony as a Christian pure.

2. I must pray and ask God for daily strength and the ability to contend successfully against trials of faith and the traps of Satan's temptation.

3. I must study and memorize the Scriptures, so that I will always remember what kind of trials my brothers in faith went through in the past and how they managed to emerge victoriously.

4. I must make sure to remain in the company of believers who seek to obtain the prize defined for us in God's Word **(Phil. 3:14)**.

Summary —
Constructive Criticism

1. The apostle Paul does not mention the incident with Simon Peter for the purpose of slandering him, or glorifying himself at the expense of a fellow apostle (1 Cor. 3:5; Gal 6:1). He does it in order to:

   a. prove to the false teachers that his apostolic authority is recognized by the other apostles. The proof: Peter accepts Paul's justified rebuke without protest.

   b. show an example of standing up for the truth and the purity of the gospel. To attain this goal Paul was ready even to confront those who were regarded as the foundation pillars of the church.

2. Simon Peter's discriminatory behavior towards the Gentile believers was in blatant contradiction to the unity Christ obtained by His blood for Jews and Gentiles who believe in Him (Eph. 2:14).

3. When Simon Peter walked on the water, he began to sink when taking his eyes off Jesus and fearing the waves (Mt. 14:30). From his failure in Antioch we learn that taking our eyes off God's truth and attempting to please man will lead to failure.

4. The apostle Paul taught that in order to please God we must obey His written Word. We were created for God's glory (Eph. 2:10; 3:21; Ti. 2:14), and the only way to bring glory to Him is to walk according to His Word.

   That is our responsibility, and it is vital that we live up to it!

The Believer in Jesus and the Mosaic Law

The Relationship Between the Law and the Righteousness of God

Galatians 2:15-16:

> ¹⁵ *We who are Jews by nature, and not sinners of the Gentiles,* ¹⁶ *knowing that a man is not justified by the works of the law but by faith in Jesus Christ, even we have believed in Christ Jesus, that we might be justified by faith in Christ and not by the works of the law; for by the works of the law no flesh shall be justified.*

Most commentators agree that Paul's admonition, directed at Peter and the other Jewish brethren in the Antioch church, runs from verse 14 through to 21. He explains to them and to us, why Simon Peter's behavior is wrong in view of Scripture. His words help us understand what the attitude of the believer in Christ should be towards the Mosaic Law.

15 *"We who are Jews by nature, and not "sinners of the Gentiles."* — By now it has become crystal clear that Paul is addressing Jewish readers. He does not imply here that they are saved because of their nationality, but that, being Jewish, they grew up knowing the Scriptures (the Old Testament).

That is how they know the difference between permitted and forbidden, pure and defiled, just and sinful, holy and abominable. After all, the average Jewish person grows up with the standards of holiness that God established in the Law (**Rom. 2:17-20; 3:1-2; 9:4-5**).

The Gentiles, on the other hand, do not know the Law of God. They live in sin and abomination without even knowing that their deeds are wicked.

 **"Justified"**

"Man is justified by faith in Christ." — The one who is justified is considered free of the guilt of sin, pure and innocent. God took upon Himself the punishment that person deserved. In return for a sincere faith in Jesus as his Lord and personal Savior, God now considers him clear of guilt. This status gives him direct access to the Creator and the eternal right to be called a son of God.

The person who has thus been given righteousness seeks to fulfill the will of God and to observe all His commandments out of love and faith, not out of compulsion **(Rom. 5; 7:6; 8)**.

"Not Justified"

"Knowing that a man is not justified by the works of the law." — The apostle is saying: "Because we, as Jews, know the Law of God and its commandments, it is obvious to us that man is not justified by keeping the Law (since no one is able to keep all the commandments perfectly). As Jews who know the Law, **even we** have believed that our salvation and righteousness come through faith in Jesus alone and not by keeping the commandments." **(See also 3:10-11; Psalm 51:5; Ecclesiastes 7:20; Isaiah 53:6)**.

"That we might be justified by faith in Christ." — "So if **even we**, as Jews, are saved and receive the righteousness of God by faith in Jesus and not by keeping the commandments, why should we teach the Gentiles that they can be saved only after keeping all of Moses' commandments? Why demand of them something we can neither fulfill nor is it required of us? What is the point?" **(Acts 13:38-39; Rom. 1:17; 3:21-26; 8:3)**.

Salvation Before the Giving of the Law

"Knowing that." — Let us look back to the early days of Bible history, in order to understand why Paul takes it as a given fact that his Jewish brethren know. What did they know from the Old Testament that supports the apostle's argument?

Well then: Methuselah, Enoch, Noah, Abraham, Isaac, Jacob, Joseph, and Moses were all saved **before** the giving of the Law. Only the two latter men are actually "sons of Israel." Three of them were fathers of the nation, and the first three — although righteous in the eyes of God — were Gentiles. It follows that Gentiles and Jews alike are saved by faith in God who pronounces them righteous, independent of the Law — and this is the way it has been since creation.

 Salvation by faith in Jesus — before Jesus came into the world?

If salvation was given on the basis of faith **before** the Law was given, what kind of faith was it that saved our fathers? On the basis of what faith did God pronounce them not guilty, innocent, righteous?

Paul says that salvation has always been granted *"by faith in Jesus Christ"* **(2:16)**. How can that be? Jesus came to Earth as Messiah and Savior 2,000 years **after** Abraham!

The answer will become apparent as we get to know…

Almighty God — El-Shaddai

The Scriptures teach us of one God in whom, in a mysterious way, exist three entities, so that in God there is at the same time unity and plurality, while all along His absolute completeness is not being compromised.

The three Persons are:

1. **The Spirit of God / the Holy Spirit**
   (Gen. 1:2; 2 Sam. 23:2; Job 33:4; Ps. 51:11; 139:7-8; Isa. 63:10; John 14:16-26; 15:26; 16:7-15; Acts 5:32; 8:29; 13:4; 28:25; Rom. 8:11, 26; 1 Cor. 2:10-11; Gal. 5:22-23; Heb. 3:7).

2. **The divine entity man cannot see face-to-face and live**
   (Ex. 33:20);

3. **The divine entity man can see face-to-face**
   (Ex. 6:2-3; 33:11; Num 12:8; 14:14).

These three Persons in the one perfect God can be seen in **Isaiah 42:1; 48:16; 61:1-3; 63:8-10.**

The divine entity that man is not permitted to see is portrayed in Scripture as God the Father. The entity man may see is God the Son (**Ps. 2; Prov. 30:1-4; Mt. 28:18-20; Jn. 5:19-24**).

The Bible records many encounters between men and God. These are occasions when He came to Earth in the form of a man and talked with people face-to-face. The meetings served to strengthen the bond between God and the persons involved, because they came to know Him personally:

- In Genesis 17 God revealed Himself to Abraham as *El-Shaddai* — Almighty God.

- In chapter 18 God appeared to Abraham in the company of two angels, all three looking perfectly human.

- God told Moses very clearly: ***"I appeared to Abraham, Isaac, and Jacob, as God Almighty** [**El-Shaddai**]"* — that is, as the entity they could see and yet live (**Ex. 6:2-3**).

Since this divine entity whom people were allowed to see face-to-face in the days of the Bible was called El-Shaddai; and since the entity we are allowed to see face-to-face is also called the Son of God (**Jn. 14:9**), it follows that El-Shaddai is none other than **Jesus the Messiah**.*

Jesus is God (El-Shaddai), and as El-Shaddai He appeared to our fathers face-to-face. They apparently did not know Him by the name Jesus, but they knew that God who was talking to them face-to-face, El-Shaddai, was their Redeemer, their Savior, who cleanses them from sin and justifies them.

God did all this for them by His grace, not as a reward for their good deeds. See **Isaiah 63:8-10**: the "Angel of God's Presence" (lit. "the Angel of God's Face") is saving His people. From Exodus 33 we learn that "God's Presence" (lit. "God's Face") is El-Shaddai, the Messiah Himself.

---

* For a more detailed treatment of this subject see the book *Jesus in the Hebrew Scriptures* by Meno Kalisher. Available at www.foi.org

Abraham promised his son Isaac — by faith in El-Shaddai — that God would provide the burnt offering to be sacrificed instead of him (**Gen. 22:8; see also Isa. 53:6; 62:11; Zech. 3**).

The faith God requires of us is a sincere faith in Him — in God who took on flesh and blood and came to the world in order to save men from their sins.

- This is the faith that leads to salvation — for Jews and Gentiles alike.
- This is the faith that allows God to reflect His holiness in the life of the believer.
- This is the faith that saved Old Testament believers before the giving of the Law.
- Only he who has such faith is regarded as righteous in God's eyes.
- This is the faith that gives life — and therefore God's Word can say:

The Just Shall Live By His Faith

Through the inspiration of the Holy Spirit, the prophet Habakkuk proclaimed one of the most important principles of Scripture:

> *"The just shall live by his faith"* (Hab. 2:4).

We need to remember that Habakkuk said this towards the end of the first Temple period, at a time when the Law was still in effect.

Habakkuk's declaration proves that the principle of faith as the basis of righteousness and salvation was not foreign to the people of Israel. Faith saves and leads to the good works that are pleasing to God. That is to say — the righteous man keeps and does God's commandments by faith and in love to God, not in order to be justified or to earn His salvation.

Look...and Live

Even while the people of Israel were still in the desert, God taught them this crucial lesson.

Numbers 21:4-9:

> ⁴ Then they journeyed from Mount Hor by the Way of the Red Sea, to go around the land of Edom; and the soul of the people became very discouraged on the way. ⁵ And the people spoke against God and against Moses: "Why have you brought us up out of Egypt to die in the wilderness? For there is no food and no water, and our soul loathes this worthless bread." ⁶ So the LORD sent fiery serpents among the people, and they bit the people; and many of the people of Israel died.
>
> ⁷ Therefore the people came to Moses, and said, "We have sinned, for we have spoken against the LORD and against you; pray to the LORD that He take away the serpents from us." So Moses prayed for the people.
>
> ⁸ Then the LORD said to Moses, "Make a fiery serpent, and set it on a pole; and it shall be that everyone who is bitten, when he looks at it, shall live." ⁹ So Moses made a bronze serpent, and put it on a pole; and so it was, if a serpent had bitten anyone, when he looked at the bronze serpent, he lived.

The people of Israel complained against God. In return, He punished them by sending a plague of poisonous snakes that bit many in the camp — *"and many of the people of Israel died."* The people cried out to Moses. They confessed their sin and pleaded with him to intercede for them to God, so He would take away the snakes.

God answered Moses' prayer and commanded him to fashion a serpent of bronze and set it up on a pole so that everyone could see it. Whoever was bitten by a snake and looked to the bronze image — was saved and lived.

The lesson is clear:

Death was averted through lifting up one's eyes in faith, not by observing any ordinances of the Mosaic Law. Those who looked at the brazen serpent did not put their faith in the symbol set up on the pole, but in **God** — the only One who can save us from death. Whoever was bitten and tried to save himself by other means, died.

This instance of the bronze serpent in the desert is an excellent example of man's spiritual status before God.

Jesus Christ used this example in His talk with Nicodemus (Jn. 3), when He explained that He would be lifted up *"as Moses lifted up the serpent in the wilderness."* That is, Jesus came in order to die as the atoning sacrifice for our sins. Whoever looks to Him in faith — whoever believes in Him as God who came to Earth in order to pay the penalty of our sin with His blood — will be saved.

We learn the following truths from the events in the desert and from Jesus' talk with Nicodemus:

- We are **all** born with the blight of sin (Ps. 51:5; Isa. 53:6; Jn. 3:18-19).

- Whoever tries to rid himself of the effect of sin in his life by his own strength, by good deeds or by keeping the commandments, however commendable his efforts may be, will fail and remain with the guilt of his sin. When he dies his soul will go to hell. There he will suffer until the day of God's judgment, when he will be sent to the Lake of Fire for eternity (Lk. 16:19-31; Rev. 20:15).

- Whoever truly and sincerely believes that Jesus Christ is his Redeemer from sin and his Savior from all its consequences, will be forgiven. The "sting" called sin, the result of which is death and eternal banishment from God's presence, will be taken away from him (1 Cor. 15:55-57).

The believer is assured of forgiveness of sins and everlasting life in God's eternal Kingdom. All this, not because he is any better than others, but because God is faithful to His promises (Rom. 10:9-10).

The above lesson on salvation by faith raises an important question:

What Is the Purpose of the Law?

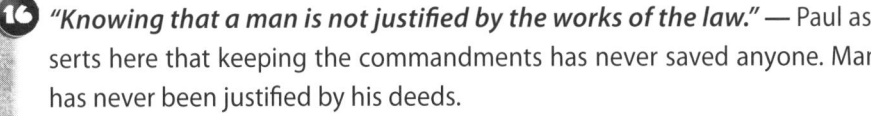

"Knowing that a man is not justified by the works of the law." — Paul asserts here that keeping the commandments has never saved anyone. Man has never been justified by his deeds.

"Knowing." — Why was Paul so sure that every Jew knew this fact? — Because this is what it says in Psalm 143:2: *"For in Your sight **no man** living is righteous."*

*If the commandments of the Law were not given in order to save people, why **were** they given?*

God gave the Law through Moses for several purposes.

1. In order to teach the people of Israel that God exists and is holy (**the Ten Commandments; Ex. 20**).
2. To define sin (**Rom. 7:7; Gal. 3:19**).
3. To make it clear that every person is a sinner and cannot have fellowship with the holy God, unless his sin is atoned for (**Dt. 27:26; Ps. 51:5; Eccl. 7:20; Isa. 53:6; 59:1-4; Rom. 3:19-20**).
4. To teach the people of Israel how to serve God as His representatives — as His witnesses to all other nations (**Ex. 19:5-6**).
5. To teach them that God is their Savior and that life is dependent on Him alone (**Rom. 3:21-28**).
6. To teach by symbolic elements about the Messiah who would save the people of Israel and those from among the nations who would believe in Him (**Gal. 3:23-25; 4:8-11; Col. 2:16-18**).

To put it simply: The Law was a mirror exposing sin, but it could not heal that deadly disease. The Law brought to light the spiritual illness of the human race, and it also pointed forward to the One who would bring healing, preparing the people for His coming.

The Tutor

The Law Moses received served as a kind of tutor to keep the people of Israel separate (or to use the biblical term, *holy*) from the other nations, as a chosen people walking in the path that would lead them to their Messiah (See commentary on chapter 3:23-25.)

A correct understanding of the Scriptures and obedience to the commandments of the Law would certainly keep the people holy and prepare them to meet Jesus their Messiah. Chapters 13 and 18 in Deuteronomy prepared the way so the people would receive the words of the prophets. Those in turn would guide the people in the way to the Messiah — Jesus. Also the rabbis realized that when they wrote, "The prophets did not prophesy except of the days of the Messiah" (Sanhedrin 99:1).

Over 2,000 years ago the Messiah did come and fulfilled all that the prophets had said about Him. The moment the people of Israel met Jesus, God required them to recognize Him, to submit to Him and to worship Him. Had they submitted to the Holy Scriptures instead of the authority of their rabbis (Mt. 23; Mk. 7), they would have recognized their Savior. They would have understood that from the moment He died, the Law (the tutor) ceased to be in effect — that is to say, all the symbolic elements in the Law that had pointed to the Messiah were now fulfilled. This is what Paul teaches in Galatians 3:23-25:

> ²³ But before faith came, we were kept under guard by the law, kept for the faith which would afterward be revealed. ²⁴ Therefore the law was our tutor to bring us to Christ, that we might be justified by faith. ²⁵ But after faith has come, we are no longer under a tutor.

Commandments That Have Expired — And Others That Have Not

Now that the apostle Paul has explained the relationship between the Law and salvation, let us continue to read and study what should be the believer's attitude toward the ordinances of the Mosaic Law.

Galatians 2:17-18:

> *¹⁷ But if, while we seek to be justified by Christ, we ourselves also are found sinners, is Christ therefore a minister of sin? Certainly not! ¹⁸ For if I build again those things which I destroyed, I make myself a transgressor.*

17—18 To put it more simply, the apostle is saying:

- At the death of Christ, the New Covenant promised by Jeremiah was established (**Jer. 31:31-34; Mt. 26:26-29; 1 Cor. 11:25-26; 2 Cor. 3:6**).

- Also at the death of Christ, the authority and validity of all the ordinances that foreshadowed Him or pointed to Him by symbolic means came to an end. From this point forward, no one is obliged to keep them, whether he be Jew or Gentile.

- Thus, if anyone was saved through faith in Christ and as a consequence stopped observing these ordinances — and if he later reverts to observing them — not because his freedom in Christ permits him this option, but because he thinks he ***must*** — then this person is saying three things:

1. All the ordinances of the Mosaic Law are still binding.

2. The atonement of Christ does not take away all my iniquities. It has not fully justified me in the eyes of God, and I am now perfecting my justification by keeping the ordinances of the Mosaic Law.

3. By placing myself once again under the authority of the ordinances, I declare that I sinned by stopping to observe them in the first place (*"I testify against myself as a transgressor"*). Jesus Christ caused me to stop observing the ordinances, therefore it is **He** who caused me to sin.

Woe to any behavior that conveys such a message!

Let us quote verses 17-18 again and add a bit of explanation:

"But if, while we seek to be justified by Christ"
> [justified by faith in the grace of God revealed in Christ Jesus and not by submitting to ordinances that are no longer obligatory]

"we ourselves also are found sinners,"
> [i.e., we go back to keeping the ordinances in order to perfect our salvation],

"is Christ therefore a minister of sin?"
> [does this mean that Jesus has caused me to sin by making me stop keeping ordinances I was still supposed to keep?]

"Certainly not! For if I build again those things I destroyed,"
> [i.e., if I return under the authority of ordinances that have been fulfilled by the death of Jesus Christ, that have fulfilled their purpose and therefore need no longer to be observed],

"I make myself a transgressor."
> [i.e., I work against the will of God and His plan, and I treat with scorn the salvation the Messiah has procured for me at the ultimate cost].

I will put My law in their minds and write it on their hearts (Jer. 31:33)

No Anarchy

The believer is no longer subject to the ordinances of the Law, but that does not mean he is free to do whatever he wants!

It is important to note that all those ordinances of the Mosaic Law reflecting the character and attributes of God continue to be observed by His children. We observe them not because we are subject to the Law but out of faith and love for God. The desire and the ability to keep these ordinances are given by the Holy Spirit who dwells within us. We have been given this promise in Romans 7:6:

*"But now we have been delivered from the law, having died to what we were held by, so that we should serve in **the newness of the Spirit** and not in the oldness of the letter."* (See also 2 Corinthians 3.)

The same God who forbids adultery in the Law (the seventh commandment), forbids it also in the New Testament (Rom. 13:8-10). Here He even goes further and considers sinful thoughts to be just as serious as the sinful act itself. Jesus warns in Matthew 5:28: "But I say to you that whoever looks at a woman to lust for her has already committed adultery with her in his heart."

Even as believers we continue to read and study the Law as part of God's Word. In this way we sharpen our understanding of His will and how He desires us to behave towards each other in this world, because *"**ALL** Scripture is given by inspiration of God and is profitable for doctrine, for reproof, for correction, for instruction in righteousness, that the man of God may be complete, thoroughly equipped for every good work"* (2 Tim. 3:16-17).

The Law is Good

From Paul's words we should learn the correct attitude towards the Law and the ordinances:

- God did not give bad ordinances. All His words are *"holy and just and good"* (Rom. 7:12.)
- The ordinances had a purpose, which was to bring us to Christ Jesus (Gal. 3:23-25.)
- As with anything that is completed when the goal is reached, the laws and ordinances of Moses have fulfilled their purpose since the death of the Messiah.

Summary — Salvation comes by faith:

1. From the beginning, people have been saved on the basis of faith in God, who atones for their sin Himself, and never because of their works. Even if in Old Testament times they did not know the Redeemer by His name Jesus, they well knew that El-Shaddai — the Person who revealed Himself to them face-to-face — was God Himself, and that He is the One who forgives their iniquities and carries them in His hands for eternity. That truth is already expressed in Isaiah 63:8-9: *"For He said, 'Surely they are My people, children who will not lie.' So He became their Savior. ⁹ In all their affliction He was afflicted, and the Angel of His Presence saved them. In His love and in His pity He redeemed them; and He bore them and carried them all the days of old."*

2. God's Law was given in order to preserve Israel and to teach the people to revere Him. The purpose of the Law was to expose sin, to emphasize our inability to conquer sin, and thus to teach us to look to the Redeemer — to Jesus Christ — and beg for His grace. It teaches that all men are convicted sinners and cannot be saved by their own strength or their own works.

> Whoever is intent on keeping the ordinances of the Law in the belief that this will save him, has misunderstood their purpose. For all his best efforts, he remains in his sin.
>
> 3. Receiving Jesus Christ as Savior and accepting His teaching as the Word of God does not contradict the Law: On the contrary, the Law was intended to lead us to precisely this decision. Our understanding of the Law of God is measured by our acknowledgement of Jesus as Lord and Savior and by our level of submission to Him. God requires these of all men — **of the Jew first** (Jn. 8:19, 42).

Dead to the Law

The apostle now shows us another aspect of the believer's relationship to the Law:

Galatians 2:19-21:

> *[19] For I through the law died to the law that I might live to God. [20] I have been crucified with Christ; it is no longer I who live, but Christ lives in me; and the life which I now live in the flesh I live by faith in the Son of God, who loved me and gave Himself for me. [21] I do not set aside the grace of God; for if righteousness comes through the law, then Christ died in vain.*

This is a firm declaration: "There is no way we can go back to keeping obsolete commandments in order to be considered righteous. The Messiah has fulfilled their purpose! We are severed from the ordinances of the Law that have been fulfilled — completely and forever. We have been justified by faith in Jesus who saves us from our sins."

12 *"For I through the law died to the law that I might live to God."* — What does this mean? Well, the Law taught me that I am a sinner, and as a sinner I am worthy of death. The Law presents God's demands and His standards of holiness and righteousness. Anyone honest with himself must realize that only the Creator can meet these standards. He will then agree with the statement of God's Word: No man in the world is so righteous that he can keep all the ordinances and not sin (**see Ps. 51:5; Eccl. 7:20**).

The Law also declares that whoever does not keep all the ordinances is under a curse (**Dt. 27:26: "Cursed is the one who does not confirm all the words of this law by observing them"** — **see also 2 Chr. 33:8**). The message of the Law to every human being is: "You are cursed because of your sin."

So what are we to do? — The Law goes on to teach: "All men are guilty before God and will never reach perfection by their own strength." We are all to strive for the perfection that comes by the grace of God alone, and not by virtue of our works.

If God were to judge mankind by the standards of justice — and justice alone — we would all be sentenced to death and be cut off from Him forever. But He does not wish to destroy us. By His grace He came to Earth as a man and died as a sin offering for mankind. The Messiah redeemed us. He took our death upon Himself and saved those who believe in Him from the punishment for sin (**Isa. 53**).

Conclusion

We now understand that the Law

- declares that I deserve to die for my sin.
- teaches me that my redemption from sin and death is a gift of grace from the Savior who gave His life for me.

Thus, my faith in Jesus as my Savior is the fulfillment of the Law. In my complete submission to Jesus Christ, the Law is perfected in me. I am dead to its requirements and now live for Christ.

The Law of Christ

Romans 8:2 reads: **"For the law of the Spirit of life in Christ Jesus has made me free from the law of sin and death."** — At the very moment I was saved by faith in Jesus Christ as my Savior, I was pardoned from the curse and separation from God, and I am now considered a new creation. **(See 2 Corinthians 5:17-21; Galatians 6:15-16).**

Since I am	●	a new creation,
I am subject to	●	a new law
within	●	a new covenant between me and God.

I am subject to the law of Christ who died for my sins and redeemed me from the punishment of death. This law of Christ is written in the Old and New Testaments, and it outlines a way of life that is holy, pure, truthful, and loving **(Mt. 5—7; Eph. 4:17-32; 1 Th. 4:1-12; 5:12-28; 1 Tim. 4—5).**

> ***God does not expect His children to achieve such virtues on their own. Therefore, life by the law of Christ is a life guided by the Holy Spirit who dwells within each believer, teaches him to understand God's Word and gives him power to obey it*** **(Jn. 14—16; 1 Cor. 3:16-17; 6:19-20; Gal. 5:22-23; Eph. 5:18-19).**

Living by the law of Christ is a way of life identical to that of the righteous men of the Old Testament, but with no obligation to those ordinances which Christ has fulfilled.

The apostle Paul elaborates on this principle in Romans 7:1-6:

> *¹Or do you not know, brethren (for I speak to those who know the law), that the law has dominion over a man as long as he lives? ² For the woman who has a husband is bound by the law to her husband as long as he lives. But if the husband dies, she is released from the law of her husband. ³ So then if, while her husband lives, she marries another man, she will be called an adulteress; but if her husband dies, she is free from that law, so that she is no adulteress, though she has married another man. ⁴ Therefore, my brethren, you also have become dead to the law through the body of Christ, that you may be married to another — to Him who was raised from the dead, that we should bear fruit to God. ⁵ For when we were in the flesh, the sinful passions which were aroused by the law were at work in our members to bear fruit to death. ⁶ But now we have been delivered from the*

law, having died to what we were held by, so that we should serve in the newness of the Spirit and not in the oldness of the letter. (See also Galatians 4:8-11; Colossians 2:11-23)

Crucified With Christ

20 *"I have been crucified with Christ; it is no longer I who live, but Christ lives in me; and the life which I now live in the flesh I live by faith in the Son of God who loved me and gave Himself for me."* — The apostle now exhorts the Galatians to look at his personal example in order to learn the **principle** (we can understand that to be part of his criticism of Peter): Life in accordance with Christ's teaching is a holy and pure life, guided by the Spirit of God who dwells within every believer. In chapter 5:22-23 Paul elaborates on the kind of life to be led by believers, in listing the qualities included in the fruit of the Holy Spirit.

The death of Christ on the cross proved to Paul that there is no hope of salvation by keeping the ordinances — by human strength — because if there was, then the Messiah would not have had to die. The death of Christ on the cross graphically demonstrates what punishment I deserve. But in His death He also gave me life and a glorious future.

"It is no longer I who live." — In other words: "When you see me living a life of purity and holiness in accordance with the will of God, know that this is not because of my own abilities or strength."

This statement is completely contrary to the understanding of religious Jews, both in Paul's time and in ours. As far as they are concerned, observance of the ordinances of Moses and the tradition of the Jewish sages is what stands between the people of Israel as the unique, Chosen People and their eradication by assimilation. To say, *We have been preserved and will continue to exist by the grace of God alone,* is foreign to the rabbinical way of thinking. What a pity that rabbinical Judaism tries with all its might to achieve spiritual perfection, but without the Spirit of God.

The apostle Paul teaches a different attitude. The fact that the believer in Christ is free from the dominion of the Mosaic Law does not mean he lives in a spiritual vacuum or outside of any spiritual framework to protect and guide him. When Paul tried to keep all the ordinances in his own strength, the Law defined him as a sinner worthy of death. Now, by Christ's atonement, Paul has received a new life, a life no longer his own but belonging to the Messiah. That is why he can say, *"It is no longer I who live."*

"But Christ lives in me." — Belonging to Christ is expressed by an absolute surrender **to the One who *gave* the Law.** The law of Christ is engraved on my heart (**Jer. 31:33**), and He Himself lives within me (**Jn. 14:20-21**). This is the only way I can live for God.

The apostle describes this in his epistle to the Ephesians 3:17-19: *"That Christ may dwell in your hearts through faith; that you, being rooted and grounded in love, ¹⁸ may be able to comprehend with all the saints what is the width and length and depth and height — ¹⁹ to know the love of Christ which passes knowledge; that you may be filled with all the fullness of God."*

"Christ lives in me" is another way of saying that the fullness of **God** dwells in me, as we read in Colossians 2:9-10: *"For in Him* [in Christ] *dwells all the fullness of the Godhead bodily; and you are complete in Him."*

If the fullness of God dwells in us, there is no reason we should desire to live a corrupt life (Rom. 6:1-6; 1 Cor. 12:13; Eph. 3:14-19; Col. 2:11-15).

Did Noah live a corrupt life? After all, in his days there **was** no written law of God! And what about Enoch, Abraham, Isaac, Jacob, or Moses? Who kept them holy if not the Spirit of Christ who lived in them? The Ten Commandments and the will of God were engraved on their hearts.

If El-Shaddai kept them before the giving of the Law, there is no doubt that He is able to keep me also, today. If this spiritual foundation was good enough for Noah and for Abraham, then it is good enough for me.

The believer in Jesus is free from any obligation to observe the ordinances that no longer have dominion over him, but he is in no way free of the obligation to live a life of holiness, purity, and truth as expressed in the Ten Commandments and the Sermon on the Mount (Mt. 5—7).

If I Can be Saved Through the Law, Who Needs a Messiah?

21 *"I do not set aside the grace of God; for if righteousness comes through the law, then Christ died in vain."* — If anyone has not yet understood what the apostle is saying, he gets a clear explanation in this verse: "If the Law was intended to save, then the death of Christ was not necessary. — Whoever thinks he can be saved by keeping the Law, is in fact saying that he does not need the grace of God."

If we look at this verse in context, the finger of accusation is pointed foremost at Peter and those who imitated his error. But the words of Paul are important also to us, the believers of today!

The Believer in the Messiah and Observance of Symbolic Ordinances

Note!

The apostle Paul does not forbid believers in Jesus to celebrate the Jewish holy days, does not free them from observing the biblical laws of family purity, and does not forbid them to keep symbolic traditions (as wearing the prayer shawl and donning phylacteries). There is nothing wrong with a believer in Jesus observing the Jewish holidays, or circumcision, or eating kosher (following the Jewish dietary laws). In fact, many believers (especially in Israel) use these and other ordinances that have been fulfilled in Jesus, teaching their children about the Messiah by means of these symbols.

A problem arises when believers in Jesus attribute a wrong significance to these ordinances:

- Whoever observes the Mosaic Law because he believes he has to — thinking that if he does not, his righteousness and even his salvation are endangered — proves that he has not understood the significance of Christ's death and the New Covenant.

- Whoever observes these ordinances out of a sense of duty, is obliged to keep them all perfectly. (See the emphasis in Deuteronomy on **"*all* the words of this law,"** Dt. 28:58-59; 29:29; 31:12-13; 32:46; 2 Chr. 33:8.)

- A Jewish believer pointing a finger at other believers who do not observe these now obsolete ordinances and accusing them of disassociating from their Jewish identity or contributing towards assimilation, simply exposes his lack of spiritual maturity and shows that he has not understood the Word of God in the epistle to the Galatians.

The Example of the Apostle Paul

Paul considers himself dead to the Law (Gal. 2:19). Next, he is going to clarify to the Galatians that the Law was a tutor that led them to the Messiah (3:23-25), and that since the coming of Christ we are no longer in need of the tutor — the Law.

> *If that is so, how can we explain Paul's actions in Acts 18:18 and 21:23-24?*

Acts 18:18: Paul shaves his head because he has taken a vow in accordance with the ordinances given in Numbers 6:2-5, 13-21.

Many commentators believe that in this way Paul expressed his thankfulness to God for keeping him safe through all the dangers and difficulties he had been exposed to during his travels, (See a partial list in 2 Corinthians 11:23-28.) Who has not heard stories of soldiers under fire, or of people who found themselves in immediate danger of death, who made promises to God at that moment?

On the one hand the apostle exercised his liberty to make a vow to God within the framework of the Law given to every Jew.

On the other hand we can be sure that Paul, as an apostle and a mature believer, knew how to make his vows conditional on the will of God (Jas. 4:13-15) and to avoid forbidden vows (Mt. 5:34-37; Jas. 5:12).

THE OCCASION

Acts 21:20-24: Paul is in Jerusalem. A rumor has spread among the thousands of believers in Jesus who are *"zealous for the Law,"* claiming that he is teaching the Jews of the Diaspora to abandon the Mosaic Law, not to circumcise their sons and to discard the traditions of Israel.

Since the elders of the church are concerned about a possible escalation in emotions and conflict to the point of bloodshed, they ask Paul to join four men who have taken vows and have now come to the Temple to shave their heads, as commanded in the Law. By joining them, Paul is to show to all those who criticized him, believers and unbelievers alike, that he does observe the Mosaic Law.

THE EXPLANATION

Regarding the accusations: Paul's doctrine never contained such teaching as he was accused of. He taught that the observance of the symbolic ordinances could not save and that salvation was by faith in Jesus Christ alone. He taught that the Messiah is the end purpose of the entire Law.

In joining the other four who had taken vows, he was not indicating that he placed himself under the authority of the ordinances. His actions were not contrary to his teaching in Galatians. As a Jew he had the freedom to act as he did — by personal choice and not by obligation.

Why did the apostle not decide to leave Jerusalem immediately, to return to the Diaspora and thus avoid conflict? After all, he had done just that in a similar situation in the past (Acts 9:29-30).

Because:

a. He submitted to the instructions of the elders in Jerusalem who wished to put out the fire of malicious slander against him.

b. He submitted to the leading of the Holy Spirit who had told him ahead of time that *"chains and tribulations"* were waiting for him in Jerusalem (Acts 20:23).

A Personal Opinion

This was an attempt to prove to both believers and non-believers in Jerusalem that Paul observed the ordinances just like everybody else. We do not know from the account in Acts 21 what the reaction of those same zealous believers was. But as far as the non-believers were concerned, this attempt was a failure. Paul, perhaps for the first time in history, came up against something that has become the norm in our day and age:

1. Paul's Jewish co-religionists saw him meticulously follow the Mosaic Law.
2. They recognized him to be a disciple of Jesus.
3. He was thrown out of the Temple in an act of physical violence (**Acts 21:26-30**).

Paul, the former Pharisee, was in effect told: "It does not matter how well you keep the ordinances or how hard you try to live as a Jew — ***you are not one of us!***"

It is important for believers today to understand this lesson:

On the one hand every Jewish believer in Christ has the right and the freedom to observe the ordinances of the Mosaic Law and the traditions.

On the other hand we must not deceive ourselves: what makes the difference in the end is the stumbling block of the cross. Those who receive Jesus will receive us; those who do not receive Jesus will not receive us, regardless of the way we dress, of what we observe or do not observe.

"***I do not set aside the grace of God.***" — Whoever believes in Jesus and insists that he is obliged to observe the ordinances of the Mosaic Law, simply has not understood the atoning death of Jesus Christ, the Son of God.

The mature believer knows that:

- **On the one hand** he is a sinner, who depends completely on the grace of God.

- **On the other hand** God attributes to him the righteousness and perfection of Jesus. He has been made perfect in Christ, and that perfection does not need any addition to please God. He is a citizen of heaven, and his identity is complete in Jesus (**Phil. 3:1-20**).

Summary of Chapter 2

1. Many of us say, *"I have been crucified with Christ,"* but how many of us truly understand and live out what is meant by the rest of the verse: *"It is no longer I who live, but Christ lives in me"* (Gal. 2:19-20)?

   - If Christ does indeed live in me, the inevitable result will be that I seek to obey His teaching — that I adopt the way of thinking of Jesus Christ (Phil. 2:5-18).

   - If Christ lives in me, then those around me must see the fruit of the Holy Spirit in my life (Gal. 5:22-23).

   We must remember at all times whom we have died with and who it is that lives in us now!

2. Whoever does not understand that the Law points us towards Jesus as our Lord and Savior — whoever does not understand that it teaches us to reach spiritual perfection by the grace of Christ alone — is reaching for an unattainable perfection. Whoever rejects the only atonement for sin that God in His grace has given to men, insists on being judged severely and condemned to the Lake of Fire for eternity.

Thanks be to God for His grace! Thanks be to Jesus Christ

— El-Shaddai —

who offered up His life for us and gave us eternal life.

Chapter 3

The Tutor, the Promise, and the Faith of Abraham

Introduction to Chapter 3

In chapters 1 and 2 Paul has established his authority as an apostle. He reminded his readers that he was appointed to this task by Jesus Christ Himself. The other apostles, without exception, recognized him as their equal in authority. Therefore, the message he brings is indeed God's message of truth.

The apostle has also proved that the teaching of the false teachers could only be a false doctrine!

Now he moves on to reprove the Galatians firmly and authoritatively for their behavior and their deviation from the truth.

In chapter 3:1-14 Paul re-emphasizes that righteousness comes by faith alone. While doing so he invokes:

1. The Galatians' personal experience (vv. 1-6);
2. The written Word of God (vv. 7-14).

Who Has Bewitched You?

Galatians 3:1-6:

> *¹ O foolish Galatians! Who has bewitched you that you should not obey the truth, before whose eyes Jesus Christ was clearly portrayed among you as crucified? ² This only I want to learn from you: Did you receive the Spirit by the works of the law, or by the hearing of faith? ³ Are you so foolish? Having begun in the Spirit, are you now being made perfect by the flesh? ⁴ Have you suffered so many things in vain — if indeed it was in vain?*
>
> *⁵ Therefore He who supplies the Spirit to you and works miracles among you, does He do it by the works of the law, or by the hearing of faith? — ⁶ just as Abraham "believed God, and it was accounted to him for righteousness."*

❶ *"Foolish!"* — The apostle calls them by a name given to someone who chooses the wrong way, even though the truth is right in front of him (**Lk. 24:25; 1 Tim. 6:9; Titus 3:3**). The Galatians' mistake was not due to limited intellectual ability, but to an irresponsible attitude to God's Word.

"Before whose eyes Jesus Christ was clearly portrayed among you as crucified." — Paul's visit in Galatia had served one sole purpose: the proclamation of the gospel — and at the center of that gospel stands the cross of Christ.

- Jesus Christ crucified is the end of the Law (**Rom. 10:4**).
- His death on the cross for the sin of man is the fulfillment of all the symbols in the Law and of all the Messianic prophecies in the Old Testament.
- Jesus Christ crucified is evidence that God is sovereign and His Word is truth.

- Jesus Christ crucified is the expression of God's victory over sin, Satan, and death.

Paul emphasizes the **crucifixion** of Jesus rather than His resurrection, because His death was the fulfillment of those ordinances of the Mosaic Law, which by their symbolism foreshadow Christ and His work. (More details on the central place of the cross in the gospel can be found in the commentary on Galatians 5:11 under the title "The Offense of the Cross.")

> *The moment of Christ's death on the cross marked the end of one thing and the beginning of something new. Here, by His spilt blood, the New Covenant promised by Jeremiah was ratified* (Jer. 31:31-34).

And as to the resurrection of Christ: It was the visual proof that the New Covenant indeed was established with His death.

The Comparison

The apostle now asks four questions:

A. *"Did you receive the Spirit by the works of the law?"*

>Paul points back to his readers' first experience in their life of faith. He is convinced that they have been saved, as they give evidence of the fruit of the Spirit (**Gal. 4:6**). But at this point they are under the influence of false teachers and have deviated from the way of truth.
>
>Every saved person in the churches of Galatia was able to testify of one thing: The Holy Spirit had begun to work in him from the moment he received Jesus Christ in faith, and not because of his observance of obsolete ordinances (**Rom. 10:17**).
>
>There is another fact that makes the question of verse two rhetorical, especially concerning the **Gentile** believers in the Galatian churches: Before they heard the gospel — whether from Paul or from another believer — they had not kept and were not even familiar with the commandments of the Law.

So the obvious answer is: "Of course, we tasted of the power of the Holy Spirit only from the moment we believed in Jesus Christ as our Savior."

B. *"Having begun in the Spirit, are you now being made perfect by the flesh?"*

"Dear brethren in Galatia, are you so ignorant as to think that you can begin the Christian life in faith (with the help of the Holy Spirit), and then reach spiritual perfection by observing ordinances (by the abilities of the flesh)? Can you see a precedence for that in the Scriptures? Does God prefer the circumcision of the flesh or the circumcision of the heart **(Dt. 10:16; Jer. 4:4)**? I think you are listening to the false teachers and not to the Law of God!"

The false teachers taught that observance of the ordinances of the Mosaic Law is a condition for salvation. There is no greater lie!

The apostle creates a clear distinction:

On the one hand: C o m m a n d m e n t s — dependence on the flesh and human ability.

On the other hand: P e r f e c t i o n — dependence on the Spirit of God and His unlimited power.

Just as the flesh is temporal, limited, and weak, so the commandments, being symbols foreshadowing the Messiah, are limited and temporal.

The Spirit of God, on the other hand, is eternal, perfect, and unlimited. It is He who comes to dwell in the person who puts his faith in Jesus **(Eph. 1:13)**.

In Galations 5:16-26 Paul draws a comparison between the "fruit of the flesh" and the "fruit of the Spirit." From his explanations it is clear beyond a shadow of doubt that the Galatians would do well to rid themselves of the false teachers with their deceptive doctrine and to adopt to themselves once again the Word of truth they had heard from Paul.

C. *"Have you suffered so many things in vain?"*

When the Galatians first believed in Jesus, each of them had personally experienced the power of God in his life. Before long they had suffered persecution from their opponents. They had stood firm in their affliction and remained faithful to their Lord, because they knew that their faith was based on truth **(Acts 14:21-23)**. Now Paul asks them: "Have you suffered all that in vain?"

The writer of the epistle to the Hebrews deals with a similar issue. From the first, his readers had stood firm in the truth of the gospel, even at the cost of heavy persecution and suffering. But as time went by, socio-religious pressure caused them to waver:

Hebrews 10:32-39:

> *[32] But recall the former days in which, after you were illuminated, you endured a great struggle with sufferings: [33] partly while you were made a spectacle both by reproaches and tribulations, and partly while you became companions of those who were so treated; [34] for you had compassion on me in my chains, and joyfully accepted the plundering of your goods, knowing that you have a better and an enduring possession for yourselves in heaven. [35] Therefore do not cast away your confidence, which has great reward. [36] For you have need of endurance, so that after you have done the will of God, you may receive the promise:*
>
> *[37] "For yet a little while, and He who is coming will come and will not tarry. [38] Now the just shall live by faith; but if anyone draws back, My soul has no pleasure in him."*
>
> *[39] But we are not of those who draw back to perdition, but of those who believe to the saving of the soul.*

D. "Therefore He who supplies the Spirit to you and works miracles among you, does He do it by the works of the law, or by the hearing of faith?"

"When you received the gospel of Jesus Christ you witnessed many signs and miracles confirming the truth of the message. What do you think was the reason for the wonders of God you experienced — a perfect obedience to the commandments, which most of you had never heard of before, or receiving Jesus in faith?" **(Acts 14:3, 8-11)**.

"Which of you has received the Holy Spirit by observing commandments?" — Paul is so amazed that his readers have been tempted into a wrong path that he asks: **"Who has bewitched you?"** (v. 1). "It does not make sense that you would choose to go back to keeping commandments which are no longer valid."

Any honest Galatian believer could have only one answer: "We did not receive the Holy Spirit by keeping the commandments but 'by the hearing of faith.'"

And that brings us to

The Faith of Abraham

Paul summarizes **part one** of this chapter (vv. 1-6: "The Galatians' personal experience") by a declaration that should stop the mouth of his opponents:

"Just as Abraham believed God and it was accounted to him for righteousness." — "Dear Galatians, I have not invented a new principle. What I am teaching you was known already to Abraham, the father of the Jewish nation.

"The false teachers claim to know the mysteries of the Mosaic Law but, please, remember what the Law teaches: Abraham, the father of the nation, was justified by faith even before the giving of the Law and while he was still uncircumcised **(Gen. 15:6)**.

"If God did not demand anything else from him other than his faith in order to be considered righteous (= saved), then He will not demand anything more from you than faith in Jesus as your Lord and Savior from sin!"

Another Comparison in Galatians:

The Gospel of Christ		The "Gospel" of the False Teachers	
3:6-9	The faith of Abraham	3:10-14	The curse
3:15-18	The testament (eternal)	3:19-22	The temporariness of the Law
3:23-29	Heirs	4:1-7	Slavery, bondage

"And works miracles among you" (v. 5)

Note! The Christians in Galatia, as in many other churches that were established in the days of the apostles, were witness to supernatural signs and miracles which God performed in order to confirm the gospel. But the Word of God does not teach that these supernatural signs **must** accompany salvation, or that they prove its genuineness.

> *Today, just as then, the presence of the Holy Spirit in the Christian will produce the fruit of the Spirit (Gal. 5:22-23). This fruit — likeness to Christ — is the mark of the saved person, not signs and wonders! Salvation itself is a miracle of God.*

Since the Word of God has been written down and the Scriptures are widely distributed and available in our day, anyone can examine the truth of Scripture in light of its historical fulfillment.

Even today God performs miracles and signs — not because He has to, but by grace and according to His sovereign will, because He wants us to know Him and to draw near to Him. However, we must not expect God to do miracles in order to confirm His Word, as He did in the days of the apostles.

Salvation by Faith

Galatians 3:7-14:

> [7] Therefore know that only those who are of faith are sons of Abraham. [8] And the Scripture, foreseeing that God would justify the Gentiles by faith, preached the gospel to Abraham beforehand, saying, "In you all the nations shall be blessed." [9] So then those who are of faith are blessed with believing Abraham.
>
> [10] For as many as are of the works of the law are under the curse; for it is written, "Cursed is everyone who does not continue in all things which are written in the book of the law, to do them." [11] But that no one is justified by the law in the sight of God is evident, for "the just shall live by faith." [12] Yet the law is not of faith, but "the man who does them shall live by them."
>
> [13] Christ has redeemed us from the curse of the law, having become a curse for us (for it is written, "Cursed is everyone who hangs on a tree"), [14] that the blessing of Abraham might come upon the Gentiles in Christ Jesus, that we might receive the promise of the Spirit through faith.

In this passage Paul uses Old Testament Scripture to explain one of the central doctrines of the Word of God: **the principle that salvation comes by faith alone**.

In verses 2 and 5, as you will remember, Paul asked a question of life and death:

Observance of the Law's commandments — or the hearing by faith?

- Which of the two leads to righteousness in the eyes of God?
- Which of the two leads to salvation?
- Which of the two leads to the indwelling of the Holy Spirit?

And now we are given two detailed answers to this crucial question: one in verses 7-9 and the second in verses 10-11:

 Answer #1: *"Those who are of faith are sons of Abraham."*

Galatians 3:7-9:

> ⁷*Therefore know that only those who are of faith are sons of Abraham.* ⁸*And the Scripture, foreseeing that God would justify the Gentiles by faith, preached the gospel to Abraham beforehand, saying, "In you all the nations shall be blessed."* ⁹*So then those who are of faith are blessed with believing Abraham.*

7—9 God promised Abraham that in him **all the nations of the world** would be blessed. To underscore this promise He repeated it several times (**Gen. 12:3; 18:18; 22:18**).

- *"Abraham believed God and it was accounted to him for righteousness."* — The promise of blessing was given to Abraham on the basis of his faith and belief in God, even before he was circumcised (**Gal. 3:6; Rom. 4:10**).

- *"So then those who are of faith are blessed with believing Abraham."* The blessing of Abraham for us depends on genuine faith in Him who has promised, not on the observance of ordinances of the Mosaic Law that were given hundreds of years after the promise (**Gal. 3:9**).

- *"God would justify the Gentiles by faith."* — Because the blessing is promised to *"all the families of the earth"* and *"all the nations,"* the condition on which it can be received is the same for Jew and Gentile: a faith such as Abraham had (**3:8**). (See also **Romans 11:16**, where Abraham's faith is likened to the root of an olive tree.)

Abraham was saved while still uncircumcised, therefore his faith is an example of salvation for all men — Jews and Gentiles alike. Whoever shares Abraham's faith, whether he be Jew or Gentile, shares also in the blessing that was given to Abraham, which is **salvation** (Rom. 2:28-29; 4:11, 16; Gal. 3:29).

The spiritual sons of Abraham receive the blessing of Abraham: Salvation!

"Abraham is Our Father!" (Jn. 8:39) — Is He Really?

7 *"Only those who are of **faith** are sons of Abraham."* — In other words, whoever believes as Abraham did, is considered by God to be a son of Abraham. He is entitled to the same righteousness God attributed to Abraham because of his faith.

Verse 7 sounds very disturbing to most Jewish ears. Not only in Paul's day were there many Jews who believed that their nationality — the physical descent from Abraham — was an entrance ticket to heaven! Also today there are many who confidently claim: "All Israel has a part in the world to come" (Sanhedrin, tractate 11:1) whenever the subject of life after death crops up.

But what does Galatians 3:9 tell us?

9 *"So then those who are of faith are blessed with believing Abraham."* — Salvation is received by **faith**. This condition is the same for both Jew and Gentile. (See also Galatians 3:28-29.)

⑧ Pay Attention to the Scripture — God's written Word! That is what we read in verse 8: *"And the Scripture, foreseeing that God would justify the Gentiles by faith, preached the gospel to Abraham beforehand, saying, 'In you all the nations shall be blessed.'"* — Whatever is in the Scriptures is God's Word **to us!** Just as God spoke to Abraham, so He speaks to us today through the Old and the New Testaments (**Jn. 10:35; 2 Tim. 3:16; 2 Pet. 1:20-21**).

Answer #2:   *"No one is justified by the law in the sight of God."*

Galatians 3:10-11:

> ¹⁰ *For as many as are of the works of the law are under the curse; for it is written, "Cursed is everyone who does not continue in all things which are written in the book of the law, to do them."* ¹¹ *But that no one is justified by the law in the sight of God is evident, for "the just shall live by faith."*

⑩ — ⑪ In these verses the apostle exposes the absurdity of the claim that man can reach perfection by keeping the commandments.

The Law was meant to show

    on the one hand   the righteousness and holiness of **God**;

    on the other hand   **man's** sin and limitations.

In doing so it was intended to cause man to run to God, his only Redeemer. The Law reflects our problem perfectly — like a mirror — but it is unable to heal. However, it can do more than a mirror: the Law shows us the way to our Healer and describes how we are to be healed.

You Have Not Kept It — You Are Cursed!   ●   ●   ●   ●   ●

⑩ *"Cursed is everyone who does not continue in all things which are written in the book of the law, to do them"* (**Dt. 27:26; 28:58-59; 2 Chr. 33:8**). — The Law is not a random collection of commandments that can be divided up into those that are important and those that are secondary. They all come together as a single package. Each individual commandment is important and serves to complete the next one. Failure to perfectly keep just one of the ordinances means complete failure at keeping the whole Law.

Whoever seeks to attain holiness and righteousness by keeping the commandments is actually trying to do the impossible, and thus he ends up accursed.

11 *"The just shall live by his faith."* — That is what God proclaims through the prophet Habakkuk **(Hab. 2:4)**. This proclamation stresses the relationship between righteousness and faith, and it was coined at a time when all the ordinances of the Mosaic Law were in effect — hundreds of years before the First Coming of Christ.

Conclusion:

- Jews and Gentiles who receive Jesus Christ in faith are considered by God to be sons of Abraham. They have been justified by their faith and are "holy" in the eyes of God.

- On the other hand, Jews who reject Jesus as the One who has fulfilled the Law and rely on their own ability to keep commandments, place themselves in grave danger: God may apply to them the maledictions spelled out in Deuteronomy 27:15-26 simply because there is no man — Jew or Gentile — who is able to perfectly keep all the commandments of the Law.

Godly People in the Old Testament ● ● ● ● ●

In Old Testament days, was the godly believer obliged to keep all the commandments of the Law?

Of course! But the keeping of the commandments was motivated by his love for God and His Word and not by a desire to be saved by perfect observance. No man has ever kept the commandments perfectly — none except one: Jesus, when He first came to Earth as Messiah.

> **Jesus Christ, before His atoning death, was subject to the Mosaic Law, just like any other Jew (Gal. 4:4).**

Did Jesus observe the commandments in order to be saved — in order to perfect His righteousness before His Father in heaven? No! But because the commandments of the Mosaic covenant were in effect, obedience to God was expressed by keeping all of them with a pure heart (Dt. 6; Hos. 6:6; Mic. 6:6-8). This is exactly what Jesus did, and He is the only one in history who did it down to the very last detail. Jesus was speaking the truth when He said: *"I did not come to destroy but to fulfill"* (Mt. 5:17).

All commandments that were a type, foreshadowing Christ and His work, lost their authority the moment the Messiah established the New Covenant in His blood (Jer. 31:31-37; Mt. 26:26-29; 1 Cor. 11:25). But although the New Covenant replaces the Mosaic covenant, there is no difference in the standards of purity, righteousness, and holiness that God requires of us.

Even so there ***is*** a difference: Whoever believes in Jesus does not act in his own strength but has the presence of the Holy Spirit in his body. By the power of God who dwells in him he can live by the moral standards God requires. The motives for such a life are love for God and the desire to obey Him and bring glory to Him — not a need to accumulate "credit" in righteousness (Rom. 7:6; 2 Cor. 3; 5).

12 *"Yet the law is not of faith, but 'the man who does them shall live by them.'"* — The Law demands exact adherence to clear instructions. It measures a man by the level of his obedience to the commandments and promises life to those who keep all of them. It says: "Whoever keeps all my ordinances perfectly — is righteous" **(Lev. 18:5)**. Galations 3: 12 reads in other words: "In theory it is possible to be justified by keeping all the commandments with no need for faith."

Is there a contradiction here to what is said in the previous verse (11)? Not likely, as the Word of God never contradicts itself.

The question is:

Is there anyone who is able to keep all the commandments perfectly?

The Word of God establishes that there is **not**. It states clearly: *"For there is not a just man on earth who does good and does not sin"* (Eccl. 7:20). (See also Psalm. 51:5; 53:3; Isaiah 53:6.) Only God Himself can keep all the commandments perfectly. This again demonstrates the purpose of the Law: It shows us the perfection and holiness of God, so that we might clearly realize our weakness and absolute dependence on Him.

Narrowing It Down

Some Basic Principles

Galatians 3:13-14:

> ¹³*Christ has redeemed us from the curse of the law, having become a curse for us (for it is written, "Cursed is everyone who hangs on a tree"),* ¹⁴*that the blessing of Abraham might come upon the Gentiles in Christ Jesus, that we might receive the promise of the Spirit through faith.*

In this one-sentence summary Paul defines the status of believers in Jesus. By doing so, he also precisely defines the condition of all who have **not** been redeemed by the perfect atoning sacrifice of Jesus Christ.

Since no man is able to keep all the ordinances of the Mosaic Law perfectly, none will ever be able to free himself from the curse the Law promises to sinners! Thus, the righteousness of any man — whether Jew or Gentile — must be founded on something **outside** the Law (Isa. 53:4-6).

The Principle of Substitution

13 *"Christ has redeemed us from the curse of the Law."* — In other words, Jesus Christ has redeemed us from the sentence of the Law that determines: *"Cursed is everyone who does not continue in all things which are written in the book of the law, to do them."* He voluntarily took that curse upon Himself, and as a result He also incurred the punishment reserved for a man cursed under the Law: hanging on a tree (or "on wood"), i.e. crucifixion **(Dt. 21:23)**.

The prophet Isaiah lived at a time when all the ordinances of the Mosaic Law were in effect and the Temple with its sacrificial system was functioning. Even so, he proclaims in chapter 53 that it is the perfect Servant of the Lord — and not some sacrificial bull or sheep — who bears the sins of men. Isaiah describes the Messiah who pays with His life — in the sinners' place — for their transgressions.

The prophet says: *"The chastisement for our peace was upon **Him**, and by His stripes we are healed"* **(Isa. 53:5)**. In other words, the Messiah took our punishment in our place. The price paid by the Son of God satisfied the requirements of God the Father. As a result He grants every believer the righteousness of Christ and His peace. The curse has been lifted from the believer. He is no longer subject to the wrath of God **(1 Th. 5:9; Rev. 3:10)**.

Galatians 3:13 and Isaiah 53 are all about the **principle of substitution**: the Messiah takes my punishment by sacrificing His life. When I believe in Him, He gives me in return His righteousness, life, peace, purity, and guiltlessness.

"He who is hanged is accursed of God"
(Dt. 21:23)

Hanging as a form of punishment was not foreign to the people of Israel. It is mentioned in the Old Testament as *lehokia*, which refers to the hanging of an offender after he has been put to death.*

It is interesting that in the two recorded instances in which people

---

* See Keil-Delitzsch on Numbers 25:4.

were hung in this manner *"before the Lord,"* their death served to remove a curse from the entire nation:

1. **Num. 25:1-4, 9:** The people of Israel "began to commit harlotry with the women of Moab," and because of this sin a plague broke out. At this point God instructed Moses: *"Take all the leaders of the people and hang the offenders before the Lord, out in the sun,"* and He promised that the immediate result of this action would be *"that the fierce anger of the Lord may turn away from Israel."*

2. **2 Sam. 21:1-14:** Here we read of seven descendants of King Saul who were *"hanged before the Lord"* in order to atone for the sin of Saul against the Gibeonites. In this instance also, the punishment the entire people of Israel was suffering (famine) was lifted following the hanging, and *"God heeded the prayer for the land."*

In **Deuteronomy 21:22-23** we have instructions from God on how to hang the body of an offender on a tree, after he has been put to death. Later, Joshua follows these instructions in the case of the king of Ai (Josh. 8:28-29). Commentators and scholars agree that in each of the cases mentioned in the Old Testament the guilty was put to death before he was hanged.*

The public display of the body was considered extremely shameful. It gave physical expression to the curse of God on the dead man.

In contrast to the Jews in Old Testament times, who hanged the body of the offender after he had been put to death, the Gentiles used the actual hanging to end the offenders' lives. Thus, the punishment of crucifixion was introduced to the Middle East by Alexander the Great of Macedonia.**

---

* See Keil-Delitzsch on Deuteronomy 21:22-23 and Joshua 8:29.

** *"The Siege of Tyre"* in Quintus Curtius Rufus, *Historiae Alexandri Magni*, iv. 2-4.
J. E. Atkinson and J. C. Yardley (comm., trans.): *Curtius Rufus — Histories of Alexander the Great*, Book 10 (Oxford; New York: Oxford University Press, 2009; Clarendon ancient history series).

In the year 90 B.C. King Alexander Yanai (a Jewish king of the Hashmonean Dynasty) crucified 800 Pharisees who had encouraged rebellion.*

Crucifixion was a common form of capital punishment among the Romans, and was considered particularly humiliating and contemptible.**

In light of the above, the priests' and Pharisees' demand that Jesus be crucified was not something unheard of. Hanging on a tree was a recognized punishment for those who blasphemed God or brought a curse upon their people — and as far as they were concerned, Jesus was guilty of both. Whether the hanging was carried out in accordance with the instructions of the Law — after putting the offender to death, or whether one used the Roman crucifixion — the outcome was the same: a contemptible death that expressed the curse of God on the culprit.

---

* Flavius Josephus: *"The Wars of the Jews or History of the Destruction of Jerusalem."* Translated by William Whiston, on Project Gutenberg (www.gutenberg.org).

** Wikipedia, "Crucifixion."

The Principle of Equality Before the Creator: ● ● ● ●

The Blessing of Abraham — Also for the Gentiles

14 *"That the blessing of Abraham might come upon the Gentiles in Christ Jesus."* — As mentioned earlier, God never gave us several ways by which to be saved, only one unique way, which is through the blood atonement of His Son, Jesus Christ, on the cross. **(See John 14:6; Acts 4:12.)**

The same principle that rejects the observance of the commandments as a condition of salvation has also rejected the idea of Jewish national preference. Now the Gentile may stand next to the Jew, both may ask in faith for Jesus' atonement, and both will receive salvation and the seal of the Holy Spirit.

This is the blessing of Abraham, in which Gentiles now share as well: **Salvation**, which includes ● the righteousness of God ● the indwelling of the Holy Spirit in the believer ● eternal life with God in His eternal Kingdom ● the child of God status.

The gifts and the calling of God are irrevocable (Rom. 11:29)

Note!

The fact that the blessing of Abraham was also intended for the Gentiles does not alter the original purpose of the people of Israel, which is — to be *"a kingdom of priests and a holy nation"* (Ex. 19:6).

This mission will be fulfilled when Jesus Christ returns to Earth to reign over the world from Zion.

The surviving remnant of Israel — all Jews who will live through the Great Tribulation — will serve the Messiah in holiness and purity and will inherit the full borders of the Promised Land in peace (Ezek. 47:13-23; Zech. 8:23; 13:8-9).

While many Gentiles do share in the blessing of Abraham (salvation), this glorious truth does not serve to incorporate them into the people of Israel. They do not become part of the 12 tribes, the descendants of Abraham, Isaac, and Jacob, and they therefore have no promise of an inheritance in the land of Israel, neither today nor during Christ's thousand-year-reign on Earth.

In the final state — God's eternal Kingdom — **Jesus Christ** will be the inheritance of all those who have been saved (Col. 1:12; 3:24; Heb. 9:15; 1 Pet. 1:4).

"That we might receive the promise of the Spirit through faith." — Here too we read of a promise (an inheritance) but not an earthly one. All those who are saved — both Jew and Gentile — will inherit the promised Holy Spirit.

The Law and the Promise

Galatians 3:15-18:

> [15] Brethren, I speak in the manner of men: Though it is only a man's covenant, yet if it is confirmed, no one annuls or adds to it. [16] Now to Abraham and his Seed were the promises made. He does not say, "And to seeds," as of many, but as of one, "And to your Seed," who is Christ. [17] And this I say, that the law, which was four hundred and thirty years later, cannot annul the covenant that was confirmed before by God in Christ, that it should make the promise of no effect. [18] For if the inheritance is of the law, it is no longer of promise; but God gave it to Abraham by promise.

The apostle now continues his argument:

- Salvation has always been rooted in faith.
- The Mosaic Law with all its commandments was never intended to change this principle.
- There is no way to change it, and trying to do so would, in fact, be illegal.

15—18 In these verses Paul describes the uniqueness of the covenant God made with Abraham. He emphasizes that there is no doubt his descendants will eventually receive their full inheritance, because God has given His word.

15 The apostle addresses his readers as "brethren," to make it clear that his hard words so far have not been rooted in hatred or a desire to cut off the believers in Galatia. On the contrary, he writes the epistle out of love for them and a deep desire that their spiritual lives should glorify Christ.

A Last Will and Testament Cannot Be Altered

From what Paul writes it is understood that there were voices claiming: "The Law given hundreds of years after the Abrahamic Covenant altered or amended the promises made to the father of the nation."

The apostle explains that while the Law is important, it was neither able nor intended to amend God's promise to Abraham. Its objective was altogether different from that of the Abrahamic Covenant.

"Though it is only a man's covenant...no one annuls or adds to it." — To demonstrate that the covenant of Moses cannot change those conditions that were fixed in the Abrahamic Covenant, Paul brings an example from life: A **will** — a signed testament of someone who has died — can never be changed (Heb. 9:17, *"For a testament is in force after men are dead, since it has no power at all while the testator lives"*).

Upon establishing a fact on which everyone agrees, the apostle describes Abraham's covenant as a will. No commandment that comes after it can add or detract anything from its promises.

From here we can ascertain that the covenant of Moses was neither a replacement for, nor an improvement on the Abrahamic Covenant. It consisted of something else.

The Seed of Abraham — the Messiah

16 *"Now to Abraham and his Seed were the promises made. He does not say, 'And to seeds' as of many, but as of one, 'And to your Seed,' who is Christ."* — The reference here is to God's promise to Abraham in Genesis 22:18, that all the nations of the earth would be blessed in his seed.

The Seed God speaks of here is the Messiah. When looking at the genealogy of Jesus Christ recorded in the Gospel of Matthew, we see that it begins with Abraham, emphasizing the fact that Jesus is the Seed of the promise (Mt. 1:1).

The Nature of the Abrahamic Covenant

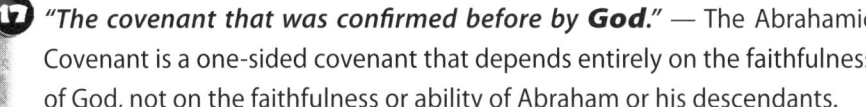 *"The covenant that was confirmed before by **God**."* — The Abrahamic Covenant is a one-sided covenant that depends entirely on the faithfulness of God, not on the faithfulness or ability of Abraham or his descendants.

This we learn from the account in Genesis 15: God commands Abraham to slaughter the sacrificial animals needed for the ratification of a covenant and to divide each one into two halves. Immediately afterwards he causes a deep sleep to fall on Abraham. In the end it is only God Himself who passes between the animal parts, thereby sealing the covenant.

In other words: only one of the parties "signed" the covenant between God and Abraham — God Himself! He is the sole guarantor for its implementation. Now we are able to establish beyond a shadow of a doubt:

 Since this covenant stands or falls with God's faithfulness to His promises, it can never be broken!

Thus the law of commandments that came hundreds of years later — a covenant that depends on both parties to fulfill its conditions — cannot alter, improve, or contradict any of the promises of God to Abraham, in the same way that a last will and testament cannot be altered after the testator's death.

 *Conclusion:*

The Abrahamic Covenant is the basis of salvation by faith. The law of commandments that came later on cannot alter that. Salvation of man has always been the result of faith in God who saves. — It does not depend on keeping the Law or belonging to the nation of Israel. After all, Abraham was saved while he was still an uncircumcised Gentile!

*"The law, which was **four hundred and thirty years later**, cannot annul the covenant that was confirmed before by God in Christ, that it should make the promise of no effect."* — About 645 years passed from the time God made His covenant with Abraham in Genesis 12, to the day the Law was given. That is, if we start counting from the year Abraham left Haran **(Gen. 12:4)**, i.e. 2090 B.C. to the giving of the Law on Mt. Sinai in the year 1445 B.C.

Is Paul wrong about the dates?

N o ! The promise of blessing to Abraham was repeated to his descendants as well: to Isaac **(Gen. 26:24)** and to Jacob **(Gen. 28:13-15** / 1928 B.C.). The latest recorded reconfirmation of God's covenant to Jacob is in **Genesis 46:2-4** (1875 B.C.), just before Jacob went down to Egypt. Calculating from that point, 430 years passed from the time the covenant was applied to Jacob and his sons, to the date the Law was given on Mt. Sinai (1875-1445 = 430).

18 *"For if the inheritance is of the law, it is no longer of promise."* — The apostle Paul supports what he said earlier by another appeal to logic:

If the promise of God is based on the Law, then fulfillment of the promise depends on *our* ability to keep the commandments:

1. If the inheritance is the Kingdom of God — there is no way we will ever get to see it, because no one is able to keep all the commandments **(Gal. 3:10)**.

2. If the inheritance is the land of Israel with the borders defined in God's promise — there is no way the people of Israel will ever get it or be able to hold on to it, since no nation is able to keep all the commandments of the Law perfectly.

*"But God gave it to Abraham by **promise**."* — God promised the inheritance to Abraham in a unilateral covenant. By this He made it clear that fulfillment of the promise depends on God's power alone, not on man's ability. Anyone who desires the complete and blessed inheritance of God must have a faith like Abraham's.

The Promise of God to the Seed of Abraham

● **The promise of the land:**

   a. **The extent of the borders** — In **Genesis 15:15-18** God promises that the land, from the river of Egypt to the Euphrates, will be given to the seed of Abraham, and that his descendants will fill the land until they are too numerous to be counted. (**See also Genesis 12:5.**)

   b. **The eternality of the covenant** — In **Genesis 17:7-8** God promises Abraham that the land will be given to his seed as *"an everlasting possession."*

● **The promise of closeness to God:**

   In **Genesis 17:8** God includes another promise, declaring that He will be the God of Abraham's seed after him — to everyone.

As of today the people of Israel, the physical descendants of Abraham, inhabit the land of Israel, but their borders are very narrow compared to those promised them. In central areas of the land lives a nation that demands ownership of a portion of their inheritance, with the support of most of the world. From the area of Lebanon and all the way to the Euphrates we see nations whose guns and missiles are aimed at the cities of Israel. So it follows that the promise of God to Abraham has not yet been fulfilled completely.

Those are the facts.

And what is the conclusion
from what we have just studied in the epistle to the Galatians?

The people of Israel have not obtained their full inheritance and do not enjoy all the blessings God promised. That is because they do not share in the faith of Abraham but rely on:

- physical descent from Abraham and the fathers of the Jewish nation.
- keeping the ordinances of the Mosaic Law by their own strength.

As long as the people of Israel reject Jesus their Messiah, attempt to hold on to their inheritance by might and military superiority, and base their righteousness on the observance of the commandments, they can only expect wars and destruction.

In other words, our dismal situation today reflects our remoteness from God (Lk. 19:41-44).

The Faithful Remnant

On the other hand, the Word of God is full of descriptions of a time when the remnant of Israel will dwell in the Promised Land *"from the river of Egypt to the river Euphrates."* This remnant will be the physical descendants of Abraham who also share the faith of the father of their nation (**Ezek. 45-47**).

The prophet Daniel (**7:27**) teaches us that the day will come when their full inheritance from God will be given to the people of Israel as an everlasting gift, unlike the situation today where they occupy only a portion of their inheritance and fight hard to hold on to it. This will happen at the beginning of the Millennium, the thousand-year reign of Jesus Christ on Earth.

In the inheritance given to the remnant of Israel — to those who survived the Great Tribulation and are saved — there will finally be peace.

Isaiah 11:6-9:

> ⁶ The wolf also shall dwell with the lamb, the leopard shall lie down with the young goat, the calf and the young lion and the fatling together; and a little child shall lead them. ⁷ The cow and the bear shall graze; their young ones shall lie down together;

and the lion shall eat straw like the ox. ⁸ The nursing child shall play by the cobra's hole, and the weaned child shall put his hand in the viper's den. ⁹ They shall not hurt nor destroy in all My holy mountain, for the earth shall be full of the knowledge of the Lord as the waters cover the sea.

Summary — Salvation by Faith:

- Paul asks: "What brought you the wonders of the Holy Spirit — keeping the commandments or faith, in Jesus as Lord and Savior?" Faith, of course!

- He proves that the promises God gave to Abraham because of his faith are like a will that cannot be breached. The commandments of the Mosaic Law could not and were not intended to change, update, or contradict any of the promises of God to Abraham.

- The salvation of Jew and Gentile depends on faith in Jesus alone. This is the way it was for Abraham. Since the Law did not change this truth, salvation is by faith also today.

- The apostle mentions the inheritance promised by God to Abraham and his seed. Since only the seed of the Messiah will enjoy the full inheritance, each and every one of us should examine his heart: Who is Jesus to me? Is He God who took on flesh and blood? Do I believe that the Lord Jesus died as an atoning sacrifice for my sins and rose from the dead? (See Galatians 3:29.)

The Physical Versus the Spiritual in Galatians 3

In the present chapter we meet various "sons of Abraham" who gain different kinds of inheritances, and it is vital that we know to distinguish between them:

- the spiritual sons of Abraham *and* - the physical descendants of Abraham
- the spiritual inheritance *and* - the physical inheritance

1. The spiritual sons of Abraham

Galatians 3:7:

"Those who are of faith are sons of Abraham."

This group of people is comprised of saved Jews and Gentiles. (See verse 8.)

Galatians 3:14:

Their inheritance is *"the promise of the Spirit,"* the Holy Spirit given to every believer at the moment he is saved.

2. The physical sons of Abraham

Galatians 3:18:

"God gave [the inheritance] to Abraham by promise."

Abraham himself never inherited the land. So the promise continued to his physical descendants through Isaac, the son of promise (Heb. 11:9). These descendants are the people of Israel.

The inheritance of the people of Israel is the land that God promised them within the borders specified in Genesis 15:18-21.

3. The Seed of Abraham

Galatians 3:16:

"He does not say, 'And to seeds,' as of many, but as of one, 'And to your Seed,' who is Christ."

Also the Messiah is the seed of Abraham — in both the spiritual and the physical sense.

The inheritance of the Messiah is defined in Hebrews 1:2, where He is called *"heir of all things."* His inheritance, then, is the entire creation (Ps. 2; 110; Mic. 5:2; Mt. 28:18-20).

What Purpose Does the Law Serve?

Galatians 3:19-20:

> ¹⁹ *What purpose then does the law serve? It was added because of transgressions, till the Seed should come to whom the promise was made; and it was appointed through angels by the hand of a mediator.* ²⁰ *Now a mediator does not mediate for one only, but God is one.*

Now that the apostle Paul has established that:

1. The giving of the Holy Spirit is not a result of the believer keeping the commandments (vv. 1-5).

2. The commandments of the Law did not alter the principle of righteousness and salvation coming by faith alone (vv. 6-9).

3. Whoever tries to base his salvation and righteousness on keeping the commandments perfectly, remains under the curse (vv. 10-12).

We should not be surprised if any thinking person, especially any Jew, should ask:

> *So why **did** God give the Law to the people of Israel after making a covenant with Abraham?*

The answer of the apostle will help us decide how we as believers should stand regarding the commandments:

 "The law ... was added because of transgressions." — So the Law was to deal with sin. How? Paul explains this further in **Romans 7:1-13** (especially v. 5). **Romans 7:7** states that: *"I would not have known sin except through the law. For I would not have known covetousness unless the law had said, 'You shall not covet.'"*

So then, the Law

1. teaches us about God's characteristics and His will. Everything (both thought and deed) that opposes the holy nature and will of God is sin.

2. was intended to define sin and the consequences of sin, how God treats sinners and how we should deal with sins (**1 Tim. 1:8-11**). The knowledge of what God hates and what He loves helps us decide what we should reject and what we should accept.

3. shows man that he cannot save himself by his own strength and is in desperate need of a Savior.

4. was not given to cure man from the disease of sin but to point him to the remedy for sin — the atoning Messiah.

What follows is this:

- In the covenant with Abraham God made a promise that cannot be earned, but can only be received by faith.

- Later on the Law was given to the descendants of Abraham, so that they would know how to conduct their lives in a way appropriate to the people of God. The apostle explains this more fully in chapter 4.

Let us continue reading in verse 19.

"***Till** the Seed should come to whom the promise was made.*" — Paul stresses the **impermanence** of the Law, which was to be in effect only until a certain person would come.

 Who is "the Seed to whom the promise was made"?

The answer was already given in verse 16. There we read that the promised Seed is Jesus Christ (**Gen. 22:18**). Therefore:

- When Jesus Christ died, the law of commandments ceased to be in force. In His blood and atoning death He established the New Covenant that was foretold by Jeremiah (**Jer. 31:31-34; see also Mt. 26:28; 1 Cor. 11:25**).

"It [the Law] was appointed through angels by the hand of a mediator." — When is a mediator necessary? When there is no contact between the giver and the receiver. When God gave the Law at Mt. Sinai, He forbade the people to draw close to the mountain. Moses was the mediator (**Ex. 19—20**), and from the Scriptures we learn that the angels were also involved in the event. (**See Acts 7:38, 53; Hebrews 2:2.**)

 *"Now a mediator does not mediate for **one** only."* — That is, a mediator is used when it is necessary to liaise between two or more parties. Moses was the mediator between God and the people of Israel.

"Now a mediator does not mediate for one only, but God is one." — Unlike what we have just said about the covenant at Sinai, God did **not** use a mediator in His covenant with Abraham (**Gen. 15**). God Himself passed between the parts of the sacrifice, and He prevented Abraham from passing. God thereby not only became the sole signatory to that covenant, He even "signed" it personally.

In other words, Paul proves the superiority of the Abrahamic Covenant in that it was given directly and not through a mediator.

- The Mosaic Covenant, which was given hundreds of years later, was not intended to replace it.
- The Mosaic Covenant was temporary. It remained in effect only until the Seed came, who is the Messiah.

An additional question arises from what has been said so far:

 Is there a contradiction between the Mosaic Law and the Abrahamic Covenant?

The apostle answers this question and continues to define the limitations of the Law:

Galatians 3:21-22:

> [21] *Is the law then against the promises of God? Certainly not! For if there had been a law given which could have given life, truly righteousness would have been by the law.* [22] *But the Scripture*

> has confined all under sin, that the promise by faith in Jesus Christ might be given to those who believe.

㉑ *"Is the law then against the promises of God? Certainly not!"* — There is no contradiction between the Mosaic and the Abrahamic covenants. The Law was never intended as a means to save man.

"For if there had been a law given which could have given life" — If it had been possible to keep the law perfectly and to be justified by it, then Jesus' sacrifice would have been unnecessary (**Jn. 14:6; Acts 4:12; Gal. 2:21**).

> **God promised that we could come to Him by faith, and the Law does not contradict this principle** (**Dt. 30; Rom. 10:9-10; Heb. 11:6**).

㉒ *"But the Scripture has confined all under sin."* — The Word of God teaches us very clearly that:

- All creation is under the curse of sin (**Gen. 3; Dt. 27:26; Rom. 8:19-21**).
- All men are sinners (**Ps. 143:2; Rom. 3:9-20, 23; 11:32**).
- Sin separates between us and God (**Isa. 59:2**).
- *"The wages of sin is death"* (**Rom. 6:23**).

In addition to teaching these principles, Scripture also set up the sacrificial system. The latter served as a visual reminder of the death threat hanging over every created being because of sin. The symbolism of the sacrifices was intended to remind people over and over: "Salvation from death is only by the grace of God and not by your own works!"

"That the promise by faith in Jesus Christ might be given to those who believe." — If all creation is under the curse of sin, then the way out of sin's vicious cycle must be provided by a sinless factor **outside** of creation — greater than creation — by God Himself.

The Law points to God — to the Messiah — as the only One who can take sin away once and for all, and that only by means of faith in Him (**Isa. 53; Heb. 7—10**).

In other words:

- The Law — like a mirror — shows you the truth about yourself.
- The mirror cannot heal you. All it does is show you exactly what the problem is: You are a sinner — and the wages of sin is death.
- The cure is given by a doctor, not by the mirror **(Jas. 1:23)**. That is why the Law points you to Jesus Christ — the only One who can give you eternal life. **(See Romans 3:19-31.)**

*"The promise given to those who **believe**."* — The apostle describes a wonderful hope:

Since the Seed of promise **(v. 16)** is Jesus Christ — son of David, son of Abraham, son of God — He will share the blessings of the promise with the believers — with everyone, with no distinction between Jew and Gentile. **(See verse 29.)**

- At God's appointed time the remnant of the Jewish people — **the physical seed of Abraham** — will receive the Messiah in faith, following which they will inherit the entire Promised Land. In the Kingdom of Christ, they will finally be true to their calling as a nation of priests. The starting point for this fulfillment will be the return of Jesus to Earth following the *"time of Jacob's trouble"* — the Tribulation **(Ezek. 47-48; Hos. 2:14-23; Rom. 11:26)**.

- Believing Gentiles — **the spiritual seed of Abraham (Gal. 3:7)** — will also be a part of the Kingdom of Christ. They will obey the will of God and enjoy the blessings of the Kingdom in the same measure as their Jewish brothers in faith **(Isa. 65—66; Ezek. 45—47; Dan. 7:27; Zech. 14:16-21; Rev. 19—20)**.

The apostle mentions *"the promise given to those who believe"* in order to support his claim that salvation is built on faith in Jesus and does not depend on perfect observance of the ordinances of the Mosaic Law.

Note:

During the 1,000 years of the Messiah's reign on Earth, there will also be believers in His Kingdom who had been taken up to heaven. All the saved of the Church Age will return with Jesus to Earth with a new body that cannot be affected by sin. All citizens of the Kingdom of Christ who have that new body — both those of the Jewish nation and those who were saved from among the Gentiles — will reign with Christ in His thousand-year Kingdom (**Zech. 14:5; 1 Cor. 15:50-58; 1 Th. 4:13-18; Rev. 5:10; 20:6**).

The Tutor

Now the apostle describes the temporary nature of the commandments of the Mosaic Covenant and of the role they fulfill with yet another picture.

Galatians 3:23-25

> [23] *But before faith came, we were kept under guard by the law, kept for the faith which would afterward be revealed.* [24] *Therefore the law was our tutor to bring us to Christ, that we might be justified by faith.* [25] *But after faith has come, we are no longer under a tutor.*

23–25 The Law was the tutor (Greek: *pedagogos*), a kind of schoolmaster that was to guide and teach the people of Israel in the ways of God. If the people had adhered to the direct verbal meaning of the Law:

- Their faith in God would have been strengthened.
- Their moral behavior would have reflected God's principles.
- They would have come to know Him as God who is sovereign, holy and pure.
- They would have realized that it is not in man's power to overcome sin and to present himself pure before God.
- Seeing the endless chain of sacrifices whose blood had to be poured out for men's sins, they would have realized that this symbol points to a future Savior.

- On the basis of this understanding they would have prepared themselves for the coming of the Messiah — Jesus Christ — who would save them once and for all from sin.

The authority of the commandments — the tutor — ended when the Messiah Jesus died as the ultimate sacrifice for sin and sealed the New Covenant with His pure blood. At this point the commandments had fulfilled the purpose for which they were given.

The authority the Law once had now belongs to Jesus Christ.
(See also 2 Corinthians 3; Hebrews 3:1-6; 9:23—10:18.)

In these three verses (**Gal. 3:23-25**) the apostle uses the word faith four times in order to underline the order of priorities. Every time he says faith he means Jesus Christ. In order to illustrate Paul's intention, let us read the verses with the name *Jesus* instead of the word *faith:*

> ²³ *But before **Jesus** came, we were kept under guard by the law, kept for **Jesus** which would afterward be revealed.* ²⁴ *Therefore the law was our tutor to bring us to Christ, that we might be justified by **Jesus** .* ²⁵ *But after **Jesus** has come, we are no longer under a tutor.*

Note!

- Whoever claims to keep the Law but at the same time rejects Jesus as Messiah, has not understood the purpose of the Law (Jn. 8:19, 42).

- Whoever studies the Law properly and strives to meet its requirements, will desire to receive Jesus as Lord and Savior from sin.

25 The apostle Paul says that the believer is no longer under the dominion of the Law. This raises the question:

What purpose then does the Law have for the past 2,000 years, ever since the coming of Jesus?

1. Just as the Law pointed to the Messiah and directed men to Him in the past, so it does today. All the commandments related to sacrifices, to holiness, to the priests and their work, to the Tabernacle and later the Temple — all of them foreshadow Christ (**Heb. 9:23-26**).

   When a believer today learns the symbolism contained in the Law's commandments,

   a. his faith is strengthened, because he sees how Jesus has fulfilled all the symbolic elements of the Law. The Law proves to him that he believes in the right Messiah — the true one.

   b. he discovers, while studying the symbolic elements, more details of the greatness, the glory, the holiness, and the divinity of the Messiah.

2. The educational value of the Law remains. The descriptions of events, portraits of believers and of sinners, the many details of the Creator's involvement in human history and in the life of the individual — all these were given us to learn from. From the picture that is drawn we can see God's plan of salvation and learn of His attributes and His expectations of man. This dimension of the Law is still in effect.

"We are no longer under a tutor." — This is a sentence every Jewish reader struggles with. It raises another crucial question:

Does that mean that I am no longer obliged to keep commandments such as "Do not steal" or "Do not commit adultery"?

No! This is certainly not what it means!

All the moral commandments were given to show us how to live according to God's standards of morality and holiness. They show us God's nature and eternal attributes, and since God never changes, these commandments are inseparable from any covenant He makes, including the New Covenant.

That is to say, I am not under the authority of the Law, *but I am under the authority of the holy God who* **gave** *the Law.* (**See Romans 8:1-17.**)

This means that

Everyone Is Under Someone

- We have learned that we are not under the dominion of the Mosaic Law, but nevertheless we are *"not ... without law toward God, but under law toward Christ"* (1 Cor. 9:21; see also Gal. 6:2; and the "law of liberty" in Jas. 1:25, 2:12).

- We have learned that no man on Earth is able to meet the requirements of the Law of God — even if it is defined as the *"law of Christ,"* that is, the laws of God in the New Covenant. Whoever tries to keep the Law of God by his own strength, discovers that he is *"in the flesh"*: His sinful nature and his weaknesses render him unable to please God.

- But to the believers, the apostle says: *"You are not in the flesh but in the spirit"* (Rom. 8:9).

And since we, as disciples of Jesus, are *"in the spirit"* — i.e. under His dominion — we should briefly mention here

The Role of the Holy Spirit

Keeping the law of Christ becomes possible for the believer because:

- The Holy Spirit dwells within him (1 Cor. 3:16).

- The Holy Spirit is a private tutor of the Word of God to each believer (Jn. 16:13; 1 Cor. 2:6-10).

- The Holy Spirit is the power that enables each believer to do the will of God: *"Who works in you both to will and to do for His good pleasure"* (Phil. 2:13). (See also John 14—16; Romans 7:6; 2 Corinthians 5:11-21.)

- The Holy Spirit changes the believer so that he hates sin and loves the righteousness and holiness of God (Jn. 16:8.)

- The Holy Spirit gives the believer the wisdom, faith, and willingness to confess sin in order to remain in pure fellowship with God and with his brothers in faith (**Gal. 5:22-25; 1 Jn. 1:6-9**).

The believer has the right to observe symbolic elements of the Law. For instance, there is nothing wrong in observing the Feasts of the Lord (the holy days of Israel — Lev. 23:2) or to eat only kosher food. Living among our people and knowing that our witness is important we must always keep two facts in mind:

1. We are free to keep this or that commandment of the Mosaic Law by choice, but it is not our duty to do so.
2. The justification or godliness of a believer is not thrown in doubt if he does not observe certain ordinances of the Mosaic Law.

In our community of believers here in Jerusalem we celebrate the biblical feasts while making sure to place Jesus Christ at the center of every event.

Summary — What Purpose Does the Law Serve?

Paul defines and explains the purpose of the commandments so that believers in Jesus would know how to stand in regard to them. He wants them to understand that:

- The commandments were not intended to save, and salvation has never depended on perfect observance of the ordinances of the Law.

> The Law was a tutor whose purpose was to keep and guide the people of Israel according to divine principles and to prepare them for the coming of the Redeemer — Jesus Christ.

We Are no Longer Under the Tutor's Authority

Every believer who sticks to the literal meaning of God's Word and says, *"We are no longer under a tutor"* (Gal. 3:25), has to deal with…

A Variety of Claims

 **"The Law will never be changed!"**

… *Response A:* The New Testament teaches that the Law **will** in fact change.

From the first days of the church the opponents of Christ raised what seemed to them a serious accusation: *"We heard him (Stephen) say that this Jesus of Nazareth… will change the customs which Moses delivered to us"* (Acts 6:14).

In Galatians 3 we learned that this accusation was actually true in two respects:

1. *"The Law… was added because of transgressions, **till** the Seed should come to whom the promise was made"* (3:19). In other words: The Law was an addition intended to deal with sin. Its validity was limited from the start to the coming of the Redeemer who saves from sin — Jesus Christ. In this sense, the coming of the Messiah **did** change the Law.

2. The accusation against Stephen was not that Jesus would **cancel** the laws but that He would *change* them — therefore:

The believer is no longer under the authority of the Law, but he is not without boundaries and discipline. He is God's child, the Holy Spirit dwells within him. As a son he willingly places himself under the will of his heavenly Father. Whoever believes in Jesus belongs to his Lord in a New Covenant that was sealed by the blood of Christ. He obeys the will of God by the help of the Holy Spirit who dwells within him (**Rom. 7:6; 1 Cor. 3:16-17; 2 Cor. 3**).

This transition

- from obedience to the written letter **in order** to obtain salvation, depending on my own ability,
- to obedience that is the **fruit of my salvation**, which is made possible by the help of the Holy Spirit,

certainly does constitute a change to the Law.

Response B: Even the rabbis teach that the Law will change.

As a second response to the common claim that the Law will never be changed, it is worth mentioning what rabbinical Judaism says about the changes to the ordinances of the Mosaic Law, or a clarification of the Law's commandments, by the Messiah.

"The Law of Messiah" According to Rabbinical Judaism

1. Rabbi Yehuda Chayun, in his book *Otzrot Acharit HaYamim* (*Treasures of the Last Days* — in Hebrew only) under the heading "Commandments will be abolished in the future," collects quotations from many rabbis who state that the Messiah will abolish certain commandments.

   Rabbi Chayun quotes from the commentaries of famous authorities such as Maimonides (the Rambam), Shlomo Ben Aderet (the Rashba), Asher Ben Yechiel (the Rosh); the Tur (an important halachic code, compiled by Rabbi Yaakov ben Asher) and the Shulchan Aruch, the code of Jewish Law.

In the mishnaic tractacte VaYikra Rabba, in Yalkut Shimoni and others, Jewish sages comment that the Messiah, at His coming, will change the Torah, or at least certain laws will be abolished or changed.*

2. Rabbi Menachem Brod, a senior rabbi of the Chabad movement in Israel, writes in his Hebrew article, "The Torah of the Messiah,"** that one of the most prominent innovations in the days of the Messiah will be in the area of Torah knowledge.

Rabbi Brod quotes (among others) the Rambam (Maimonides): "For in those days [of the Messiah] knowledge, wisdom and truth will be increased in the world. That king who will arise from the descendants of David will be even wiser than Solomon and will approach the level of Moses our Teacher in prophecy, and he will therefore [be able to] teach the people the ways of God" (Mishneh Torah — Hilchot Tshuva [The Laws of Repentance], chapter 9:9).***

The Rambam says further: "The Jews will therefore be great sages and know the hidden matters" (Mishneh Torah — Sepher Shoftim [The Book of Judges], Hilchot Melachim [The Laws of Kings], chapter 12:8).****

The Jewish sages reached this conclusion from the words of the Lord in Isaiah 51:4: **"Listen to me, My people; and give ear to Me, O My nation: For law will proceed from Me, and I will make My justice rest as a light of the peoples."** (Parallel verses: 2:3; 11:9-10; 12:4-6; Mic. 4:1-2.) And about this it is written in Yalkut Shimoni

---

*   Taken from the Hebrew website www.aharit.com.
**   www.ascent.co.il/?CategoryID=303&ArticleID=497.
***   In English at: http://www.panix.com/~jjbaker/MadaT.html — quoted from last paragraph of chapter 9.
**** In English at: http://www.panix.com/~jjbaker/rmbmesia — quoted from last paragraph of chapter 12.

(Isa. 26; Remez 429): "In the future, God will sit...and expound a new Torah which will be given through Messiah."

Rabbi Brod infers: "From all this we can see that in the days of Messiah the knowledge and the wisdom of the Law will increase and be thought of as a 'New Law.'"

Under the heading "Hidden Secrets" Rabbi Menachem Brod continues: "The 'New Torah' to be revealed by the Messiah is divided into two parts:

1. *Revelation of the mysteries of the Torah.* Today we study the revealed portion of the Torah, but our understanding of its mysteries is miniscule. In the days of the Messiah the inner secrets of the Torah will be revealed in abundance, so that it will be considered a 'New Torah'.

2. *Changes and new interpretations in the laws of the Torah.* The Midrash describes how we will eat the Leviathan and the giant beast: 'How will the Leviathan and the giant beast (shor habar) be slaughtered? The beast will gore the Leviathan with its horns and tear it up, and the Leviathan will tear the beast with its fins.' The Midrash asks: 'How could that be a kosher form of slaughter?' and answers that in those days there will be a 'Renewal of Torah', according to which such a slaughter will be kosher."

.... ***Response C:*** Also the Old Testament teaches that the Law will change.

The Law of Christ
According to the Scriptures

Now that we have read samples of what the rabbis say about the "Torah of the Messiah" — let us see what the **Word of God** says about the *law of Christ*:

1. **Jeremiah 31:31-32:**

   > ³¹ *Behold, the days are coming, says the L*ORD*, when I will make a new covenant with the house of Israel and with the house of Judah —* ³² *not according to the covenant that I made with their fathers in the day that I took them by the hand to lead them out of the land of Egypt, My covenant which they broke.*

   The change in the Law is clear here. God tells the people of Israel:

   - "In the past I made a covenant with you that depended on you keeping the Mosaic Law."
   - "You broke that covenant by failing to keep the commandments of the Law."
   - "Now I am making another covenant with you — a new one. Keeping it will depend solely on Me, not on you."

   And then Jeremiah lists the differences between the Old and the New Covenant — between the Law that is no longer in effect and the new Law that is written on the hearts of believers:

2. **Jeremiah 31:33-34:**

   > ³³ *But this is the covenant that I will make with the house of Israel after those days, says the L*ORD*: I will put My law in their minds, and write it on their hearts; and I will be their God, and they shall be My people.* ³⁴ *No more shall every man teach his neighbor, and every man his brother, saying, "Know the L*ORD*," for they all shall know Me, from the least of them to the greatest of them, says the L*ORD*. For I will forgive their iniquity, and their sin I will remember no more.*

Jeremiah describes the days in which the Messiah will sit in the house of God in Jerusalem, and all the nations will go up to hear the Word of God from Him. **(See also Isaiah 2:3; 11:9-10; 12:4-6; Micah 4:1-2; Zechariah 14:16-21)**. In the Millennium of Christ's reign on Earth, Satan will be bound in Hades, and sin will be restrained. The way of life, especially at the beginning of Messiah's reign, will be like in the days of Genesis, before sin destroyed the good in man and in nature **(Isa. 11:4-9; Mic. 4:3; Rev. 20:1-3)**.

 **"If the people of Israel will not observe the Mosaic Law, they will lose their Jewish identity!"**

 *Response A:*

What should characterize the Jewish nation is their identification with Jesus the Messiah, their Savior and Redeemer. That is the purpose God determined for His people, and it will eventually be fulfilled in the future. When a Jew reaches true spiritual maturity, it will be evidenced by faith in Jesus Christ and submission to His will **(Jn. 8:19, 42; 15:23)**.

The nation of Israel was chosen to represent God before all other nations; therefore the attributes and nature of God must be reflected in the life of each one of the people of Israel — just as in the life of every child of God.

Jesus Christ is the fulfillment of all the laws of the Torah. Whoever claims that he observes the Law but rejects Jesus Christ, is admitting that he does not understand the Law and actually opposes it **(Gal. 3:23-25)**. To believe in Jesus as Lord and Savior and to live according to **His** Law, is God's objective and purpose for the nation of Israel in particular and for all men in general **(Eph. 2:10)**.

- If you keep the Law but at the same time reject Jesus, the Savior and Redeemer from sin, you will have only a religious veneer and an identity of your choosing, but you will remain without atonement for sin, cut off from God because of the guilt of your sins **(Jn. 3:16-18; 8:19, 42; 14:6-7)**.

- If you believe with all your heart that Jesus is the promised Messiah, the Savior, then you will have atonement for sin and God will attribute to you the righteousness of the Messiah (**Acts 4:12; Rom. 5:1-11; 10:8-10; 2 Cor 5:21**). That is the only identity that has any importance in God's eyes.

Response B:

The above second claim raises a counter question:

What do people ***mean*** when they say "Jewish identity"?

1. A religious Jew using this term would mean:

   - keeping the ordinances of the Oral Law — even though he knows he will never be able to keep them all perfectly. The emphasis will be on a set of laws that constitute the three pillars of Judaism: **a.** Sabbath, **b.** keeping kosher (observing dietary laws) and **c.** family purity.
   - wearing "Jewish" clothes — in particular a head covering and *Tsitsit* (a fringed vest).
   - observing the Jewish holidays.
   - circumcision, bar mitzvah, a Jewish wedding.
   - donning phylacteries (*Tefillin*), praying in the synagogue, and from the prayer book (*Siddur*).

2. A secular Israeli speaking about his Jewish identity would mean:

   - observing the Jewish holidays at a level of his own choosing.
   - circumcision, bar mitzvah, a Jewish wedding.
   - living in the land of Israel.
   - being a good citizen and serving in the Israel Defense Forces.

The above do not cover all the components of "Jewishness," as understood in the various strata of Israeli society, but they are a rather accurate sample.

So which of the two lives in a way that leads to salvation?

What is more important, to be true to the traditions and the general consensus of the society we live in, or to obey the demands of God? — Does God command me to preserve my Jewishness, or is it more important that I obey Him?

Jewish identity must be expressed by belonging to the Messiah and in a daily close walk with Him. There is a price to pay in a life of obedience to Christ! Whoever believes in Jesus — even if he does his best to satisfy the expectations of the society he lives in — will always be considered different, just as Jesus Himself was.

Rejection and scorn from our people is part of the price to pay for walking with Jesus and identifying with Him. The Scriptures prepare us for this: *"Yes, and all who desire to live godly in Christ Jesus will suffer persecution"* **(2 Tim. 3:12; see also Mt. 19:29-30).**

If only we would all desire first and foremost to live a life of **Christian** identity — or better: of **Christ-likeness**. Only in this way will we fulfill the law of God:

Romans 2:28-29: *For he is not a Jew who is one outwardly, nor is circumcision that which is outward in the flesh; ²⁹ but he is a Jew who is one inwardly; and circumcision is that of the heart, in the Spirit, not in the letter; whose praise is not from men but from God.*

Romans 9:6: *For they are not all Israel who are of Israel.*

Being Jewish, Believing in Jesus — and the Question of Identity

Many Messianic Jewish families struggle with the definition of Jewishness when raising their children. Our children want to be like their friends. There is very strong peer pressure to be like everyone else and to take on the kind of identity that meets the majority's consensus. In this respect Israel's predominantly Jewish society is no different from any other society in the world.

Parents often ask: "What is our identity, really? What should we, as believers in Jesus, teach our children while they are young, so that they do not go through an identity crisis in their teenage years?"

1. I believe that our only and complete identity is in Jesus Christ, and we must at all costs persist in living in a way that demonstrates this identity in our way of life as individuals and as a family (**Phil. 3:1-11**).

2. Our children will experience pressure from the society we live in (persecution, ostracism by the family, and more). They will examine the validity of our faith as they watch us endure antagonism from family and surrounding, brought on by our faith in the Messiah. Our children will remember how we, their parents, stayed true to Jesus in every situation, and how He helped us because of that. We, the parents, must bring the problem in prayer to God, with pleadings and thanksgiving (**Phil. 4:6**), so that our children also will learn that He answers prayer and all our help comes from Him. They must understand that our faith is not some abstract psychological exercise, it is the real thing.

3. If we vacillate — on the one hand identifying with the believers in Jesus and on the other hand teaching our children that we live under the authority of the ordinances of the Law (that are, actually, no longer in effect) — then we will have difficulty explaining our faith to them, as well as the motives behind what we do. Thus we will risk our children going through a much more intense crisis of identity.

4. Even if we follow all these guidelines and give our children the best support we can, we cannot guarantee that they will come through all stages of their development without an identity crisis. We are required only to submit to the Messiah and to lovingly obey His Word. In the process we must present every need and

problem before God. He in His grace will work out His purpose in each of our lives — including the lives of our children.

None of us chooses which nation to be born into. If you are an Israeli, then your belonging to the Jewish nation and being a citizen of the State of Israel is not a coincidence. It is part of God's perfect plan for you, and you must fulfill His will in your life as part of this special people. If you were born into any other nation, God had a purpose in that, too. No one has reason to glory in his national identity — we have received it as a **tool** from God, and in it we must serve Him, bringing glory to His name. That is the end for which we were created **(Eph. 3:21)**.

Our purpose is to proclaim the gospel of Jesus *"to the Jew first, but also to the Gentile"* **(Rom 1:16)**, to grow in faith, to build the body of Christ, to be a faithful witness to the truth of the gospel, to pray for the salvation of Israel and for the salvation of all people. All this, in order to bring glory and honor to the name of our God **(Rom. 13; Eph. 2:10; Ti. 2:14)**.

> *Man's salvation — be he Jew or Gentile — is more important than his nationality or his earthly identity. The purpose of our life is fulfilled in our salvation!*

Who and What Are We?

1. We are children of God, saved by the grace of God in Christ Jesus. We belong to the body of Christ — the church — which consists of all those who have been saved — both Jews and Gentiles **(Eph. 2:10; 4:12-16; Ti. 2:14)**.

2. We are all citizens of our respective countries, and we will observe faithfully all the laws of our state **(Rom. 13)**. Should it ever happen that the laws of the land contradict the principles of the Holy Scriptures, we must remain true to the Word of God but accept the judgment of the state **(Dan. 6)**.

3. Those of us who are Jewish belong to the physical seed of Abraham. But more important: All of us — regardless, of our nationality — are saved by the same faith Abraham had.

THIRD CLAIM — "**Intermarriage between a Jewish believer and a non-Jewish believer leads to assimilation of the people of Israel!**"

.... *Response:*

Not so! — Belief in Jesus is the ultimate purpose of the law of God. God forbade His people to marry idolaters, but He did not forbid marriage with someone from another nation who adopts the law of God and identifies with the people of Israel. There is no criticism of Rahab the prostitute, or Ruth the Moabitess, who joined the congregation of Israel, as both women adopted the faith in the God of Israel. Both are even included in the genealogy of Jesus Christ (**Mt. 1; Lk. 3:23-38**).

All believers must pray and ask God for grace to know whom He has chosen as their partner. What the Creator puts together is a source of great blessing. A saved couple is one which has the promise of living with God for eternity. While it is true that the people amongst whom they live may reject them for not maintaining the man-made traditions and customs that are standard in their society, such couples are nevertheless a tool that brings glory to God.

The purpose of our lives is to fulfill the will of God and not to give in to public opinion where it contradicts God's Word. *"Our citizenship is in heaven"* (**Phil. 3:20**), therefore problems of national identity should not trouble Christian believers.

It would be arrogant to claim that the people of Israel have ensured their continued existence throughout history by upholding the rabbinical traditions. Every day our people continue to exist — whether in the Diaspora or in the State of Israel — is a gift of grace from God. It is God who preserves the chosen nation! And that is not because of anything we do, but because He will never break His promises (**Ezek. 36:21-32; Rom. 11:29**).

The reader may be wondering whether we have not digressed too far from our study of the epistle to the Galatians. — I do not think so, because the false teachers who influenced the churches in Galatia raised similar objections to those we have just discussed. Also they asked:

What Will Preserve Us If Not the Law?

"The ordinances of the Mosaic Law have kept us unique, gave us our moral lifestyle, and preserved our position as a separate nation. If the authority of the ordinances is abolished, what will preserve us from being assimilated into the nations of the world, who are ungodly and immoral?" This is what many Jews have asked in the past and still ask today.

To those among the inquirers who are believers the apostle Paul says:

Galatians 3:26-29:

> ²⁶ *For you are all sons of God through faith in Christ Jesus.* ²⁷ *For as many of you as were baptized into Christ have put on Christ.* ²⁸ *There is neither Jew nor Greek, there is neither slave nor free, there is neither male nor female; for you are all one in Christ Jesus.* ²⁹ *And if you are Christ's, then you are Abraham's seed, and heirs according to the promise.*

Since verses 23-25 have portrayed the Law as a tutor that completed its task with the death of Jesus Christ, we must ask ourselves:

If the dominion of the Law has come to an end, under whose dominion do we live now?

The answer is:

 You are all sons of God through faith in Christ Jesus. — We have not come out from under the dominion of the Law (those ordinances that were fulfilled by the death of Christ) to a life of lawlessness and immorality. We are not free to share the lifestyle of those who have not been saved. The saving faith in the Lord Jesus, who atones for our sins, has given us the status of sons of God, whether we be Jew or Gentile. This status places us in a life of holiness, not of lawlessness (**Rom. 7:6; 8:12-39; 1 Cor. 3; 9:21**).

When someone rejects Jesus Christ, that has a grave spiritual significance: He chooses to live under the influence and dominion of Satan (**Mt. 13:38; Jn. 8:38, 41, 44; Acts 13:10; Eph. 2:3; 1 Jn. 3:10; 5:19**). As long as a person lives, that spiritual state can change.

The Law identifies sin as the factor which separates us from God (**Isa. 59:2**), but faith in Jesus has done what the Law could never do: it has taken away the guilt of sin and the curse it brings (**Isa. 53:5**), giving us the status of **"sons of God."** This is not a new principle! It has been that way ever since sin entered creation (**Rom. 8:15-17; Gal. 3:26-29; Jas. 2:23**).

The New Framework

27 *"As many of you as were baptized into Christ have put on Christ."* — This is how the apostle describes the new framework that is to keep us holy and moral. All those who have given their lives to Jesus, witnessed to their faith through baptism, and now live in obedience to Christ — their lives are to reflect the behavior, attitude and thoughts of El-Shaddai, Jesus Christ, God who has taken on flesh and blood and come to Earth (**Phil. 2:5-18**).

Paul uses the verb *to be baptized* as an image that explains our full identification with Christ — He is in us and we are in Him (**Rom. 6:3-5; 1 Cor. 6:17; Gal. 2:20**).

All believers are commanded to be unified with one purpose: to be likened to Christ — and that by the power of the Holy Spirit who dwells within each and every one (**1 Cor. 3:16-17**). Can there be a holier way of life than that?

Receiving God's Messiah in faith not only draws you nearer to God, it also transforms your body into a temple of the Holy Spirit (**Rom. 5; 1 Cor. 3:16-17; 2 Cor. 5:18-20**).

	true	false
I am no longer under the authority of the commandments that have been fulfilled by Christ	✓	
I am no longer under the authority of the Scriptures		✓

The believer in Jesus is no longer under the authority of the Law and has walked straight into the arms of his Creator. It is the presence of God within him that now keeps him holy and pure.

And there is another characteristic of a true believer: his dedication to learn and to obey the Word of God.

"You ... have put on Christ." — This is not a temporary condition for the sake of a certain occasion — it is a transfer of ownership, a new identity. Whatever was before I was saved has ceased to be. From the moment of salvation my life is dedicated solely to doing the will of God. The same new identity is given to both Jew and Gentile who believe. That is why all believers in Jesus are called Christians — people who belong to Christ and resemble Him (**Acts 11:26; Gal. 6:16**).

Already in Galatians 2:19-20 Paul has gone into detail on what it actually means to "put on Christ." Let us look again at those important verses: ***"For I through the law died to the law that I might live to God. I have been crucified with Christ; it is no longer I who live, but Christ lives in me; and the life which I now live in the flesh I live by faith in the Son of God, who loved me and gave Himself for me."***

 "There is neither Jew nor Greek, there is neither slave nor free, there is neither male nor female; for you are all one in Christ Jesus." — These differences exist no longer among those who are in Christ.

 What does that mean?

- We all alike need atonement for our sins, and we all need salvation.

- All of us, with no exception, are called to receive salvation in the blood of Christ.
- Jesus Christ paid with His blood the same price for every one of His children. Each one of us — male or female, Jew or Gentile — is a sinner saved by grace.
- We all receive the same new identity: We become members of one body, whose head is Jesus Christ **(1 Cor. 12)**.

True, God gives different spiritual gifts (abilities to serve) to each believer **(Rom. 12; 1 Cor. 12, 14; Eph. 4:11-13)**, but each believer is equally His child. Just as parents do not play favorites with their children, so in the eyes of God there is no difference between His children **(Col. 3:10-11)**.

There are some who claim that this verse abolishes all differences between men and women in all capacities of service in the church. But that is not the writer's intention.

Paul here teaches equality in salvation, not equality in ministry.

There is a difference between men and women when it comes to the gifts of service and their active use **(Rom. 16:1-2; 1 Tim. 2-3; Ti. 2)**.

29 *"And if you are Christ's, then you are Abraham's seed, and heirs according to the promise."* — Rabbinical Judaism claims that the promises of God belong to every Jew because he is a descendant of Abraham, Isaac, and Jacob. Whoever adds to this advantage of belonging to the Chosen People by keeping the commandments of the Torah, will even improve his preferential status before God. Rabbinical Judaism rejects with scorn the most important part of the promise: *"If you are Christ's."* — However, If you do not belong to Jesus Christ there **is no** eternal inheritance.

In order to receive the inheritance, we need more than a biological connection to Abraham — we must be partners to his **faith**. Your spiritual standing is the most important thing to God, therefore everyone who belongs to Jesus (everyone who has been saved and *"put on Christ"* [v. 27]) has a part in the Kingdom of God **(Rom. 9:1-7; Gal. 6:16)**.

Also those who do not believe in Jesus the Messiah have a part in eternity.

It will be in the eternal Lake of Fire, in an irreversible state of separation from God's presence and His inheritance (**Rev. 20:11-15**).

Summary of Chapter 3:

1. The apostle Paul teaches that the believer in Jesus is no longer under the dominion of the Law. The presence of the Holy Spirit in every believer is what keeps him holy and pure. A true Christian learns the will of God, obeys His Word and lives according to His direction.

2. The apostle speaks of baptism as a parallel to salvation. As people who have been called to be like Christ, let us not put off this first step of obedience! Whoever knows clearly that he has been saved and determines to follow His Lord and Savior in faith, should not delay his baptism in water.

3. There isn't a believer who has never thought of Paradise, the eternal Kingdom of God. However, the apostle Paul makes it very clear that our genealogy is not a ticket to heaven, only our belonging to Jesus! — Is Jesus Lord of your life? If so, you have a part in the

inheritance of Christ.

Chapter 4

The Adoption as Sons

In verses 1-7 Paul continues teaching the principle to which he had dedicated most of the previous chapter: The Law served the people of Israel as a tutor. It kept the people within parameters that prepared them to recognize Jesus Christ as the promised Messiah when the day came. The Law was not an end in itself — Jesus Christ was the end of the Law. From the moment we were saved, we ceased to be subject to the ordinances of the Mosaic Law.

The apostle now gives another illustration from life that exemplifies this spiritual principle:

Heirs of God

Galatians 4:1-7:

> ¹Now I say that the heir, as long as he is a child, does not differ at all from a slave, though he is master of all, ²but is under guardians and stewards until the time appointed by the father. ³Even so we, when we were children, were in bondage under the elements of the world. ⁴But when the fullness of the time had come, God sent forth His Son, born of a woman, born under the

> law, ⁵ to redeem those who were under the law, that we might receive the adoption as sons.
>
> ⁶ And because you are sons, God has sent forth the Spirit of His Son into your hearts, crying out, "Abba, Father!" ⁷ Therefore you are no longer a slave but a son, and if a son, then an heir of God through Christ.

❶—❷ "The heir, as long as he is a child." — It is obvious to us all that a small child cannot look after himself or make his own decisions concerning his life and future. He is immature and definitely lacks the wisdom needed to manage his inheritance. If children were to decide what to do with the money of their inheritance, no doubt before long they would be left penniless!

Because this is so, the legislators have decreed that if a child loses both his parents and has no living relative to care for him, he is to be given a guardian (ἐπίτροπος / *epitropos* in Greek). This is an adult who is appointed executor of the child's property and affairs until the child comes of age. As long as the child is a minor, he is under the authority of his guardian and may not manage his property by himself, even though it is legally his. Paul draws a picture of a wealthy heir. While a minor, he is under the authority of his guardian and differs little from a servant, who has to do whatever he is told.

"Until the time appointed by the father." — When the child comes of age legally, or reaches the age his parents appointed in their will, he receives sole control over his inheritance. From this point on the guardian has no authority to make any decision in the child's life or regarding his property.

The purpose of this illustration is not to teach us civil law. It is to explain that the Mosaic Law's commandments are like a guardian responsible for the training and welfare of the people of Israel, until the coming of the promised Messiah. As the guardian is temporary, so this example emphasizes the temporariness of the Law. Just as the authority of the guardian is over once the child has grown up, so the authority of the Law in the life of all believers — Jewish and Gentile — has ended with the coming of Jesus the Messiah and the establishment of the New Covenant in His atoning blood (**Gal. 3:19, 23-25**).

❸ ***"Even so we, when we were children, were in bondage under the elements of the world."*** — The term *the elements of the world* indicates that the commandments of the Law laid the foundations. That is very important, but no builder who knows what he is doing will occupy himself indefinitely with this first stage. His purpose is to construct a building on the foundations he has laid (**Gal. 4:9; Col. 2:16-20**).

Paul warns us in verses 9-10 against returning ***"to the weak and beggarly elements."*** He is warning those who wish to return to the observance of holy days in order to be saved. These holy days were given us as symbols, foreshadowing the Messiah (**Col. 2:8, 16-17**). Going back under the dominion of these commandments as if they were the whole purpose of the Law — that is, keeping commandments out of obligation — is like returning under the authority of the guardian after one is fully grown and independent.

All According to Plan

❹ ***"When the fullness of the time had come."*** — The coming of Jesus Christ was no surprise. God had determined in the Old Testament Scriptures when the Messiah would come, where He would be born, His identity, and many other details about Him:

- As early as Genesis 3:15 God says that the Seed of the woman would crush the head of Satan.
- The prophet Isaiah foretells that the Messiah would be born of a virgin (**Isa. 7:14**).
- In another prophecy, Isaiah identifies the child we would receive as God Himself (**Isa. 9:6-7**).
- In chapter 53 Isaiah tells us that the Messiah would die as a lamb for our atonement.
- In Micah we read that the Messiah must be born in Bethlehem Ephrathah (**Mic. 5:2**).

- Zechariah prophesies that the Messiah will enter Jerusalem riding on the foal of a donkey (**Zech. 9:9**).

- The prophet Daniel defines a time frame (69 weeks of years) at the end of which the Messiah will be cut off and the Temple destroyed. According to the details Daniel provides, the point for the cutting off of the Messiah was the month of Nisan in the year A.D. 32 (**Dan. 9:24-27**).

  At precisely this time Jesus Christ entered Jerusalem and was received with honor by the inhabitants of the city. In the same week, during the Feast of Passover, Jesus was put to death. In the year A.D. 70 the Temple was destroyed and Jerusalem lay in ruins. The only One who claimed to be the Messiah and performed God's miracles during the time Daniel specified for this event was Jesus, who was born in Bethlehem Ephrathah in accordance with Micah's prophecy.

- The wise men from the East (**see Mt. 2**) knew enough to interpret these prophecies. That is why they came to Judah once they learned that the King of the Jews, whose coming they awaited, had been born.

In the political arena, the Roman Empire created the ideal conditions for the spread of the gospel after the coming of Christ. The Romans developed an extensive network of paved roads, and the borders of the known world were open, so that the gospel was able to reach even the remotest regions and peoples of the Empire in a relatively short time.

Jesus Christ has already fulfilled all the prophecies concerning the First Coming of the promised Redeemer and Messiah of Israel. No other person in history has fulfilled Old Testament Messianic prophecies to the extent Jesus has — in fact, no one comes anywhere **near** Him in that respect.

The Divinity of Christ

"God sent His Son." — Here is a list of verses in which Jesus Himself tells us that He was sent by the Father: **John 5:30, 36-37; 6:39, 44, 57; 8:16, 18, 42; 12:49; 17:21, 25; 20:21.**

The Scriptures tell us that God **sent** His Son, not that He **created** His Son, in order to teach us that Jesus existed *"from of old, of everlasting"* **(Isa. 9:6; Mic. 5:2; Rom. 8:3-4; Phil. 2:6-7; Heb. 1:3-5).**

The Humanity of Christ

Why was Jesus "under the Law"?

"Born of a woman, born under the law." — As long as Jesus Christ had not tasted death, as long as He had not yet paid the price of atonement for man's sin, as long as He had not established the New Covenant by His blood — all the ordinances of the Mosaic Law, with no exception, were still in effect. So while He was alive on Earth and until He was crucified, He was also obliged to keep all that the Law required of a Jewish man **(Mt. 5:17).**

Those observing Jesus were eyewitnesses of how God had intended the ordinances of the Mosaic Law to be kept — to be kept **perfectly**. Jesus is the only Jew — the only person — in history who can claim complete and flawless observance of the entire Law **(Jn. 8:46; 2 Cor. 5:21; Heb. 4:15; 7:26; 1 Pet. 2:22; 1 Jn. 3:5).**

The Law demands that the sacrificial offering be pure and without blemish in order to be acceptable to God. Jesus was indeed perfect according to the Law's requirements — perfect and pure physically and pure of sin in a spiritual sense — and was therefore accepted as a worthy and perfect sacrifice for our sins. His righteousness and holiness are imputed to us from the moment we are saved **(Isa. 53; Jn. 1:29; Rom. 5:1-5; 2 Cor. 5:21).**

Jesus was born of a woman, like all of us, so that He could atone for the sins of mankind. The writer of the epistle to the Hebrews enlarges on this:

Hebrews 2:14-17:

> ¹⁴ *Inasmuch then as the children have partaken of flesh and blood, He Himself likewise shared in the same, that through death He might destroy him who had the power of death, that is, the devil,* ¹⁵ *and release those who through fear of death were all their lifetime subject to bondage.* ¹⁶ *For indeed He does not give aid to angels, but He does give aid to the seed of Abraham.* ¹⁷ *Therefore, in all things He had to be made like His brethren, that He might be a merciful and faithful High Priest in things pertaining to God, to make propitiation for the sins of the people.*

- In order to fulfill all the ordinances of the Mosaic Law perfectly, Jesus (*Immanuel* — "God with us") had to be **God** (**Lk. 1:32; Jn. 1:1, 18**).
- To be an acceptable sacrifice for man's sin, He had to be at the same time 100 percent **man** (**Isa. 7:14; Mt. 1:20-25; Lk. 1:35; Jn. 1:14**).

The Redeemer

5 *"To redeem those who were under the law"* — When someone redeems a possession or a slave, he needs to pay a set price. In our case, the required price was paid in order to redeem us from the slavery of sin and death. God determined that price in the Law: The life of a perfect sacrifice (**Lev. 17:11**). Jesus Christ paid this price with His life. This holy and costly price satisfied the requirements of God the Father (**Isa. 53:10**), so that now all who believe in Jesus as their Lord and Savior from the curse of sin receive atonement, and by the grace of God are considered righteous in His eyes (**Rom. 5; 10:9-10**).

When the price of redemption is paid, all rights to the redeemed object (or person) are transferred to the redeemer. Whoever is redeemed from the curse of the Law that was hanging over him because of his sins (**see commentary on Gal. 3:10, 13**), now becomes the property of the Redeemer —

God. God does not treat the saved people as slaves or lifeless objects. He lovingly considers them His sons — partners in the inheritance of Jesus Christ.

Sons of God

"That we might receive the adoption as sons." — What is involved in being adopted as sons of God? What rights and duties go with that amazing title?

1. Sons of God enjoy the indwelling of the Holy Spirit because their sins have been forgiven (**Gal 4:6; 1 Cor. 3:16-17; 2 Cor. 6:14-18**).

2. Since the Holy Spirit dwells within them, they experience His involvement and His help in every area of life (**Jn. 14:16; Rom. 8:12-39; 1 Cor. 10:13**).

3. Sons of God have the promise of eternal life and of a share in God's eternal inheritance (**Gal 4:7; see also Rom. 8:15, 23; Eph. 1:5**).

4. They have been saved from the wrath of God (**1 Th. 5:1-11; Rev. 3:10**).

DUTIES

1. Fulfilling God's will and obeying His Word are the highest priorities in the life of the believer (**Eph. 2:10; Ti. 2:14**).

2. This necessitates an intentional and consistent yielding of one's own will to the will of God (*"Present your bodies a living sacrifice, holy, acceptable to God,"* **Rom. 12:1-2; Gal. 2:19-20**).

And here is a word of encouragement to those who are repulsed by the prospect of having to fulfill duties: There is no happier person than the one who does the will of God!

6—**7** *"And because you are sons, God has sent forth the Spirit of His Son into your hearts, crying out, 'Abba, Father!' ⁷Therefore you are no longer a slave but a son, and if a son, then an heir of God through Christ."* — In verse 6 we are taught a very important principle: Beyond the truth that Jesus Christ, God the Son, came to Earth to die in order to atone for our sins, also the **Holy Spirit** is involved in the salvation of man.

We know that the Holy Spirit:

- opens our eyes to understand the Word of God (**1 Cor. 2:10-16**).
- teaches us and reminds us of the Word of God (**Jn. 14:16-26; 16:5-15**).
- gives us the power to obey (**Jn. 3:1-21, 31-36**).

In Galatians 4:6-7 we learn that:

1. The believer in Jesus Christ is spiritually reborn by the **Holy Spirit**. Thus he is adopted as a "son of God."
2. He receives **Jesus Christ** through faith in Him as his Savior and Lord of his life and is therefore found innocent and pure before God (**Rom. 5:1-5**).
3. The full extent of his salvation will be reached in the future, when he comes into the presence of **God the Father** and receives the eternal inheritance (**Rom. 8:16-18; Eph. 1:10-11; Col. 1:12; 2 Th. 2:14; 1 Pet. 1:3-4**).

So then, God the Father, Jesus Christ, and the Spirit of God (Three who are One) are all involved in man's salvation! How great and loving our God is (**Ps. 8:3-6**) (See what the Bible says about the three entities of God as one: **Isa. 48:16; 42:1; 61:1; 63:8-10**.)

The New Is **Instead** of the Old

After the death of Christ, the New Covenant took effect. The beginning of the New Covenant marked the end of the previous one — the Mosaic Covenant that was given at Mt. Sinai (**Jer. 31:31-34; 2 Cor. 3**). The only way to glorify God and to do His will is to acknowledge Jesus as Lord and Savior and to understand that by His blood He sealed the New Covenant, in which each of His children takes part. To ignore the New Covenant or to adopt it only partially are expressions of ignorance, or even contempt, towards God.

It would be a mistake to assume that after Jesus established the New Covenant the Mosaic Covenant is still in force. God does not permit the Jew (or anyone else) to choose which covenant he wishes to belong to. From the moment the New Covenant was established, **every person** is required to receive Jesus in faith as his Redeemer, who saves him from the punishment of sin. This is a must also for Jewish people because, after all, the Law of Moses was designed to lead the people of Israel to Jesus the Messiah (**Gal. 3:23-25**).

If there was another way to perfection and salvation, then Jesus was a liar and His death was unnecessary (**Jn. 14:6; Acts 4:12; Gal. 2:21**).

Just as the authority of a guardian ends when the child comes of age, so the dominion of the ordinances of the Mosaic Law came to an end when Jesus sealed the New Covenant.

There are some who claim that, though Jesus inaugurated the New Covenant, this was not the end to the Mosaic one. They see it rather as a kind of re-confirmation and updating of the existing covenant. The Scriptures stand against such a claim:

1. We must remember that the New Covenant was first promised to the people of Israel by Jeremiah. He prophesied that God was about to make a New Covenant that would be **different** from the one Israel had broken (**Jer. 31:31-34**). The author of the epistle to the Hebrews quotes from this passage in Jeremiah and adds: *"In that He says 'a **new** covenant,' He has made the first obsolete. Now what is becoming obsolete and growing old is ready to vanish away"* (**Heb. 8:13**).

It would be well worth reading chapters 7—10 of the epistle to the Hebrews. There the author explains unequivocally that the laws of the Mosaic Covenant were temporary and have been fulfilled in Jesus Christ.

2. The apostle Paul uses various illustrations in chapters 3—4 of Galatians to teach us that the authority of the first covenant (the commandments of the Law of Moses) ends completely with the inception of the New Covenant.

Summary — The Adoption as Sons in Jesus

1. Whoever knows the Law well, knows that the purpose of the Law was fulfilled completely in Jesus Christ. Since Jesus has established the New Covenant, the ordinances of the Mosaic Law are now obsolete. The spiritual maturity of a believer is measured by his personal knowledge of Jesus as Lord and by his obedience to the Word of God.

2. Whoever rejects Jesus Christ as the One who has fulfilled the Law and as his personal Savior, proves that he has not understood the essence of the Law. The curse is hanging over him, which says "Cursed is everyone who does not continue in all things which are written in the book of the law, to do them" (3:10), and he can only expect the wrath of God.

3. The believer in Jesus as Lord and Savior is adopted as a son of God. He receives many blessings — but also has duties. As children of God, we have the responsibility to be a light and a worthy example to the world (Mt. 5:13-16).

Let us pray that God will use us to bring the message of salvation to those around us.

Back to the Beggarly Elements

Now the apostle Paul takes his gloves off to teach a painful truth. Every word is a blow to the works of the flesh:

Galatians 4:8-11:

> *⁸But then, indeed, when you did not know God, you served those which by nature are not gods. ⁹But now after you have known God, or rather are known by God, how is it that you turn again to the weak and beggarly elements, to which you desire again to be in bondage? ¹⁰You observe days and months and seasons and years. ¹¹I am afraid for you, lest I have labored for you in vain.*

The apostle sorrowfully explains to the Galatians that with salvation and spiritual maturity God also gave them responsibility. It is neither a worthy nor a sensible decision to go back to the weak foundations — i.e. to keep symbolic commandments as if they were obligatory or a condition of salvation. The behavior of the believers was a disappointment to Paul. He felt they had not understood anything he had taught them, because now he saw them unreservedly and without hesitation submit to false teaching (**Lk. 12:48**).

"Then, indeed, when you did not know God, you served those which by nature are not gods." To whom is he talking here? — The letter was written to both Jews and Gentiles together, so this sentence must be true regarding both of them:

- **The Gentile believer,** before he received Jesus as Lord and Savior, served false gods in every sense of the word.

    Let us take, for example, the account in **Acts 14**: When Paul and Barnabas visited the cities Lystra and Derbe and the surrounding area (the region of Galatia), they healed a man who had been paralyzed from birth. When the local people saw what had happened, they began to shout: *"'The gods have come down to us in the likeness of men!' And Barnabas they called Zeus and Paul, Hermes"* **(Acts 14:11-12)**.

It is clear that no form of idol worship can justify a Gentile in the eyes of God **(Eph. 4:17-19)**.

- **The Jewish believer,** if he had continued to observe the ordinances of the Mosaic Law in order to be justified before God and had never come to a personal knowledge of Jesus Christ as his Savior by the grace of God, would have been in the same situation as the idolatrous Gentile. All his efforts to keep the Law would not have saved him. The description in verse 8 would have suited him, too: *"When you did not know God, you served those which by nature are not gods."*

In Jesus' debate with the Pharisees, He told them: "If you do not know **Me**, you do not know **God**" **(Jn. 8:19, 42; 14:6-7)**.

9—**10** *"How is it that you turn again?"* — The apostle writes with a tone of despair. "How can it be that after the truth was explained to you — after Jesus Christ was demonstrated to you clearly and beyond any doubt as the Messiah, after you learned that He fulfilled the commandments of the Mosaic Law and their purpose — you return to your previous state, to serving the shadow and the symbols in order to be saved **(Col. 2:16-20)**? What you are doing is no different from a Gentile going back to the worship of statues and rocks!"

11 *"I am afraid ... lest I have labored for you in vain."* — The ease and speed with which the Galatians left the way of truth led the apostle Paul to fear that the efforts he had invested in them had been in vain. **(See also 1 Thessalonians 3:5.)**

Can it be understood from Paul's words that a believer can lose his salvation?

No! — There is a reason verse 9 places emphasis on God's choice: *"You are known by God!"* He knows His children, His elect. No power on Earth can take them out of His hands **(Jn. 10:29-30; Rom. 8:38-39; Eph. 1:4;** see also the example where the word *to know* expresses God's election of Abraham in **Gen. 18:19)**.

God Is the One Who Chooses

"You...are known by God." — All the descendants of Adam, the first sinner, are infected by sin and are born into a state of alienation from God (**Ps. 51:5**). This being so, we all begin life in a lost state. Were it not for the grace of God, we would stay in that state for eternity (**Jn. 3:17**). As sinners by nature we have no way to overcome sin, and our salvation depends entirely on God and His power.

God is the sovereign Ruler, and He chooses whom He wills. No one can claim: "I am saved because I am smarter or better than others."

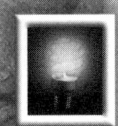

Conclusions:

1. Since God is the one who chooses — and He cannot err in His choice — we can say that the desire of a believer to go back to serving the *"weak and beggarly elements"* does not mean he has lost his salvation. It does indicate a deviation from the truth due to faulty teaching, or some inhibition of a new believer's spiritual growth, or a bad example of spiritual leadership that affects him negatively. Such failings are evident among God's children today, too, and Paul wishes to correct them by the power of the Holy Spirit. (See verses proving that salvation bestowed by God is irrevocable: John 10:1-21; Romans 8:34-39; 1 Peter 1:3-5). See also pages 51-54 about God's election of His sons from before time.

2. In contrast to believers who are caught up in error, there are also those who **persist** in a way of sin. A way of life that consistently defies the principles of God's Word and the nature of Christ is evidence of a person who has never been saved (1 Jn. 2:19).

Days and Seasons

10 *"You observe days and months and seasons and years."* — This verse explains what the term **beggarly elements** refers to: observing days and times as a means of justification before God (**Col. 2:16-18**). These elements are called beggarly because they cannot save us. All they are meant to do is teach us about the identity of the Messiah, His nature and work. Our brothers in Galatia gave the type and symbol the same authority in their lives as they should have given the Messiah (**Acts 4:12**).

Every holiday or Sabbath the Old Testament commanded us to observe foreshadowed something the Messiah has fulfilled — or will fulfill in the future — in God's plan of redemption:

1. **Passover and the Feast of Unleavened Bread:**

    - The type of the paschal lamb was fulfilled in the death of Jesus on the cross as the atoning sacrifice for us:

        Exodus 12:13: *"And when I see the blood, I will pass over you."*

        John 1:29: *"Behold! The Lamb of God who takes away the sin of the world!"*

        Romans 6:23: *"The wages of sin is death, but the gift of God is eternal life in Christ Jesus our Lord."*

    - The spiritual purity granted us by Christ's atonement is symbolized by the *matzoh*, the unleavened bread (**1 Cor. 5:6-8**).

2. **The Sheaf of the Firstfruits:**

    This holiday takes place on the Sunday following the Sabbath included in the week-long Passover holiday. It was fulfilled in the resurrection of Jesus — *"the beginning, the firstborn from the dead"* — on exactly that day (**Lev. 23:9-11; Jn. 20:1; Col. 1:18**).

3. **Pentecost** — (Heb. **Shavuot** — the celebration of the new grain harvest)**:**

    The symbolic meaning of *Shavuot* was fulfilled when the Holy Spirit fell on the first believers, and the church was established precisely on this holiday (**Acts 2**).

4. **The Sabbath:**

   The seventh day of every week is a symbol of: ● peace with God ● rest in salvation ● Christ's Kingdom of peace on Earth ● eternal life with God (**Mt. 11:28-29; Heb. 4:1-14**).

The other Feasts of the Lord

   5. **The Feast of Trumpets,**
   6. **The Day of Atonement,**
   7. **The Feast of Tabernacles,**

will be fulfilled by the return of Jesus Christ to Earth at the end of the Great Tribulation, and by the setting up of His earthly Kingdom (**Zech. 11:11-17; 12; 14:16-21**).

Note!

Even in our modern times Jewish people take tremendous pains to clean their houses of the smallest crumb of bread in order to celebrate the Feast of Passover free of leaven. If only all of us would make the same effort in our inner man to acknowledge our sins, confess them and ask for the atonement of Christ — that is, cleanse our lives of the "leaven" of sin! It is our personal sin that separates us from God (**Isa. 59:2**), not the crumbs of bread in our home. God prefers obedience to His Word over any ritual or sacrifice (**1 Sam. 15:22; Isa. 1; Hos. 6:1-2; Mic. 6:6-8**).

Is there anything wrong with keeping the Sabbath and the holidays?

Certainly not! But it is important to assign them their proper place. Remember: Jesus Christ has already come to Earth and fulfilled the meaning and the prophetic symbolism of these holy days. The symbols are wonderful, but the Word of God itself calls them "beggarly" in comparison to the One they represent — the Messiah Himself.

It is delightful to celebrate the biblical feasts and holidays — on condition that the focus of the holiday is on Christ, not on the symbol. It is not the holiday that saves, not the physical cleanliness, not the fast on the Day of Atonement. It is a sincere faith in the Savior Himself, Jesus the Messiah, and belonging to Him that saves.

Where Is Your Joy Now?

Galatians 4:12-16:

> [12] *Brethren, I urge you to become like me, for I became like you. You have not injured me at all.* [13] *You know that because of physical infirmity I preached the gospel to you at the first.* [14] *And my trial which was in my flesh you did not despise or reject, but you received me as an angel of God, even as Christ Jesus.* [15] *What then was the blessing you enjoyed? For I bear you witness that, if possible, you would have plucked out your own eyes and given them to me.* [16] *Have I therefore become your enemy because I tell you the truth?*

Paul again reminds his readers of their beginnings, their first steps in the grace of Christ. He begs them to reject the destructive doctrine of the false teachers:

[12] *"Become like me, for I became like you!"* — That is to say: "In the past I was a Pharisee who kept all the commandments and traditions scrupulously. I based my righteousness on perfect observance of the commandments (**Phil. 3:4-6**). But after I knew Jesus as Lord and Savior from God's righteous wrath against sinners, I understood my mistake. I stopped trusting in my own strength and began to trust the power and grace of God exclusively (**Phil. 3:7-9**). I understood what was a shadow and a symbol and focused on what was important."

"Become like me," — completely free of the chains of obsolete ordinances and traditions of men. Depend entirely on the grace of God. *"Become like*

me," — filled with the Holy Spirit who teaches us to understand and do the will of God in our lives!

Paul says: "Please, understand the Law as I do. I have nothing against the Law. My criticism is of your faulty understanding of the **purpose** of the Law."

Through the Law Paul learned what was right and good in the eyes of God. When he was saved, the character and nature of God were engraved on his heart. Ever since, he is doing the will of God through the power of the Holy Spirit within him, not by his personal ability or desire to keep written commandments.

"For I became like you!" — The apostle is not subject to obsolete ordinances. He keeps them as necessary, within the parameters of his freedom in Christ, in order to avoid being a stumbling block to others weaker in the faith than himself:

- When among Gentiles, he eats whatever he is served, together with them. That is how he behaved among the Galatians.

- When he is among Jews, he respects them and acts as they do in order not to be a stumbling block to them **(Rom. 14; 1 Cor. 8:13; 9:20; 1 Pet. 2:16-17)**. Paul does not keep commandments in order to justify himself in God's eyes. His righteousness and holiness were received through faith in Jesus as his Redeemer from sin — his faith in the One who is the end of the Law.

"You have not injured me at all" can be understood in two ways:

1. "You did me no harm during my visit to Galatia" **(Acts 13—14)**. When Paul was persecuted and even stoned by the Jews of the area, it was the Gentiles who received his words with an open heart and showed him hospitality with joy and great honor **(Acts 13:42-50; 14:19)**.

2. "Even now, when I hear that you have strayed from the truth, I do not consider you to be enemies" **(Gal. 4:16)**. The apostle's harsh words could have been understood by the Galatians as something personal against them. Here he stresses that everything he says comes from a pure and loving heart that cares for their spiritual welfare, which is why he calls them *brothers* and *my children* **(v. 19)**.

13—**14** Paul recalls with fondness the loving concern the Galatians had shown him in the past. They had recognized him as a spokesman for God and honored him as if he were Christ Himself (**see Mt. 18:5-10**).

"And my trial which was in my flesh you did not despise or reject." — We do not know what illness, injury, or handicap Paul suffered from during his visit. His words imply that the ailment was clearly visible, and it may have been the result of the stoning he suffered at Lystra (**Acts 14:19**).

Paul's handicap tested their love. He acknowledges that their arms were wide open, and their expressions of love towards him showed that the Galatians had the right priorities. They understood that the main thing was the divine message he brought, not his physical appearance.

15 *"If possible, you would have plucked out your own eyes and given them to me."* — This sentence speaks first and foremost of the love of the Galatians and their willingness to sacrifice for the apostle. Perhaps it is also a hint as to the kind of physical handicap he suffered from — problems with his sight. (See also **2 Corinthians 12:7** and his words to the Galatians in **6:11**: *"See with what large letters I have written to you with my own hand!"*)

"Where then is that sense of blessing you had?" (v. 15 NASB) — "Look at the side effects of your return to the weak foundations. Pay attention to what happened when you ceased to depend on Jesus Christ, on His atoning blood, as the only means of salvation: **You lost out on your blessing!**"

When we try to base righteousness and holiness on our ability to keep the commandments, we find ourselves in debt — always! In such a state our blessing and our joy disappear.

Since Jesus is the source of peace and joy (**Jn. 14:27; 15:11; 1 Jn. 1:3-4**), focusing ourselves on something or someone else will lead to the antithesis of peace and joy.

16 *"Have I therefore become your enemy because I tell you the truth?"* — When the eyes of the Galatians were on Jesus, they received the apostle Paul with joy and love, but now — after they have strayed from God's ways — the truth seems to threaten them (**Prov. 27:5-6**). Now Paul is not welcome among them in the way he was before.

Summary — Return to the Beggarly Elements

1. Keeping the commandments by all the technical rules, but without faith that is according to the will of God, will have no better result than idol worship. Such worship does not draw man nearer to God, because it is an attempt to establish righteousness by human strength. The person who constructs an illusion of righteousness for himself does not see his need to leave the way that leads to hell (Rom. 9:30—10:4).

2. Every holiday and festival God has commanded in the Bible was intended to remind us of some part of His plan of salvation, which God has prepared for man through Jesus Christ. It is good to celebrate each holiday, on condition that this is done in faith in Jesus, and with the understanding that Jesus has fulfilled the meaning and symbolism of each of the holy days. (See, for example, 1 Corinthians 5:7-8.)

3. True joy is in Christ. Our joy comes from our assurance of salvation, which we received through faith in Jesus.

False Teachers — Then and Now

Galatians 4:17-20:

> [17] They zealously court you, but for no good; yes, they want to exclude you, that you may be zealous for them. [18] But it is good to be zealous in a good thing always, and not only when I am present with you. [19] My little children, for whom I labor in birth again until Christ is formed in you, [20] I would like to be present with you now and to change my tone; for I have doubts about you.

The apostle explains what motivated the false teachers to heap useless commandments and tasks on the believers in Galatia. It is important to understand these verses, because they will help us identify false teachers today.

"They zealously court you." — "The false teachers give the impression that they are most interested in your welfare. They seem to be dedicating time and effort to you, but all their investment in you is designed to create dependency. They draw you to themselves, not to Christ. They are trying to block the direct approach you have to Christ and take away your spiritual freedom in Him.

"They teach you that you need them and their guidance in order to be justified in the eyes of God. They do not teach you how to become like Christ in your behavior, speech, and thinking — all they seek is that you imitate **them** in their religious zeal and thereby satisfy their pride."

"They want to exclude you." — To exclude you from what? — From the truth of course!

In what ways did the false teachers exclude the Galatians from the truth?

First of all, they did their utmost to destroy Paul's reputation. Verse 16 reveals that Paul is no longer welcome in the churches of Galatia, even though in the past they held him in high respect.

1. Paul says he is an apostle:
    - The false teachers claim he is not. By doing so they appear to be saving the Galatians from following an impostor (**Gal. 1:11-12**).

2. Paul emphasizes that salvation comes by faith in Jesus alone and is the same for both Jew and Gentile.
    - The false teachers assert that salvation is based on keeping the ordinances of the Law and that the Gentiles must also keep these commandments in order to be justified. By this they give Jewish believers an advantage and tempt them to the sin of pride.

3. Paul teaches that our spiritual and moral strength depend on the presence of the Holy Spirit within us. We keep the Law of Christ by faith and love and by the leading of the Holy Spirit who dwells within us and teaches us the truth of the Scriptures.

- The false teachers claim that shaking off the authority of the Law and its ordinances will lead to a life of immorality and cause the Jew to look and live like an idolatrous Gentile.

In effect, all the claims made by the false teachers sound convincing, serious, and deeply devout. But Paul knows by the wisdom of God that their motives are far from pure.

*"They want to exclude you" **from Jesus Christ!***

We have learned that the false teachers opposed the apostle Paul, who was an apostle of Christ. If so, then the false teachers were leading the Galatians away from Jesus, the fulfiller of the Law.

The moment the false teachers caused the believers to stray from God's truth, they made them dependent on **their** words and their personal opinions. In the absence of the standard of God's Word the Galatians became the disciples of the false teachers and began to imitate their ways with religious fervor. In their eyes the false teachers became the standard of righteousness and holiness.

This did not only happen in Paul's day! The prophet Isaiah had condemned such behavior generations earlier (**Isa. 29:13-14**):

> [13] *Therefore the Lord said:*
>
> *"Inasmuch as these people draw near with their mouths and honor Me with their lips, but have removed their hearts far from Me, and their fear toward Me is taught by the commandment of men,* [14] *therefore, behold, I will again do a marvelous work among this people, a marvelous work and a wonder; for the wisdom of their wise men shall perish, and the understanding of their prudent men shall be hidden."*

As early as in the days of the first Temple the prophet lamented that the people were far from God and occupied themselves with the traditions and commandments of men.

What is happening today? — The spiritual leadership of the people of Israel is continuing down the same path. The Jew is required to accept in faith the interpretations of his sages and has no right to query their judgments. The opinion of the rabbi is what determines the truth and must be accepted as if it were the Law from Mt. Sinai. Whoever doubts the words of the sages risks rejection and ostracism.

The Characteristics of False Teachers Are:

1. Wrong teaching that springs from bad intentions, rather than from an honest mistake.

   - A teacher of the truth can make a mistake, but as a faithful and humble servant of God he will be willing to hear correction that is based on the Word of God.
   - A false teacher will respond differently when his error and his deviation from the truth is pointed out: he will insist on justifying his claim and will avoid any admission that may hurt his honor and pride.
   - False teachers **"want to pervert the gospel of Christ"** (Gal. 1:7). They deceive intentionally.

2. *"That you may be zealous for **them**."* — False teachers aspire to steal the hearts of the believers. They want everyone's eyes to be fixed on them in admiration, rather than on Christ.

3. They are concerned with their personal good, not the good of the church.

18 *"But it is good to be zealous in a good thing always."* — Paul is not speaking of religious fervor, but of the concern and empathy each one of us is supposed to show towards others. It is good to be zealous for the welfare of our brothers and to do good to each other.

This desire for good aspires to draw our brothers to God and to nothing else. We must make sure at all times that we are dependent on the power of God and His grace alone, not on man or on tradition of any kind.

"Not only when I am present with you." — "Galatians, please, show spiritual maturity. Be always zealous for one another with a holy zeal, not only when I am there with you. Show your maturity by exposing the false and destructive zeal of the false teachers, and rid yourselves of them!"

"My little children, for whom I labor in birth again until Christ is formed in you." — The apostle points out the Galatian believers' sad state, but at the same time expresses his hope for improvement:

1. He shows his love for the Galatians by calling them *My little children*. All along the way he has proven his love by his concern and his sacrifice for the churches. The false teachers, on the other hand, behaved (and always will behave) in accordance with their own best interests.

2. The time and investment necessary from the time a new church is founded to the time it functions maturely and independently, is described by Paul as birth pains.

    During the first missionary journey, Paul had personally founded churches in Galatia and had then guided the young believers, teaching them over a period of several weeks and perhaps months (**Acts 13—14**). He had shared his heart with them and had been involved in every aspect of their lives. The apostle's calling this process birth pains teaches us that much pain and effort was involved in establishing those congregations.

    Since the false teachers struck at the foundation of the Galatians' faith, it was necessary to go back to the beginning and rebuild these foundations. Paul — the spiritual father of the churches in Galatia — initiated this process of restoration by writing his epistle and accompanying it with prayer. He could well say, *"for whom I labor in birth again."*

3. *"Until Christ is formed in you."* — The false teachers had managed to displace Jesus Christ from the center of the lives of the believers, but Paul did not lose hope. He believed, and certainly prayed, that his

spiritual children would return to the right way, would reject the false doctrines and would once again give Jesus Christ His rightful place. Jesus — and not man's ideas and ideologies — is the purpose of every believer's life (**Gal. 2:20; Phil. 1:6**).

Summary — False Teachers Versus True Teachers

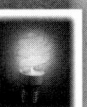

Over the past three and a half chapters Paul has responded to the accusations against him, while remaining firmly rooted in the Scriptures. In the second half of chapter 4 he proved that the motivation of the false teachers was completely self-serving — the goals set before them were their honor, their status, and their personal good.

Whereas a **faithful teacher**

- teaches the Scriptures carefully and meticulously,
- humbly receives correction,
- teaches the believers to set their eyes on Christ and to serve Him with all their heart,

a **false teacher** acts out of only one intent:

- gaining attention and personal benefits.

The means by which to defend ourselves against false teachers are:

- a personal knowledge of Jesus Christ — and as a result, the presence of the Holy Spirit within us.
- a thorough knowledge of the Word of God.
- the desire to do the will of God above anything else.

If Christ dwells in us — then false teachers will not be able to dwell in our church.

Let us examine ourselves: Whom are we serving? Whom do we look up to as an example? To whom do we surrender our lives? The correct answer to each one of these questions is: *"Jesus, the author and finisher of our faith"* (Heb. 12:2).

The Son of the Bondwoman Will Not Inherit With the Son of the Freewoman

Galatians 4:21-31:

> ²¹ Tell me, you who desire to be under the law, do you not hear the law? ²² For it is written that Abraham had two sons: the one by a bondwoman, the other by a freewoman. ²³ But he who was of the bondwoman was born according to the flesh, and he of the freewoman through promise, ²⁴ which things are symbolic. For these are the two covenants: the one from Mount Sinai which gives birth to bondage, which is Hagar — ²⁵ for this Hagar is Mount Sinai in Arabia, and corresponds to Jerusalem which now is, and is in bondage with her children — ²⁶ but the Jerusalem above is free, which is the mother of us all. ²⁷ For it is written: "Rejoice, O barren, you who do not bear! Break forth and shout, you who are not in labor! For the desolate has many more children than she who has a husband."
>
> ²⁸ Now we, brethren, as Isaac was, are children of promise. ²⁹ But, as he who was born according to the flesh then persecuted him who was born according to the Spirit, even so it is now. ³⁰ Nevertheless what does the Scripture say? "Cast out the bondwoman and her son, for the son of the bondwoman shall not be heir with the son of the freewoman." ³¹ So then, brethren, we are not children of the bondwoman but of the free.

Now the apostle describes the danger in failing to detach ourselves from the old ordinances. He uses principles taught in the Bible.

21 *"Do you not hear the law?"* — Pay attention to his manner of speaking: "Tell me, you who claim the ordinances are still valid: have you not heard what the Law says?" — In other words, "You are actually doing the opposite from what the Law teaches! — If you had obeyed the Law from the beginning, you would now be faithful disciples of Jesus, without returning to live under the dominion of obsolete commandments."

22—31 *"Abraham had two sons: the one by a bondwoman, the other by a freewoman."* — Paul uses an allegory as an example here. In order to better understand it, we need to know the events recorded in **Genesis 12—21**:

1. When Abraham was 75 years old, he was called to leave Ur of the Chaldeans and to go to the land of Canaan. Already at this point God promised him descendants, a promise that was fulfilled only about 25 years later.

2. Ten years after he had left Ur, when Abraham was 85 years old, Sarah proposed he father a child by her slave girl, Hagar. This was accepted practice in their day, but such a step was contrary to the will of God **(Gen. 16)**.

3. Ishmael was born to Hagar a year later.

4. When Abraham was 99 years old, God repeated His promise: "You will have a son from Sarah your wife." God even gave the child a name: Isaac **(Gen. 17—18)**.

5. Isaac was born when Abraham was 100 years old **(Gen. 21)**.

6. *"So the child [Isaac] grew and was weaned. And Abraham made a great feast on the same day that Isaac was weaned"* **(Gen. 21:8)**. During the festivities it became apparent that the differences between Sarah's son and the son of the bondwoman were unbridgeable. Scripture says that Sarah saw Ishmael *"scoffing"* **(Gen 21:9)**. She understood that Ishmael's actions were endangering God's promise to Abraham that *"in Isaac your seed shall be called."*

The Hebrew word translated *"scoffing"* (*metsachek* / מְצַחֵק) in the Genesis 21 account has sexual connotations in several other places in Scripture:

- **In Genesis 26:8** it describes Isaac *"caressing"* (NASB) his wife (NKJV: *"showing endearment to Rebekah"*).

- **In Genesis 39:14, 17** Potiphar's wife twice uses this same Hebrew word when she accuses Joseph of *"mocking"* her, claiming that this was in fact an attempt to "lie with her."
- **Exodus 32:6** describes the debauched festivities around the golden calf by saying that, after eating and drinking, the people *"rose up to play,"* using the same word. In **1 Corinthians 10:7-8** the apostle Paul clarifies that "rising up to play" in that instance describes "committing sexual immorality."

In light of this fact, Sarah demanded that Abraham banish Hagar's son with his mother, so that he would not inherit together with Isaac (**Gen. 21:10**). Abraham was dismayed. It was a terrible step to take. After all, Ishmael was his **son!**

7. God confirmed Sarah's demand to Abraham, *"Cast out this bondwoman and her son."* Indeed, the son of the slave would not share in the inheritance of the son of promise.

"He who was of the bondwoman was born according to the flesh." — The birth of Ishmael was the fruit of Abraham's lack of faith. After all, he and Sarah had been given a promise by God, and they should have waited patiently in faith for its fulfillment. Even while God was planning to give them a son in miraculous fulfillment of a spiritual promise, Ishmael was conceived by the will of man and in the strength of the flesh.

Problems came the moment the *"son of the bondwoman"* was forced to live with the son born as a result of the spiritual promise. It turned out that both could not live under the same roof. The son born of the flesh had to be sent away. The one to stay was the son born according to the promise of God.

In other words, what is done in our own strength and contrary to the will of God will never produce the blessing that God wants to give. We will have to get rid of it.

How does the story of Abraham and his sons reflect the situation of the Galatians (and, in fact, the situation of every believer in Jesus)?

- Hagar is a picture of the Law of ordinances — that is, the temporary works of the flesh.

- The birth of Isaac to Sarah, after she had been barren her entire life, was a miracle from God. It happened by the grace of God and in fulfillment of His promise. The birth of Isaac parallels the New Covenant that was established by the blood of Jesus Christ and grants us salvation by faith in His atonement. The new birth of every believer is also a miracle given by the grace of God in fulfillment of His promise.

- Just as it is obvious to every Jew that Ishmael could not remain together with Isaac, so it should be obvious to every believer that the authority of the Mosaic Covenant ended with the establishment of the New Covenant in the blood of Jesus, poured out for the forgiveness of our sins.

- Just as Abraham obeyed God and sent Ishmael and Hagar away, so the Galatians (and all of Israel, too), are required to obey God, to stop living in subjection to the old commandments and to accept Jesus as their Lord and only Savior, because He is the end of the Law. The false teachers and their doctrine must be rejected without hesitation.

24—26 *"Which things are symbolic [of]...the two covenants."* — Paul continues to use names and terms familiar to all. He creates a comparison that reveals the senselessness of returning to observe ordinances of the Law once Jesus Christ had fulfilled them in His death:

1. Hagar the bondwoman ➤ Mt. Sinai ➤ earthly Jerusalem ➤ the Mosaic Covenant ➤ observing the commandments by the strength of the flesh ➤ **slavery**.

2. Sarah the freewoman ➤ the heavenly Jerusalem ➤ the New Covenant ➤ doing the will of God by the power of the Holy Spirit ➤ **freedom**.

25 The Bondwoman (The Condition of the People of Israel in Paul's Day)

"Jerusalem which now is, and is in bondage with her children." — The people of Israel rejected Jesus Christ and chose to obtain their righteousness by observing the ordinances of the Law. The people chose the strength

of the flesh and rejected the power of the Spirit. For this reason they are suffering and deprived of their freedom.

The apostle points at the Jerusalem of his day, which sighs under Roman occupation, and he says: "The people of Israel today have chosen to reject the Son of promise — Jesus Christ — and have remained with the son of the flesh — the old Law. Now look at the physical consequences of your spiritual mistake: Jerusalem, the capital of the Jewish nation, is 'in bondage with her children' — occupied and under a foreign yoke." This example was like the stab of a knife in the live flesh of every Jew in the days of Paul.

26 **The Freewoman** (The Sons of the New Covenant)

"But the Jerusalem above is free, which is the mother of us all." — Those who understood that the Law was intended to prepare us to recognize and meet the Messiah Jesus, turned in faith and love to fulfilling the law of Christ. It was clear to them that their salvation was by the power of God — a gift of grace that only God can give — just like the birth of Isaac to a barren mother and a 100-year-old father.

The believers in Jesus who serve Him with no foreign yoke in their lives, are citizens of the heavenly Jerusalem **(Phil. 3:20)**. This city will never suffer occupation. It is under God's rule forever and ever. The children of God from among all the nations will live there in perfect freedom, and the Holy Spirit will be their guide in a life of holiness and purity **(Heb. 12:22; Rev. 21—22)**.

27 *"Rejoice, O barren, you who do not bear! Break forth and shout, you who are not in labor! For the desolate has many more children than she who has a husband."* — Paul is quoting from **Isaiah 54:1**. This verse was written to encourage the people of Israel after their exile to Babylon. God is assuring them: "The blessings of the future will be greater than those of the past!" The land of Israel will not remain desolate forever. The people of Israel will return to their land. They will be fruitful and multiply in it.

What does this quotation have to do with the problem the Galatians were facing? — Paul uses it to encourage the believers:

- Rejoice, sons of the promise, who have been born by the power of

God's Spirit. Do not be afraid, because you will see the day when you will outnumber the sons of the flesh.

- Rejoice, sons of the promise, because you will receive more and greater blessings than those received by all who work in the flesh — by those who choose to remain under the dominion of obsolete commandments.

28 To reinforce his words he says, *"Now we, brethren, as Isaac was, are children of promise."*

29 *"But, as he who was born according to the flesh then persecuted him who was born according to the Spirit, even so it is now."* — The conflict you witness is not new, and you must not let it surprise you. Just as the son of the flesh, Ishmael, troubled and endangered Isaac (**Gen. 21:9**), so those who reject the New Covenant that God sealed in the blood of Christ trouble the disciples of Jesus.

Remember the principle:

30 *"Cast out the bondwoman and her son, for the son of the bondwoman shall not be heir with the son of the freewoman"* (see **Gen. 21:10**). — In other words:

- Just as Ishmael could not remain under the same roof with Isaac,

in the same way,

- The believer cannot serve Jesus in freedom while at the same time submitting to obsolete commandments.

For this reason, Paul expects the Galatians (and us) to cast out the false teachers, together with their distorted teachings. There is no room for compromise when we face misrepresentation of the gospel and deviation from the truth!

31 *"So then, brethren, we are not children of the bondwoman but of the free."* — Dear brothers, make up your minds! Do you want to live as sons of the heavenly Jerusalem, or as sons of the slave? This is a difficult, emotionally charged decision, but sharp as a razor. To obey God means to understand that Christ has fulfilled the Law, and we must now serve Him without placing ourselves under the dominion of the ordinances of the Old Covenant.

- Have you chosen to remain under the dominion of these commandments? — Then you voluntarily place yourself under the curse pronounced in **Deuteronomy 27:26**. (See also **2 Chronicles 33:8**.)

- Have you received atonement for sins from the "Perfecter of the Law" — Jesus Christ? Then you have received the full grace of God and are freed from the curse. As a consequence you will aspire to live in a way that reflects Christ every day of your life.

Summary of Chapter 4:

It is not easy for individuals or nations to turn their backs on ordinances that have been a part of a 1,400-year-long tradition. However, the people of Israel in the days of Paul needed to decide:

- Would they continue to live under the dominion of ordinances that had fulfilled their purpose and were now obsolete?

   Or

- Would they obey Christ in faith, according to the conditions God determined, and as a result enjoy the freedom God gave? — And would they do so even at the possible price of rejection by family and persecution by the authorities?

There is no room for both in the same person, just as Ishmael and Isaac could not continue to live under the same roof.

This decision is necessary today also:

- either live by the rules of man-made religion and in bondage to men,
   or
- live in submission to Jesus Christ and taste of

God's freedom!

Chapter 5

Freedom in Christ

 *Why not keep all the ordinances of the Law and **also** serve Christ?*
Would that not make us twice as good?

The Word of God gives an answer to that:

Galatians 5:1-12:

> *¹Stand fast therefore in the liberty by which Christ has made us free, and do not be entangled again with a yoke of bondage. ²Indeed I, Paul, say to you that if you become circumcised, Christ will profit you nothing. ³And I testify again to every man who becomes circumcised that he is a debtor to keep the whole law. ⁴You have become estranged from Christ, you who attempt to be justified by law; you have fallen from grace. ⁵For we through the Spirit eagerly wait for the hope of righteousness by faith. ⁶For in Christ Jesus neither circumcision nor uncircumcision avails anything, but faith working through love.*

⁷ You ran well. Who hindered you from obeying the truth? ⁸ This persuasion does not come from Him who calls you. ⁹ A little leaven leavens the whole lump. ¹⁰ I have confidence in you, in the Lord, that you will have no other mind; but he who troubles you shall bear his judgment, whoever he is.

¹¹ And I, brethren, if I still preach circumcision, why do I still suffer persecution? Then the offense of the cross has ceased. ¹² I could wish that those who trouble you would even cut themselves off!

So far Paul has used many examples from life and the Scriptures in order to show the Galatians that returning under the authority of the commandments — now that Jesus has established the New Covenant — is like returning to slavery.

Which slave would prefer slavery over freedom?

As you will recall, these were the main examples:

The tutor

In chapter 3 the apostle explained that the commandments were a tutor that taught us and prepared us for the coming of the Messiah. Now that the Messiah has come, we are no longer under the authority of the tutor.

The guardian

In chapter 4 we learned that until the coming of the promised Messiah the Law served much like a guardian watching over a minor, but with the Messiah's arrival came maturity. We are now no longer under the authority of the guardian. We now know Jesus personally, and the symbols that pointed forward to Him ceased to have any bearing on us.

 ## The son of the bondwoman and the son of the freewoman

Chapter 4 presents another example: Hagar and Sarah. Ishmael — the son of the flesh — could not stay in the same home as Isaac — the son of the promise. Likewise, there is no room for both the authority of commandments that are now obsolete and the New Covenant established by Jesus through His death.

Since Paul has explained to his readers that they are no longer sons of Hagar but sons of Sarah — sons of the promise — he urges them to live in a manner worthy of sons of the promise and to enjoy the freedom granted them by their salvation:

 *"Stand fast therefore in the liberty by which Christ has made us free."*

 How is this freedom in Christ given expression?

1. **By a close relationship between God and me:**

    a. I am a child of God (**Gal. 4:1-6**). My faith in Jesus as Lord and Savior from God's righteous wrath over sinners has been tested by God and found to be true and sincere. God examines my heart. Because He knows the truth, He has accepted my plea for forgiveness and salvation. From this moment on God sees me as His son, and this can never be reversed (**Rom. 8:12-39**).

    b. As a child of God, I am indwelled with the Holy Spirit and granted all the tools I need to serve Him in purity and holiness (**Jn. 14—16; 1 Cor. 3:16-17; 2 Cor. 6:14-18; Eph. 1:13-14**).

    c. As a child of God I have been delivered from His wrath, and I am assured life in His presence in His everlasting Kingdom. There I will serve Him forever (**1 Th. 5:1-11; Rev. 21—22**).

    d. As a child of God I have direct access to the throne of God to receive mercy and help in time of need (**Heb. 4:16**).

All these rights are wonderful reasons not to lose our peace and our inner joy — anytime, anywhere.

2. By the abolition of symbolic works that demanded time and energy:

> *For He Himself is our peace, who has made both one, and has broken down the middle wall of separation, ¹⁵ having abolished in His flesh the enmity, that is, the law of commandments contained in ordinances, so as to create in Himself one new man from the two, thus making peace* (Eph. 2:14-15).

When the Mosaic Covenant was still in effect, it was the duty of every Jew to obey all the ordinances of the Law. Israelites were required to be separate from the other nations and to even look different, so that they could be a holy nation — a witness of God to the Gentiles. The differences in their lives involved:

- wearing different dress. For instance, mixing linen and wool when making cloth was forbidden;
- beards could not be shaved and hair had to be cut a certain way;
- the observance of strict dietary laws (keeping kosher);
- observance of laws regarding ritual purity;
- circumcision of all males;
- an elaborate system of sacrifices taking place in the Tabernacle and later in the Temple;
- the observance of holy days and feasts that required pilgrimages to the Temple in Jerusalem and the offering of sacrifices.

Observing the ordinances of the Law required a substantial investment in time and effort of every Jewish person. In this way the Israelites fulfilled their duty of showing to the world that they belonged to God, were faithful to His covenant and were part of His Chosen People.

The establishment of the New Covenant in the blood of Jesus Christ has fulfilled all the ordinances that were symbolic of the Messiah and His work. These ordinances are no longer in force **(Gal. 3:23-25)**, and the sons of the New Covenant are free from the tasks and requirements they entailed. They are now free to fulfill the will of God within the framework of the body of Christ, the church — without the yoke of obsolete commandments and man-made traditions.

What can limit our freedom in Christ?

Unnecessary Activity

"Stand fast ... and do not be entangled again with a yoke of bondage." — This is a warning to believers that their freedom in Christ is in danger. — In danger from what?

The false teachers tried to bring the Galatian believers back into bondage to the yoke of commandments that were now obsolete. In that way they shifted their attention away from what was crucial and deprived them of the time and freedom they were given to do God's will.

Had the Galatians given in to this distorted gospel they would have:

- avoided all contact with the Gentiles around them who desperately needed the gospel of salvation.
- cut off any fellowship with saved Gentiles who served the Lord Jesus in purity and in holiness.
- spent their time with unnecessary things that are contrary to the will of God.

Their lives would have been full of religious activity, but empty of the presence of God and His blessing.

Examples:

1. *Keeping the Jewish dietary laws (kosher):* The believer in Jesus is not required to observe these.

> **On the one hand,** a believer who lives among religious Jews is allowed to keep kosher, for the sake of his witness among the unbelievers (**Rom. 14; 1 Cor. 8—10**).
>
> **On the other hand,** if a believer in Jesus places himself under the authority of the kosher laws, he is limiting his ability to fellowship with believers who do not keep kosher, or to evangelize and fellowship with Gentiles who know nothing about such things. In this case the believer limits the scope of his service. He is not an instrument ready to serve God anywhere and in any situation. So, eat kosher when necessary, but do not set these commandments up as a condition for salvation or as an indication of greater spirituality than that of one who does not observe dietary laws!

2. *Refraining from driving on the Sabbath:* The believer in Jesus is under no such obligation.

> **On the one hand,** the believer who lives among religious Jews can choose to avoid traveling on the Sabbath, for the sake of his witness among the unbelievers around him.
>
> **On the other hand,** if this self-imposed restriction prevents him from meeting with other believers on the day intended for such fellowship, he limits his service to God and withholds from himself the spiritual food that is necessary for his growth.

The same is true regarding the prohibition to light fire on the Sabbath, or any number of other ordinances and traditions.

Freedom in Christ — A Definition

In light of the above we can now define freedom in Christ Jesus:

1. I am saved from bondage to sin and death.
2. Jesus alone is at the center of my life, and I am free from any yoke preventing me from doing the complete will of God — doing it by the help of the Holy Spirit.

3. I am free to keep certain ordinances as part of my testimony among unbelievers, on condition that:

   a. I realize they have no authority in my life.

   b. I do not allow them to inhibit me in serving Jesus Christ.

The Lord Jesus had a good reason for saying: *"If you abide in My word, you are My disciples indeed. And you shall know the truth and the truth shall make you **free**"* (Jn. 8:31-32). Spiritual freedom comes from knowing the truth — knowing Christ.

2 *"I, Paul say to you that if you become circumcised, Christ will profit you nothing."* — The apostle makes it clear to the Galatians and to us, what a serious thing it is to put oneself back under the authority of the ordinances of the Law, now that they have been fulfilled by the atoning death of Jesus Christ. He aims his words at those who choose to live under the authority of obsolete commandments and yet claim to be disciples of Jesus. (See a more detailed explanation in verse 3 below.)

3 — **4** *"And I testify again to every man who becomes circumcised that he is a debtor to keep the **whole** law. You have become estranged from Christ, you who attempt to be justified by law; you have fallen from grace."* — Those are sharp words!

What does it mean, "You have become estranged from Christ, you have fallen from grace"?

It Does **Not** Mean
You Have Lost Your Salvation • • • • • •

There are two possible interpretations:

A temporary estrangement — A believer who has been born again cannot lose the salvation God has given him by His grace and according to His sovereign will (**Jn. 10:28-29; Rom. 8:12-39; Eph. 1:4; 1 Pet. 1:5**). If a saved person strays from the truth and falls for the twisted doctrine of false teachers, he will suffer much and his life will lack God's blessing, but he will not lose his salvation. God in His grace can restore him to the way of truth.

Eternal separation — *"You have become estranged from Christ, you have fallen from grace"* can also describe a person who for a while has fellowshiped with believers but **has never been saved**. Should such a person choose to walk in a way that strays from the truth, he will reap the fruit of his decision. By turning his back on the truth of God's Word, he will find himself walking farther and farther away from Christ and His grace. Such a man does not lose his salvation, because he was never saved. It is impossible to lose what you have never had (1 Jn. 2:19).

"You Have Fallen From Grace," That Is, You Have not Utilized Your Gift

As saved children of God we have access to Him and to all He owns. As long as we are faithful in our walk with Him, He grants us all we need in order to do His will in our lives and in the world (**Ps. 37:4-5; Eph. 1:7-9; Phil. 4:19; Col. 2:3; 2 Pet. 1:3**). These gifts and abilities cannot be acquired, nor do we get them as something we deserve — they all come to us because of Christ's grace. They are at our disposal through the work of the Holy Spirit within us and under the condition that we obey God's will.

"You Have Fallen From Grace," That Is, You Have Gone Backwards

I fall from grace and miss out on the blessings that flow from walking in the truth, when I return to walking contrary to God's will, while depending on my own strength. Keeping commandments that Jesus has already fulfilled is not something God desires, when done out of a sense of obligation. Whoever walks in this way proves that he has not understood the purpose of Christ's death, and, sadly, his actions express contempt for the grace of God.

Life under the authority of commandments which are no longer valid wastes time and effort that could and should be invested in doing the will of God. Our witness is damaged, and we can become a stumbling block to others. Therefore, a follower of Christ who believes that he is still under the authority of the commandments, cannot expect the full blessing of his Savior. He finds himself taking on his shoulders the full burden of doing God's will — but without the help of God.

That is why Paul now turns to those of the Galatians who had undergone circumcision in order to gain an advantage in God's eyes or in the eyes of men. He tells them: *"Christ will profit you nothing!"*

3 *"And I testify again to every man who becomes circumcised that he is a debtor to keep the whole law."* — Paul never forbade any believing Jew or Gentile to be circumcised. He himself had Timothy circumcised (**Acts 16:3**).

What he is teaching here is: "If you undergo circumcision

- in order to gain for yourself a better standing in the eyes of God,

    and

- because you believe that the Law obliges you to do so,

then you must also obey all the other ordinances of the Law."

The apostle is not presenting a principle new and strange to Jewish ears. Circumcision should only be the outward sign of a life totally committed to doing the will of God. In fact, circumcision that is not accompanied by the "circumcision of the heart" is not acceptable to God. It is not the outward act that saves, but the circumcision of the heart, which only God can perform (**Dt. 10:16; 30:6; Jer. 4:4; Ezek. 11:17-20; 18:31; 36:26**).

"For in Christ Jesus neither circumcision nor uncircumcision avails anything"

5—**6** In contrast to those who try in vain to keep obsolete commandments, the apostle Paul presents himself as one of those who live by the Spirit of God: *"For we through the Spirit eagerly wait for the hope of righteousness by faith. ⁶ For in Christ Jesus neither circumcision nor uncircumcision avails anything, but faith working through love."*

"Faith working through love." — Spiritual life is demonstrated by love for

God and man. Whoever loves God studies His Word and obeys His instructions — and this obedience has nothing to do with wanting to obtain salvation or receiving any personal advantage.

For we through the Spirit." — The believer who lives by the guidance of the Holy Spirit is one whose life and behavior reflect the grace of Christ. After all, the spiritual person **wants** to be controlled by the Holy Spirit. When this is happening and we do not impede His work by our egoism or fleshly desires, then He uses us as tools to bring glory and honor to God. Remember: True spirituality is expressed by treating others in the same way Jesus treats us.

"We... eagerly wait for the hope." — The hope of every believer is life in the Kingdom of God with a new body — a perfect body like that of Christ, which will make it possible for the believer to live for God without sin. **(See Romans 5:1-11; Ephesians 4:17 — 6:24; Hebrews 11:1.)**

"Righteousness by faith." — The hope that one day we will stand justified before our Father in heaven springs from our faith in Jesus Christ. Its foundation is saving faith, not perfect observance of the Law **(Gen. 15:6; Hab. 2:4)**. That is why Romans 5:17 calls it *"the **gift** of righteousness."*

"For in Christ Jesus neither circumcision nor uncircumcision avails anything." — Paul again stresses that the gift of salvation makes no difference between Jew or Gentile. The Holy Spirit dwells in both, and both enjoy His guidance. Both have the same purpose: to live in holiness and purity and to testify of the salvation of Jesus Christ that is offered to all men — to the Jew first and also to the Gentile **(Rom. 1:16-17; 2 Cor. 5; Gal. 3:26-29)**.

National background has no bearing on a person's salvation. The only thing that counts is his faith in Jesus the Messiah as his Lord and Savior from sin **(Jn. 14:6; Acts 4:12; Rom. 10:9-10)**.

Note!

In verses 5-6 Paul mentions three foundations: **faith**, **hope,** and **love**:

- *"Having been justified by **faith**"* (Rom. 5:1);

- we are now *"looking for the blessed **hope** and glorious appearing of our great God and Savior Jesus Christ"* (Ti. 2:13).

- And we are commanded to love, *"For **love** is of God, and everyone who loves is born of God and knows God"* (1 Jn. 4:7).

These are meant to identify the believer in Jesus — not only in Galatia in the days of the apostles, but in all our churches today. That is why Paul states elsewhere: *"And now abide faith, hope, love, these three; but the greatest of these is love"* (1 Cor. 13:13; see also Col. 1:4-5; 1 Th. 1:3).

You Ran so Well!

7 — **11** The apostle calls upon the Galatians to abandon their error and to return to the way of Life — to a walk with Christ:

> *⁷ You ran well. Who hindered you from obeying the truth? ⁸ This persuasion does not come from Him who calls you. ⁹ A little leaven leavens the whole lump. ¹⁰ I have confidence in you, in the Lord, that you will have no other mind; but he who troubles you shall bear his judgment, whoever he is.*
>
> *¹¹ And I, brethren, if I still preach circumcision, why do I still suffer persecution? Then the offense of the cross has ceased.*

"You ran well." — When Paul first visited the region of Galatia and taught about the New Covenant that Jesus had established in His death, the Galatians obeyed the truth and lovingly adopted it.

God was not indifferent to their spiritual diligence. By the signs and wonders done among them He confirmed that the message of Paul and other believers was indeed the truth, and He showered blessings on them **(chap. 3)**.

"You ran." — Paul depicts the life of a believer as a race in the service of God. It is not enough to **begin** the race well, because the wreath of victory is given only to those who complete it **(1 Cor. 9:24-27; Gal. 2:2; Phil. 3:13-14; 2 Tim. 4:7)**. — "Dear Galatians, you walked in the way of truth and tasted of all its blessings! Who led you astray?"

 **Who is the source of "this persuasion"?**

8 *"This persuasion does not come from Him who calls you."* — This is a hint to what every child of God knows from experience: Satan is not pleased to see us serve our Savior in purity and holiness, and he does not remain idle (**1 Pet. 5:8**). Wherever the way of Jesus is adopted, Satan will sow seeds of doubt, lies, and dissension, trying to put an end to the spread of the Light. **He** is the one who tempts us so we would fall, and you can be sure that temptation never comes from *"Him who calls you"* (i.e. God — **Jas. 1:13**).

Paul never taught the people of Galatia a false doctrine. The false doctrine that caused them to stumble came from the false teachers who acted in the wisdom of Satan rather than in the wisdom of God. Their presence and their becoming entrenched in the congregations of Galatia was the temptation to which the Galatians had fallen (**chap. 1**). Had the believers stuck to the truth of God, they would have been able to identify the false brethren immediately and get rid of them.

False teachers do not come with a sign on their forehead marking them as evil. All believers are required to examine every doctrine and all teaching by comparing them to the written Word of God. That is the only way to know whether the teacher is guided by the Holy Spirit or by Satan. **Acts 17:11** commends the Jews of Berea for comparing Paul's words to Scripture when he taught in their synagogue.

"Purge Out the Old Leaven" of Sin! (1 Cor. 5:7)

9 *"A little leaven leavens the whole lump."* — This is a warning to believers not to take in even the tiniest bit of the doctrine of false teachers (**1 Cor. 5:6**). Jesus used the same vocabulary when He warned His disciples of the false teaching of the Pharisees (**Mt. 16:11-12; 23**). Just like Jesus, Paul understood how dangerous false teaching is for God's children:

- When a mistake in doctrine is identified in the church, it must be corrected.

- When false teaching is spread on purpose and with evil intent, it must be uprooted from the church together with those who teach it. In such cases we must follow the guidelines given in **Matthew 18:15-20**.

Paul's allegory is clear: The amount of yeast we add to a dough is very small compared to the amount of flour and other ingredients — but still, the yeast acts on all the dough and causes it to rise. In the same way a little false teaching will affect the whole church if we allow it to stay.

"A little leaven." — The observance of ordinances that are obsolete with the conviction that it is one's duty to do so, is sin! Sin has no place in the life of a believer in Jesus and no place in the house of God. We must repent of it and get rid of it. If we fail to do so, the sin will spread and contaminate all who come in contact with it.

The believer in Jesus must understand that the death of Christ has established the New Covenant. Ever since, what saves a person is his faith in Jesus as Lord and Savior from sin. **Nothing else** is required (**Jer. 31:31-34; Rom. 10:9-10; 1 Cor. 11:25; 2 Cor. 3; Eph. 2:1-10**).

Why Such Harshness?

If the believers in Galatia had remained focused on Jesus and kept the commandments as a cosmetic addition, Paul would not have bothered to write the epistle. But in actual fact we see the apostle criticizing the false teachers harshly and even wishing that they be cut off (v. 12: *"I only wish that they who trouble you would cut themselves off!"*). Why such harshness? Because they were leading the believers away from salvation! The doctrines of the false teachers had no life. Paul calls them *"a different gospel"* (Gal. 1:6) — which leads to death!

The false teachers taught that it was necessary to do something else in order to be saved. As far as they were concerned, the death of Jesus Christ was not enough to save.

> Such a view holds God and His grace in contempt and further, denies the divinity of Jesus.
>
> *Such another gospel does not show the way to salvation.*
>
> - It has no power to save non-believers;
> - Believers who follow it are being led into error.

10 *"I have confidence in you, in the Lord."* — Paul expresses his confidence that the current deviation in the churches of Galatia will be corrected. He knows that God will complete the work He has begun in those He has chosen from before time. The same confidence is expressed in Philippians 1:6: *"Being confident of this very thing, that He who has begun a good work in you will complete it until the day of Jesus Christ."*

"He who troubles you shall bear his judgment." — God is not indifferent towards those who trouble His children's faith. Everyone will stand in judgment before the Creator and give an account of all he has done. The enemies of God will be sentenced to eternal banishment from His presence and to everlasting shame **(Dan. 12; Lk. 17:1-2; Rev. 20:11-15)**.

The Offense of the Cross

11 *"And I, brethren, if I still preach circumcision, why do I still suffer persecution? Then the offense of the cross has ceased."* — This sentence helps us understand why some of the believers jumped on the bandwagon of keeping the old ordinances. The false teachers promised them:

1. **salvation** — because they believed in Jesus;
2. **first-class status as believers** — because they would add extra virtues to their salvation by keeping the commandments;
3. **the chance to get rid of the offense of the cross** — because the focus in their personal testimony and their gospel would no longer be on the crucified Messiah — God who came in the flesh — but on observance of the commandments.

Paul describes the true gospel by saying: *"We preach Christ crucified, to the Jews a stumbling block and to the Greeks foolishness"* (1 Cor. 1:23). However, with a "gospel" that does **not** proclaim God the Son dying on a cross for our sins, one can be accepted by both Jew and Greek.

"Why do I still suffer persecution?" — Paul was persecuted and rejected by his unbelieving nation because he taught that the ordinances of the Law had fulfilled their role and had become obsolete. Now he began to suffer persecution within the church of Christ also, because of the spiritual poison the false teachers were spreading against him and against his doctrine.

If Paul had kept silent and adopted the false teaching, he would have been welcomed everywhere. But he preferred to be acceptable before God, to proclaim the gospel of salvation the way God intended it to be told and to suffer at the hands of men (**2 Tim. 3:12**). He knew that nothing is more important in life than to please God.

"If I still preach circumcision." — Close to the time Paul wrote this epistle to the Galatians, he had Timothy circumcised (**Acts 16:3**). It is quite possible that the false teachers were spreading a rumor that Paul was doing exactly what they did and agreed with their teaching. However, the apostle had Timothy circumcised by choice and convenience, not out of duty or submission to the authority of obsolete commandments. After all, he did **not** have Titus circumcised. (See a detailed explanation under the title "Circumcision of Believers — When is it Acceptable…When is it Not?" in the commentary on Galatians 2:5.)

Now Paul asks: "If I do indeed hold to the same opinion as the false teachers, then why am I still persecuted for my faith?"

The cross of Jesus is a stumbling block. Whoever tries to get around that by hiding the cross may be accepted by men — but not by God.

Note!

> When I say we must not hide the cross of Jesus, I do not mean every believer should wear a cross on a necklace.

The meaning is:

- to live in obedience to the Scriptures;

- to refuse to deny my faith in Jesus as Lord and Savior, even at the cost of persecution.

Carrying the cross of Jesus means doing God's will for my life in faith, submission, and love.

A Sharp Reaction to Serious Sin

12 *"I could wish that those who trouble you would even cut themselves off!"* — In his epistle to the Galatians Paul mentions (relatively) often the punishment that awaited the false teachers and his hope that they would meet the end they deserved **(1:9)**. There are two reasons he used such harsh language:

1. He saw the damage caused by these teachers. He saw with his own eyes how people left the truth and adopted a lie. Paul saw how the gospel of Jesus Christ — the gospel that gives life — was exchanged for empty words, for a "gospel" that is unable to save.

2. Jesus Christ gave His life for us, but the doctrine of the false teachers turned His sacrifice into something cheap that is not enough to save us.

The false teachers led believers from a state of blessing to a curse, and unbelievers who trusted in their "gospel" were led to destruction. The apostle Paul could not remain indifferent in the face of such damage. *"I could wish that those who trouble you would even cut themselves off [be killed]"* is an extremely harsh thing to say, but it expresses the apostle's pain and his concern for the church of God and the believing souls in Galatia.

There is another explanation for the words *"cut themselves off."* They could express the desire of the apostle that the Galatians would rid themselves of the false teachers by the process prescribed in **Matthew 18:15-20**.

 Why do we not find a single invitation throughout the entire epistle, calling upon the false teachers to repent?

Those who had turned out to be false teachers and false brethren were all claiming to believe in Jesus. They had participated in the life and activities of the various congregations of believers they came out of, and there they had been exposed to the true gospel. Most likely, some of them had even sat under the teaching of the apostles themselves. They had then decided that the simple gospel was not enough.

Any person who is presented with God's full truth and rejects it denies himself an opportunity to repent and receive forgiveness of his sins. That is a dangerous thing to do, because such opportunity may never return (Heb. 6:4-8).

If only we, the believers today, would show the same kind of concern and alertness in all that has to do with the purity of the gospel and a life of holiness. Paul's warning to Timothy is relevant to us today:

2 Timothy 3:12-14:

> *¹² Yes, and all who desire to live godly in Christ Jesus will suffer persecution. ¹³ But evil men and impostors will grow worse and worse, deceiving and being deceived. ¹⁴ But you must continue in the things which you have learned and been assured of, knowing from whom you have learned them.*

Summary — Do not Limit the Freedom That Is in Christ!

1. The apostle Paul gives us a clear, decisive message: The ordinances of the Law were fulfilled in the atonement of Jesus. Therefore, whoever decides to limit himself by those commandments limits the scope of his service to God. Freedom in Christ means being free to serve God with no strange yoke.

2. When you act contrary to the will of God, you have only your own strength and ability to lean on. But when you live by the guidance of God, the Holy Spirit will give you His power and wisdom. Such a life — the life of freedom

— is a life of power. It is lived by the grace of God, it honors God and it brings forth blessed fruit.

3. Today as in Paul's day, believers in Jesus who are faithful to the gospel of truth ("who bear the cross of Christ") are not accepted and are often rejected by society.

Let us remain faithful in prayer, in the study of God's Word and in asking Him to help us not to deny Jesus. As we mature in faith we come to know Him better. We will learn that rejection, persecution and ostracism because of our faithfulness to Jesus — with all the pain they may cause — are an honor to the believer, because *"all who desire to live godly in Christ Jesus will suffer persecution."*

Called to Freedom

Galatians 5:13-15:

> ¹³ *For you, brethren, have been called to liberty; only do not use liberty as an opportunity for the flesh, but through love serve one another.* ¹⁴ *For all the law is fulfilled in one word, even in this: "You shall love your neighbor as yourself."* ¹⁵ *But if you bite and devour one another, beware lest you be consumed by one another!*

13 The apostle informs the Galatians that they are free in Christ.

Can you imagine what would happen if we told our children they are **free** and left it at that? Wouldn't we immediately have to define the limits within which they are free? Why? Because a child usually understands freedom as a license to go and do whatever comes into his head to do. If he is not given boundaries, he will most likely harm himself or those around him.

In my own life I have learned that there is little difference between adults and children in their grasp of the concept of freedom. For most, the word *freedom* describes a situation where they can satisfy all their selfish desires, without any regard for the interests of others. Paul knows all about this faulty understanding, which is why he adds:

"Only do not use liberty as an opportunity for the flesh." — That is to say: "Beware of interpreting the freedom Christ has given you as a permission to indulge in wrong desires."

So what is the right way of implementing the freedom Jesus has given us?

To Serve — But in Love

13—**14** *"Through love serve one another."* — "Dear Galatians, you who wish to be slaves to the obsolete ordinances of the Law, why do you not invest your efforts in something positive? Be slaves to one another in love, because *'love is the fulfillment of the law'* **(Rom. 13:10)**." Freedom in Christ Jesus, then, is expressed by serving others in love **(Jn. 13:34-35; 1 Cor. 13; 1 Jn. 4:11)**.

Why didn't the apostle simply say, *"Serve one another!"*? Why did he need to specify that this had to be *"through love,"* and why did he add emphasis by saying, *"For all the law is fulfilled in one word, even in this: 'You shall love your neighbor as yourself'"* **(Lev. 19:18)**? — Because serving others without love is not service. It is work done to earn money, to gain respect, or to earn some other kind of reward. Such service will be temporary, continuing as long as it yields some kind of personal gain, and it is done in the strength of the flesh. It does not bring full satisfaction, it lacks the blessing of God, and in the end it will be a disappointment. This is the kind of service the Galatians received from the false teachers.

In his first epistle to the Corinthians Paul dedicates an entire chapter to defining *love*: *"Love suffers long and is kind; love does not envy; love does not parade itself, is not puffed up;* ⁵ *does not behave rudely, does not seek its own, is not provoked, thinks no evil"* (**1 Cor. 13:4-5.**) And these are just **some** of the qualities of love!

14 *"For all the law is fulfilled in one word."* — Since true love gives the welfare of others top priority, wherever it reigns there is no need for laws that threaten with punishment in order to regulate the life of society (**Lev. 19:18; Mt. 7:12; 19:19; 22:39-40**).

"Love your neighbor as yourself." — Who is my neighbor? Is he the neighbor next door, a relative, or someone I care for? — Not necessarily. From the parable of the Good Samaritan (**Lk. 10:25-37**) we learn that my neighbor is also anyone else nearby — anyone in need, including the foreigner.

How do I get such love that cancels out my ambition for personal gain, puts others before myself, and fulfills the Law?

There is only one way to be filled with such love:

- *"The love of God has been poured out in our hearts by **the Holy Spirit** who was given to us"* (**Rom. 5:5**).

- *"The fruit of **the Spirit** is love"* (**Gal. 5:22**).

It originates with the Holy Spirit. It is not something I can produce myself. From the moment God has verified my belief in His truth as sincere, His Holy Spirit takes up residence within me. From Him I receive a new nature and the gifts of the Holy Spirit. The ministry of the Holy Spirit within me will bear fruit — the fruit of the Spirit — and the foremost fruit of the Spirit is love. (See more on the gifts and the fruit of the Holy Spirit in the commentary on Galatians 5:22-23, pp. 221-226.)

This is the love of God, the same love that motivated God the Father to give His Son to be a sacrifice for me: *"For God so loved the world that He gave His only begotten Son, that whoever believes in Him should not perish but have everlasting life"* (**Jn. 3:16**). Only the love given by God can enable us to serve consistently and sacrificially without selfish motives.

Conclusions:

- Whoever desires to live a life of freedom for Christ needs the guidance of the Holy Spirit.
- Freedom in Christ is expressed in service to each other, motivated by the love of God in our hearts.

15 *"But if you bite and devour one another beware lest you be consumed by one another!"* — This describes the state of affairs in the Galatian churches, at the time the epistle was written.

A lack of love and hurting each other, are a direct result of the works of the flesh. From the moment the Galatians took their eyes off Christ, they lost their joy of salvation. From the moment they turned to another way they began to pay the price of moving away from God's grace, involvement, and power in their lives. Instead of serving one another in love, trusting that the Lord Jesus gives each one of us all we need, they began to serve themselves at the cost of harming each other.

Under the influence of the false teachers, the believers descended into a miserable state of hatred, jealousy, and squabbling. The testimony they were supposed to bear for Jesus had hit rock bottom **(Jas. 4:1-10)**.

From verse 16 onward, Paul explains what the missing ingredient of their life is. His aim is to heal the spiritual gangrene that has started to spread throughout the Galatian congregations.

Walking in the Spirit

Galatians 5:16-18:

> ¹⁶*I say then: Walk in the Spirit, and you shall not fulfill the lust of the flesh.* ¹⁷*For the flesh lusts against the Spirit, and the Spirit against the flesh; and these are contrary to one another, so that*

you do not do the things that you wish. ¹⁸ But if you are led by the Spirit, you are not under the law.

 "Walk in the Spirit" — what does this mean?

¹⁶—¹⁷ We can widen our scope by looking at what the apostle writes to the believers in Ephesus on the same subject: *"Do not be drunk with wine, in which is dissipation; but be filled with the Spirit, ¹⁹ speaking to one another in psalms and hymns and spiritual songs, singing and making melody in your heart to the Lord, ²⁰ giving thanks always for all things to God the Father in the name of our Lord Jesus Christ"* **(Eph. 5:18-20)**. Here is the commandment to *"be filled with the Spirit."*

 *What does **this** mean? Doesn't the Holy Spirit already dwell within the body of the believer from the moment he is saved* **(1 Cor. 3:16; Eph. 1:13-14)**?

What both passages mean is that the believer is completely given to the guidance of the Spirit of God — and the guidance of the Spirit of God will **always** be according to the Scriptures. — It means a way of life characterized by doing the will of God and by submission of our will and opinions to Him **(Prov. 3:5-8)**.

Let us look at some components of walking in the Spirit and being filled with the Spirit — of living a life guided by the Spirit of God:

Walking in holiness — The Scriptures make it absolutely clear what should characterize a child of God. All of us, with no exception, are to live pure lives, as befits citizens of heaven. (See the Sermon on the Mount in **Matthew 5—7; Ephesians 4:17 — 6:24; 1 Timothy 4:6 — 6:21**.)

Walking according to God's will — Still, we are sometimes called to make decisions or do things that the Bible does not mention specifically. When that happens we must use the other tools God has given us, in order to determine what is right to do:

1. prayer;
2. systematic and consistent reading of the Word of God, so that we will learn His principles and live by them;
3. the counsel of mature believers (**Prov. 11:14**).

When we place our lives in God's hands we receive (through the Holy Spirit) understanding, power, faith, and courage to live according to the will of God.

Walking in confidence — When the Holy Spirit guides us, we receive an additional privilege: the ability to see reality through God's eyes. Here are a few examples:

1. **Family conflict, marital crisis, or conflict with brothers in the faith**

   Believers in Jesus are not immune to problems and difficulties of this sort. Just like everyone else, we try to solve them in our own strength and by leaning on our own wisdom and goodness. But God teaches us to approach conflicts in a different way.

   When we are guided by the Holy Spirit, we can lay all our problems, worries, and suffering before the Lord. He gives us the strength to forgive and to yield and the wisdom to understand where we have failed and where we are duty-bound to apologize and confess our sins. When we take on the ways of the Holy Spirit to solve crises in our personal and family lives, we discover we have achieved peace and harmony in a worthy manner that ensures good relations over the long term.

   Our *"**walking in** [the ways of] **the Spirit**"* brings glory to the name of Christ and makes us faithful witnesses of Him (**Mt. 18:15-20; 2 Cor. 5:20; Eph. 4:17ff.**).

2. **What are the chances of finding a job in a place plagued by unemployment?**

   Chances "through the eyes of the flesh": I examine the chances against my personal ability, scan the job offers in newspapers, the Internet, and at the employment office, consult friends, send my resumé to as many potential employers as possible. However, when nothing works, my self confidence dwindles and my heart fills with despair.

   Chances "through the eyes of the Spirit": I take all the steps mentioned above, but as a saved person I have an additional resource, which is superior to all the rest: I trust in God, because He has promised to provide all my needs. I believe and trust that He will grant me the right solution at the right time. I pray that He will guide me to the right places and direct my search according to His will. As I pray, I am already thanking Him for the workplace that I believe He will give me when the time is right in His eyes (**Ps. 37:4-5, 25; Mt. 6:25-34; 1 Jn. 3:22; 5:14-15**).

   I am aware of all the circumstances (which may be very dismal) but compare the size of the problem with God's power and His promises.

   As a child of God I am undergoing a shaping process at the hands of the Creator. Some of the difficulties in my life are intended to bring me to greater spiritual maturity, to cause me to lean on the grace of God, and to experience His power and providence on levels and in areas I had not known before. (**See for instance 2 Chronicles 14:9-12: King Asa; 2 Chronicles 20: King Jehoshaphat**).

   In addition, God has given me a spiritual family — the church — that stands by me in times of need and difficulty.

3. **The 12 Spies** (Num. 13—14)

   - **Ten spies** described what they saw in the Promised Land and reached conclusions based on a comparison of the obstacles with their human abilities. They advised the people to return to Egypt.

- **Joshua and Caleb** saw the same reality but evaluated it in light of what they knew of God and His promises. They knew that it was possible to conquer the land, because they saw the reality through the eyes of God!

By their faith in God the two continued to walk in the desert throughout the entire 40 years. In the end their faith in God's promises was rewarded: They entered the land of Canaan, whereas all the other spies died in the desert. (For a definition of faith see **Hebrews 11:1**.)

4. **David and Goliath**

- All the soldiers under King Saul fled. They felt inferior and were afraid because they compared their strength to Goliath's.

- David, on the other hand, stood up to Goliath and won. After hearing Goliath's words of scorn, David knew that the Philistine had maneuvered himself into a lose-lose position: Goliath was fighting against God!

David assessed his chances by the difference between Goliath's strength and God's strength:

1 Samuel 17:45-47:

> *⁴⁵Then David said to the Philistine, "You come to me with a sword, with a spear, and with a javelin. But I come to you in the name of the LORD of hosts, the God of the armies of Israel, whom you have defied. ⁴⁶This day the LORD will deliver you into my hand, and I will strike you and take your head from you. And this day I will give the carcasses of the camp of the Philistines to the birds of the air and the wild beasts of the earth, that all the earth may know that there is a God in Israel. ⁴⁷Then all this assembly shall know that*

> the LORD does not save with sword and spear; for the battle is the LORD's, and He will give you into our hands."

5. Elisha and the Syrian army (2 Ki. 6)

When the enemy army surrounded his house, the prophet Elisha was at peace. Through the eyes of his spirit he saw the army of God surrounding the army of the enemy. He acted in the knowledge that God was with him — and was saved.

2 Kings 6:16-17:

> ¹⁶ *So he answered* [Elisha to his servant], *"Do not fear, for those who are with us are more than those who are with them."* ¹⁷ *And Elisha prayed, and said, "LORD, I pray, open his eyes that he may see." Then the LORD opened the eyes of the young man, and he saw. And behold, the mountain was full of horses and chariots of fire all around Elisha.*

16 *"But if you are led by the Spirit."* — The Galatians were confronted with a difficult choice: to return under the authority of the Law and thus to *"fulfill the lust of the flesh"* (5:16), or to move forward in the freedom of Jesus and to be *"led by the Spirit"* (v. 18).

- From a human point of view, choosing Jesus meant: social pressure, ostracism, going against one's emotions.

On the other hand,

- whoever considers opting for Jesus on the basis of what he has read in the Bible,
- and whoever asks God in prayer to guide him to make the right decision,

will eventually give his life to Jesus. From that point on he will experience the protection of God, who is able to confound any attempt to harm His children **(Ps. 37:4-5; Prov. 2:7; Nah. 1:7; 1 John 5:14-15)**.

Intermediate Summary —

Freedom, Service, and the Holy Spirit:

1. Freedom in Christ is expressed by a life that does not submit to the authority of obsolete ordinances, or to man's traditions. At the same time it involves a mission that is beyond human capabilities: obedience to God in all things, in faith and in love.

Conclusion: A life of freedom in Christ is possible only by the guidance of the Holy Spirit and in His strength.

2. Life in the Spirit is diametrically opposed to life in the flesh.

- **Life in the flesh** is a life with no real confidence in God. Everything is measured by man's ability, not by God's limitless power. Such a life is sure to bring loss, fear, and failure.

- **Life in the Spirit** is a life led by faith in God and His sovereignty and by looking at all things through God's eyes. For instance, our ability to overcome difficulties is measured by God's power, not man's. We trust in God, know Him personally and allow Him to dictate the direction our life takes. This makes for a life full of joy and blessing and free of fear.

Spiritual life is, in fact, supernatural life.

In light of the above conclusions, everyone can examine to what extent he is living in the freedom of Christ and to what extent his life is guided by the Holy Spirit.

Works Of the Flesh

Now Paul lists the characteristics the Galatians will exhibit if they continue to walk in the flesh, that is, continue to live their lives contrary to God's will and without the guidance of the Holy Spirit. The apostle's diagnosis is true not only of the Galatians but of any group of people who reject Jesus Christ as their personal and only Savior.

Galatians 5:19-21:

> ¹⁹ *Now the works of the flesh are evident, which are: adultery, fornication, uncleanness, lewdness,* ²⁰ *idolatry, sorcery, hatred, contentions, jealousies, outbursts of wrath, selfish ambitions, dissensions, heresies,* ²¹ *envy, murders, drunkenness, revelries, and the like; of which I tell you beforehand, just as I also told you in time past, that those who practice such things will not inherit the kingdom of God.*

Remember:

In Galatians 5:18 we learned that *"if you are led by the Spirit, you are not under the law."*

So if the Holy Spirit dwells within me and influences my personality, my thoughts, my strength, and my will, then I will not murder, or covet, or steal, and so on. My works will be holy, not because the Law forbids impurity, but because I am sanctified by the Holy Spirit within me, and by His help I am becoming more and more like Jesus.

Ever since I was saved and gave my life to the Lord, my actions are no longer motivated by the flesh, but by the will of God (**Rom. 7:6; 2 Cor. 3**).

This should be so ideally, but what I actually do face in my daily life is:

The Struggle

Since I have not yet received my perfect body, the flesh — my old nature — is active within me and pulls me against the will of the Spirit. This struggle will continue until I am delivered from my earthly body **(Rom. 7:14-25; 1 Cor. 15:50-58)**.

The Holy Spirit who dwells within me gives me the strength to resist the urges of the flesh. However, I often fail.

When this happens:

- The Spirit of God awakens my conscience and leads me to confess my sin **(Jn. 14:16-26; 15:26-27; 16:5-15)**.
- I receive God's forgiveness on the basis of the sacrifice of Jesus Christ and by His grace only **(1 Jn. 1:9)**.
- I try with all my might not to fall again into the same sin **(Rom. 6; 2 Pet. 2:22; Jude 17-25)**.

As a saved person, my life is filled with God's peace and love. Increasingly, these replace evil and cause the character and nature of Christ to be developed within me.

This does not happen because I am good, but by the grace of God and for His glory.

The apostle Paul teaches:

- If my righteousness is based on the saving grace of God, then the Holy Spirit dwells within me and gives me the strength to deal with the desires of the flesh **(1 Cor. 10:13)**.
- If I try to reach perfection by perfectly keeping the ordinances of the Law, I will fail. My flesh will cause that failure. When I try to keep the commandments of God in the ability of the flesh, all that will be revealed in my life are the *"works of the flesh"* — as listed in **verses 19-21** — and not the *"fruit of the Spirit."*

19 *"Works of the flesh"* — is a name for our efforts when they do not involve God, when we are cut off from His grace. Whenever I give in to ways of behavior and to ideas that are contrary to the character and nature of God, that's when I perform *"works of the flesh."* By doing so, I find myself walking in the footsteps of the enemy of God — Satan.

The sad fact is that all of us, with no exception, are guilty of the sins listed in verses 19-21, regardless whether we actually commit them, or just allow them to take place in our thoughts. We are subject to the pressures of sin as long as we live in a body contaminated by sin and influenced by it. In the future, when we are changed and receive our perfect body, we will be completely free from sin and its consequences **(1 Cor. 15:35-58)**.

"The works of the flesh are evident."

- As a believer, I cannot hide sin. If I manage to conceal it today, it will be discovered tomorrow. God sees my sin at once, and those around me will see the consequences of it before long.

- If I am an unsaved person in fellowship with believers, I will not be able to play the role of a "look-alike" indefinitely. A person who does not have the indwelling of the Holy Spirit will inevitably reveal this in one way or another: *"The works of the flesh are **evident**."*

"Which Are":

(The definitions given in italics are taken from Babylon English Dictionary*)*

Adultery (Greek: μοιχεία / *moicheia*):

Adultery: infidelity, fornication, sexual relations with someone other than one's spouse.

Fornication (Greek: πορνεία / *porneia*, from which we have the word "pornography"): This refers to any sexual activity that is contrary to God's way: extra-marital sex of all kinds, homosexual relations, sex between people and animals, incest and, prostitution.

Fornication: sexual intercourse between two people who are not married to each other.

Porneia in a wider sense is: dissoluteness, indulgence, intemperance, licentiousness, dissipation, lechery, debauchery, immoral self-indulgence; promiscuity, prostitution, lust.

Uncleanness (Greek: ἀκαθαρσία / *akatharsia*): a deviation from purity in the widest sense — in thought, word, and deed **(Eph. 5:3-5)**.

Impurity of mind, immodesty; depravity, defilement, contamination; abomination; decay; corruption; that which is forbidden to eat;

Unclean: not clean, dirty, soiled; morally impure, wicked; ceremonially impure (biblical).

Lewdness (Greek: ἀσέλγεια / *aselgeia*): openly acting out the perversions listed above **(Rom. 13:13; 2 Cor. 12:21)**.

Excess, licentiousness, absence of restraint, indecency, wantonness; one of the evils that proceed from the heart [Mk. 7:22-23] (*Vine's Expository Dictonary*).

Lewd: obscene, indecent, vulgar; lustful, licentious, lecherous.

20 Idolatry (Greek: εἰδωλολατρία / *eidōlolatria*):

   a. Bowing before idols with religious faith. The religious rites of idol worship in the time we are discussing involved fornication, adultery and lewdness.

   b. Any kind of spiritual worship that is not according to the specific guidelines given by God in the Scriptures is idolatry.

An example: In the days of Elijah the prophet, most of the Israelites have strayed from God's truth. God tells Elijah that among his entire nation there are only 7,000 *"whose knees have not bowed to Baal"* **(1 Ki. 19:18)**. It is likely that not all the people of Israel bowed the knee to Baal physically, but their deviation from the truth and their mixing of the truth with foreign beliefs was idolatry.

Sorcery (Greek: φαρμακεία / *pharmakeia*, from which we have the words *pharmaceutics* and *pharmacy*): Idol worship in ancient Greece involved the use of drugs concocted to bring the worshiper into a state of trance. All forms of ecstasy were considered expressions of a lofty spirituality and a means of drawing near to the level of the gods.

We see the same phenomena in today's idol worship. Already the book of Revelation foretold that men would refuse to learn from the experience of the past. In fulfillment of that, we witness people around us despise the grace of God, preferring to do the same things that brought destruction on their forefathers throughout human history (**Rev. 9:21; 18:23**).

S o r c e r y : casting of magic spells, witchcraft, black magic.

Hatred (Greek: ἔχθραι / *echthrai*):

Extreme dislike, enmity.

Contentions (Greek: ἔρεις / *ereis*):

C o n t e n t i o n : struggle, strife; claim, assertion, argument; belligerency, aggressiveness; act of contending; discord; rivalry, competition.

Jealousies (Greek: ζῆλος / *zelos*): a dissatisfaction or self-torment at seeing the success of someone else, a negative competitiveness.

J e a l o u s y : envy, covetousness, resentment; vigilance, zealousness; intolerance.

Wrath (Greek: θυμός / *thumos*): anger, fury, rage, animosity toward someone.

Selfish ambitions (Greek: ἐριθεία / *eritheia*): rivalries (*Green's Literal Translation*), ambitions which take no account of anyone besides myself; unwillingness to see good come to others.

Dissensions (Greek: διχοστασία / *dichostasia*): stubbornly clinging to opinions that cause trouble among the believers. The source of dissensions is pride and the refusal to submit to the authority and truth of God's Word.

D i s s e n s i o n : conflict of opinion, argument, dissidence, disunity, discord, quarrel, strife, trouble, wrangles, struggle and rifts.

Heresies (Greek: αἵρεσις / *hairesis*): the denying of the truth, splitting up into groups as a result of contentions and in-fighting;

㉑ Envy (φθόνος / *phthonos*): The feeling of displeasure produced by witnessing or hearing of the advantage or prosperity of others. — *Zelos* (see "jealousies" above) is to be distinguished from *phthonos*. The distinction lies in this, that "envy" desires to deprive another of what he has, whereas "jealousy" desires to have the same or the same sort of thing for itself (*Vine's Expository Dictonary*).

Murders (Greek: φόνος / *phonos*)

Drunkenness (Greek: μέθη / *methē*): giving way to a strong desire for alcoholic drinks, to the point of confusion and loss of one's clarity of mind. Habitual intoxication (*Vine's Expository Dictonary*).

Revelries (Greek: κῶμος / *kōmos*): frivolity, mischief, licentiousness, dissipation, moral abandonment; the concomitant and consequence of drunkenness.

All these traits, whether singly or together, can damage or destroy unity and cause grief, pain, and loss. They are characteristic of a person who is self-centered, does not consider others and for the most part even works against them. They demonstrate a complete absence of love and are therefore very obviously the fruit of the flesh under the influence of sin and Satan.

These traits are a recipe for personal disaster and for the disintegration of the family unit and society in general.

"Those who practice such things will not inherit the kingdom of God." — Whoever rejects the righteousness of God, which is given by His grace through faith in Jesus Christ, will find himself enslaved to the characteristics that Paul defines as *"works of the flesh."* Whoever rejects Jesus rejects the Holy Spirit, and it is only by the Holy Spirit that we are able to overcome the works of the flesh.

In other words, even the best that man can do in his own strength leads to disaster and destruction of the human race. History has proven that time and time again.

Most important:

Whoever seeks to make his way into the Kingdom of God in his own strength — in the strength of the flesh — will fail. Eternal life in His Kingdom is a gift of grace given by God through faith in Jesus Christ alone (**Jn. 14:6; Acts 4:12; Rom. 10:9-10**).

The Fruit of the Spirit

Galatians 5:22-26:

> *²² But the fruit of the Spirit is love, joy, peace, longsuffering, kindness, goodness, faithfulness, ²³ gentleness, self-control. Against such there is no law. ²⁴ And those who are Christ's have crucified the flesh with its passions and desires.*
>
> *²⁵ If we live in the Spirit, let us also walk in the Spirit. ²⁶ Let us not become conceited, provoking one another, envying one another.*

22 — 23 The apostle tells us that the indwelling of the Holy Spirit is not something abstract, but very real and practical, and that He gives every believer perfect character attributes. Paul lists them as:

- *"love, joy, peace, longsuffering, kindness, goodness, faithfulness, gentleness, self-control."*

None of these are talents or vocations. They are the framework within which we serve Christ. These nine qualities must characterize all those saved by grace, whose hearts are filled with the Holy Spirit.

Salvation is not something theoretical. It must be evident in the life of every saved person (Jas. 3:13-18).

Let us have a look at the "fruit" that evidences the presence of the Holy Spirit in one who claims to be a disciple of Jesus.

"The fruit of the Spirit." — It is important to understand what this expression means:

- A believer can exhibit these wonderful qualities **only** by the help of the Holy Spirit who dwells within him. **(See John 15:1-8.)** He cannot develop them by himself.

- The word is in the singular — fruit — as in, for instance, a cluster of grapes that holds many grapes. There are several qualities, but they come as a package deal.

- Remember that these are characteristics of God Himself. He gives them to His children and desires to see all of them expressed in every area of their lives. After all, God wants us to live as citizens of the heavenly Kingdom, as Jesus did. **(See Matthew 5—7; 2 Corinthians 3:18; Philippians 1:21.)**

This is the Fruit of the Spirit — Slice by Slice

Love (Greek: ἀγάπη / *agapē*): Paul lists love as the first quality, because it is the basic ingredient of all the others. *Agape* is love by choice, demonstrated by unselfish sacrifice. This is not physical love, which is *eros* in Greek. *Agape* is not the love we have for friends and for our children, which is named *philo*. *Agape* can absorb hurt from others without giving back in kind (**1 Cor. 13; 1 Pet. 4:8:** *"Love will cover a multitude of sins"*).

God is love. He expressed His love when He gave His Son Jesus Christ as a sacrifice, who bore God's wrath against sinners and died for us, in order that we might receive atonement for our sins and live with Him forever. God loves — that means He gives sacrificially. We also are commanded to behave towards each other following this example (**Jn. 3:16; 13:34-35; 15:13; Rom. 5:8; 1 Jn. 2:10; 3:16-17; 4:8, 11-12, 16-21**).

Joy (Greek: χαρά / *chara*): This joy comes from knowing that God dwells within me and has forgiven my sins. I am not destined to wrath but to eternal life in God's everlasting Kingdom. This joy does not depend on the changing circumstances of life. It leans on the promise of God that He is with me everywhere and watches over me in every situation (**Jn. 15:11; 16:20-22; Rom. 8:28; 14:17, Phil. 4:4; Jas. 1:2-4; 1 Jn. 1:3-4**).

Peace (Greek: εἰρήνη / *eirēnē*): the absence of hostility between God and man; the inner peace that comes from the security of belonging to God. This is true rest and calmness, even in the face of threat and danger, because God is with me. He is my shield and my refuge. This peace comes because God Himself turns my eyes to His sovereign power, so that any earthly challenge or danger is dwarfed by comparison. Whoever has the peace of God in his heart cannot hide it. The peace of God is evidenced clearly in the lives of those in whom God lives (**Num. 6:22-26; Jn. 14:27; Phil. 4:7**).

God's peace does not assure us of a life with no battles! In Judges 6 God sends Gideon to war against the overwhelmingly numerous army of the Midianites. At the end of this encounter with God, Gideon calls him the God of Peace. As he prepares for battle, and later on while facing the enemies, Gideon enjoys the peace of God. He knows that God is not his foe, but that He is standing by his side and is protecting him.

True peace is possible only between two parties who enjoy the peace of God. Any other peace is only a temporary truce.

Longsuffering (patience — Greek: μακροθυμία / *makrothumia*): restraint, patience, self-restraint, forbearance, self-control; tolerant, uncomplaining. — Being able to wait for God to act in His own time during times of trouble and the willingness to continue to live until then in purity and holiness according to the will of God. Longsuffering is a characteristic based on all the qualities listed before (**Rom. 5:1-5; 2 Cor. 6:6; Eph. 4:2; Col. 1:11; 3:12; 1 Tim. 1:15-16**).

Kindness (Greek: χρηστότης / *chrēstotēs*): Caring about others that is expressed by solicitude for others and by giving generously. Generosity is required of the believer, because God Himself treats us with unspeakable generosity (**Mt. 11:28-29; 19:13-14; Rom. 2:4; 2 Cor. 6:6; Eph. 2:7; Col. 3:12; 2 Tim. 2:24**).

Goodness (Greek: ἀγαθωσύνη / *agathōsunē*): A pure and clean way of thought that is expressed by doing good to others, even in cases where the one we help is unworthy or not entitled to our help.

Faithfulness (Greek: πίστις / *pistis*): a quality characterizing a person who keeps his word and can be depended upon in any situation (**Lam. 3:22; Phil. 2:7-9; 1 Th. 5:24; Rev. 2:10**).

23 Gentleness (Greek: πραότης / *praotēs*; in other translations: "meekness," "humility"): A gentle, meek or humble person submits unconditionally to the will of God. This kind of humility is rooted in a sincere fear of God. It recognizes that everything good and worthwhile that I do is by the grace God has showered upon me. Humility is shown by considering others to be more important than myself (**Prov. 15:33; 22:4; Rom. 12:10; Gal. 6:1; Col. 3:12; 2 Tim. 2:25; Jas. 1:21**).

Self-control (Greek: ἐγκράτεια / *egkrateia*): restraint exercised over one's own impulses, emotions, or desires. This is the ability to do everything in moderation without going overboard in a negative way, as well as to resist the desire of my flesh to do something against the will of God (**1 Cor. 9:25; Gal. 5:16; 2 Pet. 1:6**).

"Against such there is no law." — In other words, whoever lives by the guidance of the Holy Spirit and in His power will not break the commandments of the Law. He does the will of God, not because of a written "Do" or "Do not" in the Law, but because the Holy Spirit lives within him and controls his impulses (**Rom. 7:6; 2 Cor. 3; 1 Jn. 2:27**). The Law in effect confirms that whoever evidences the "fruit of the Spirit" in his life does indeed belong to God.

 **What is the difference between the fruit of the Spirit and the gifts of the Spirit?**

The Holy Spirit not only endows disciples of Jesus with **character qualities** (with the *fruit of the Spirit*), He also gives **abilities** that are called the *gifts of the Holy Spirit* **(Heb. 2:4)**. God expects us to serve one another in the body of Christ (the church) by means of these abilities. They include the gifts of teaching, encouragement, leadership, giving, and more **(Rom. 12; 1 Cor. 12; Eph. 4)**.

How Then Are the Two Connected — The Gifts and the Fruit — And What Is Their Purpose?

- The gifts of the Holy Spirit are **abilities** — they are things I am able to do in order to serve God and the body of Christ (the church) and to bring glory to my Savior. They are the technical and practical part of the package. Not all believers receive the same gifts.

- The fruit of the Spirit, on the other hand, consists of **character qualities** that enable us to employ those gifts in a way that honors God and edifies the church. We are all expected to use the various abilities given to us by the Spirit of God, but it is essential that the character traits of the Holy Spirit (i.e., the fruit of the Spirit) are expressed at the same time. Every use of the gifts of the Spirit that is not governed by love, patience, kindness, self-control, etc. turns very quickly into a souce of arrogance and spiritual pride.

- We now understand the **purpose**, both of the fruit and of the gifts: Both combined enable the believers to edify each other, build up the church of Christ and serve God in a way that brings honor to His name **(Eph. 3:21; 4:11-16)**.

Because this is such an important principle, let's jot it down once again under three key words:

The gifts:

- The Word of God teaches that the church is the body of Christ and that Jesus is the head (**Eph. 5:23:** *"Christ is the head of the church; and He is the Savior of the body"*).

- Every believer in the church is a member of the body of Christ (**1 Cor. 12**).

- God — through the Holy Spirit — gives every believer different abilities with which to fulfill his particular calling. After all, the finger is different from the eye, and each has a different function in the body (**Rom. 12:6-8; 1 Cor. 12:8-10; Eph. 4:11-16**).

- God is the giver of all these abilities, and each one is necessary for the body to function well and healthily (**1 Cor. 12:11; Eph. 4:12**).

The fruit:

- Whereas the gifts of the Spirit differ from one believer to another, the fruit of the Spirit must be evident with identical characteristics in each of the children of God. — Why? — Since there is one head and one unified leadership (through the Word of God and by the guidance of the Holy Spirit), the character qualities must point to the same head — to Jesus Christ!

The purpose:

- God expects us, His children, to live our daily lives at home, at work and in the church by the instructions of the Scriptures, just as Jesus would have done in our place, so that anyone who sees us will say: "I see a true disciple of Jesus!" The world will recognize us as brothers and sisters, because in certain crucial points we will all be alike. Brotherly love will characterize us for all to see, and it will be obvious to everyone that we have **one** Lord (**Jn. 13:35**).

There is one interesting conclusion to be drawn from what we have said so far: If Jesus is the head, and every member of the body acts under the guidance of the head, is there any room for my own will? — **No!**

This is why Paul goes on to teach us to:

"Crucify the Flesh" — Every Day Anew

24 *"Those who are Christ's have crucified the flesh with its passions and desires."* — We cannot claim to live a life guided by the Holy Spirit and at the same time do as we please! There is a conflict between the two, as we have read in Galatians 5:17: *"For the flesh lusts against the Spirit, and the Spirit against the flesh; and these are contrary to one another, so that you do not do the things that you wish."*

25 *"If we live in the Spirit, let us also walk in the Spirit."* — Whoever knows God's Messiah — El-Shaddai, Jesus Christ — in a personal way has been **born again**. Jesus Himself calls that being *"born of the Spirit"* **(Jn. 3:5-7)**. Since it is the Holy Spirit who gives us new life, it is quite reasonable to expect that we give Him the authority to use those new lives of ours and to direct them according to God's plan **(Rom. 12:1-2**; see also "Walking in the Spirit" — **Gal. 5:16-18** above). This is the purpose for which Christ has redeemed (bought) us: that we will *"walk in the Spirit"* **(3:13; 4:5-6)**.

26 *"Let us not become conceited, provoking one another, envying one another."* — Whoever does not know Jesus personally as His Lord and Savior will not turn his life over to Him. He will try to do everything in his own strength. This is what the Galatians were doing, and this is what the world does. The results can be seen around us every day: People *"bite and devour one another"* **(Gal. 5:15; Jas. 4)**.

"Let us not become conceited." — What were the Galatian believers conceited about? We know that some boasted over their physical descent and others over their zeal in observing certain commandments. But God considers neither of the two as contributing to salvation. The honor of the false teachers and their disciples was only imagined. They thought they were better than other believers, but in actual fact they were adding judgment to themselves for the Day of Judgment **(Rom. 2:5)**.

Summary of Chapter Five:

1. The apostle Paul was accused of encouraging believers to shake off the authority of the Law, thus causing them to slide into immorality.

   We have learned that Paul was actually teaching that:

   - Believers in Jesus are no longer subject to the ordinances of the Law, which have fulfilled their purpose and are now obsolete. Believers are subject to the New Covenant established by Christ.

   - From the moment of their salvation, they are indwelt by the Holy Spirit. He gives them power and faith to live in holiness and purity according to the will of God.

     If Jesus Christ is my head, how could I possibly live a lawless life? How could I possibly immerse myself in immorality while God is living and working within me? The opposite should be true: Life in the Spirit of God must be a life of holiness and purity.

2. Throughout history, God has been advancing an important project: The plan of salvation for man — and by His wonderful grace, He lets us participate in working out this plan.

   Since this is **God's work**, and there is no way we can do it on our own, the Creator has given us abilities, as well as a character that reflects His image. And there is another condition for successfully doing God's work: I must be a submissive and obedient

   # child of God.

Chapter 6

The Law of Christ and the New Creation

The apostle Paul proves to the Galatian believers that a disciple of Jesus does not leave the authority of the Law only to find himself in a dangerous spiritual vacuum. He moves right into the hands of Christ — the fulfiller of the Law and Creator of the world **(2 Cor. 3:12-18)**.

In chapter 6 the apostle breaks down the overarching principles into practical examples from daily life. He explains how we should practically *"walk in the Spirit"* within the framework of the church:

1. in interpersonal relationships
2. in the use of money and property

1. Interpersonal Relationships

Galatians 6:1-5:

> ¹*Brethren, if a man is overtaken in any trespass, you who are spiritual restore such a one in a spirit of gentleness, considering yourself lest you also be tempted.* ²*Bear one another's burdens,*

> *and so fulfill the law of Christ.* ³*For if anyone thinks himself to be something, when he is nothing, he deceives himself.* ⁴*But let each one examine his own work, and then he will have rejoicing in himself alone, and not in another.* ⁵*For each one shall bear his own load.*

Verses 1-10 describe a way of life strikingly different from the current behavior of the Galatians, which we have seen described as "biting and devouring one another" **(5:15)**. Two subjects stand out in these verses:

- Mutual help
- Sharing and cooperation

❶ *"If a man is overtaken in any trespass."* — A brother in faith falls into sin. — What are we to do?

Having pointed out the unloving, inconsiderate treatment by which the Galatians were presently harming each other, Paul now teaches them what behavior is expected of believers who have the Spirit of God dwelling in them **(2 Cor. 3:4-6)**.

"You who are spiritual." — The apostle turns to those who claim to have been saved by a sincere faith in Jesus as their Lord and Savior and think they are living in accordance with the Scriptures.

If my actions are directed by the Holy Spirit, then the way I treat a brother who has fallen into sin will reflect the fruit of the Spirit **(Gal. 5:22-23)**. The spiritual person will try to raise up the fallen brother and restore him to the good and right way. Our reaction to a member in the body of Christ who has failed should be an attempt to help him, pick him up and restore him. That is, after all, how we treat our natural body: When a bone is broken, we do all we can to heal it, not amputate it **(Heb. 12:12-13; Jas. 5:19-20)**.

"Restore such a one in a spirit of gentleness." — We all fail at times. There is no one who does not make mistakes, so we should all act in humility and sensitivity.

"Considering yourself lest you also be tempted." — You or I could fall tomorrow, so I should treat my brother as I would wish him to treat me.

"Considering yourself." — Before I can correct a brother, I must examine myself and make sure I do not harbor a similar sin in my heart.

Help given *"in a spirit of gentleness"* is extended discreetly without condescension, but from the heart and with one purpose — the good of one's brother. For occasions where correction is needed, Jesus describes how we should approach a sinning brother in **Matthew 18:15-18**.

Paul teaches a behavior that is the complete opposite to what false teachers and those who consider themselves righteous exhibit. (See for example **John 8:3-12**, the Pharisees and the woman taken in adultery; **Acts 21:21-27**.)

Note!

God does not command us to restore the brother to fellowship at all costs. If he refuses to return to God's ways and persists in his error, the Scriptures say he must be expelled from the congregation (Mt. 18:15-20).

Two Kinds of Burdens

2 *"Bear one another's burdens, and so fulfill the law of Christ."* — This is a logical continuation of the commandment to restore the fallen brother. Help one another, support those without strength, encourage the oppressed; let the strong give a hand to the weak; let the rich support the poor. Remember that *"the law of Christ"* calls you to love one another. This love will show everyone that you are disciples of Jesus (**Jn. 13:34-35; Acts 2:38-42; 1 Jn. 4:7-11**).

3 **But how does this go** with Galatians 6:5, which says: *"Each one shall bear his own load"*? — We will quickly see that verse 5 does not contradict the commandment in verse 2 to help one another. The *"load"* (Greek: *fortion*) that each of us is called to bear by himself is different from the *"burden"* (Greek: *baros*) that we are instructed to help each other with.

God gives each of us a *"load"* of obedience that is intended to mature us spiritually. This *"load"* is not evil, it is part of the process by which we draw nearer to God and experience Him and His power in a personal, intimate way. The meaning of the commandment that *"each one shall bear his own load"* is that we must faithfully and consistently fulfill our personal obligations in various areas of life: in holiness, faithfulness in marriage, responsibility to work and earn a living, and so on. If we are faithful in carrying the load God has placed upon us, we will see our prayers answered, and we keep our joy even in hard times.

Each one must pass these tests of spiritual maturity on his own, since they are his personal tests of faith. Let us not be alarmed by the trials that are bound to come in these areas, but always remember Christ's words of comfort: *"Come to Me, all you who labor and are heavy laden, and I will give you rest. Take My yoke upon you and learn from Me; for I am gentle and lowly in heart, and you will find rest for your souls. For My yoke is easy and My burden is light"* **(Mt. 11:28-30)**.

The apostle Paul comforted the believers in Corinth with the promise that God never burdens His children with more than they can bear. He always gives enough power and grace to carry and endure the hardships He permits in our lives **(1 Cor. 10:12-18; see also Rom. 8:26-30)**.

The Law of Christ

"And so fulfill the law of Christ." (Gal. 6:2) — What is the *"law of Christ,"* and how do we fulfill it by "bear(ing) one another's burdens"?

1. In 5:14, the apostle said: *"For all the law is fulfilled in one word … 'Love your neighbor as yourself,'"* thus quoting a principle that Jesus Himself taught **(Mt. 22:39-40)**. Since carrying my brother's burden is an act of love, it is an expression of the law of Christ. Sincere love between believers identifies them as disciples of Jesus **(Jn. 13:35; 1 Jn. 2:9-10)**.

2. Just as Jesus bore the heavy burden of my sins and gave me life and freedom, so I should help relieve my brother of the weight of his burden **(Rom. 8:2)**.

3_4 *"For if anyone thinks himself to be something, when he is nothing, he deceives himself. But let each one examine his own work, and then he will have rejoicing in himself alone, and not in another."* — To understand these verses we must take the context into account: Paul is teaching mutual help and cooperation, which are an expression of "walking in the Spirit." So then these verses warn us of reasons that would **prevent** us from helping our brothers:

- pride, conceit;
- comparing my achievements to those of my brother.

There are two ways to deal with these dangers:

1. **Humility**

   Humility is, first of all, one of the characteristics of the fruit of the Spirit. **(See commentary on chapter 5:22-23.)** Humility honestly acknowledges the fact that all I have and all my achievements are by the grace of God, not because of my own strength and abilities. Humility understands that I serve God in the position in which He has placed me, and that the other children of God are exactly equal to me, even if they have been given other work to do. I am not competing with them, their success is to the glory of Christ, and it will not endanger my own position or progress **(Rom. 12:3)**. With such an attitude, nothing prevents me from helping my brother.

2. **Focusing on Jesus Christ**

   Comparing myself with others can cause one of two things: Frustration and despair — or pride **(2 Cor. 10:12-18)**. It is not necessarily bad to compare data, but such a comparison must never serve a desire to humiliate someone or to bring honor to myself.

   Since our lives belong to the Messiah and we are busy serving Him, our actions must conform to the standards of the Kingdom of heaven **(Phil. 3:20)** — and those were set by the earthly life of Jesus Himself. Measuring my "successes" against the person of Jesus and His sinless perfection, I realize that I can never be good enough. Thus Jesus always remains the center, not I myself.

- Any help I extend to my brother will glorify Christ, therefore I am **obliged** to help.
- As long as I depend totally on the Messiah and desire to glorify Him in everything I do, I will also **want** to help and build up my brother.

After we have seen how "walking in the Spirit" is given practical expression in the day-to-day affairs of the church through the interpersonal relationships of its members, let us now consider how walking in the Spirit governs:

2. The Use of Money and Property

Galatians 6:6-10:

> ⁶ *Let him who is taught the word share in all good things with him who teaches.*
>
> ⁷ *Do not be deceived, God is not mocked; for whatever a man sows, that he will also reap.* ⁸ *For he who sows to his flesh will of the flesh reap corruption, but he who sows to the Spirit will of the Spirit reap everlasting life.* ⁹ *And let us not grow weary while doing good, for in due season we shall reap if we do not lose heart.* ¹⁰ *Therefore, as we have opportunity, let us do good to all, especially to those who are of the household of faith.*

Primary meaning: Paul explains that walking in the Spirit is characterized by mutual help, cooperation, and giving, by investing both in the spiritual and in the physical fields. When we study these verses in their context and compare them to what Paul wrote to the Corinthians (**1 Cor. 9; 2 Cor. 8; see also Heb. 13:16**), the main sense of the verses is clear: The apostle expects the believers to use their money and their property in a certain way.

Secondary meaning: There is a second interpretation to these verses: When believers learn the wonders of God's Word, they should share with their teachers the spiritual blessings they have received through their teaching. Such positive feedback encourages the teachers to persevere and to study even more deeply, in order to teach and equip the believers for spiritual service (**Eph. 4:12**).

6 *"Let him who is taught the word share in all good things with him who teaches."* — The general principle in Galatians 6:6-10 is: Just as the teachers share with the congregation everything good and edifying that is at their disposal, so should the members of the congregation share everything good they have with their teachers. This is what is said here to the Galatians. The Corinthians were told even more clearly and in greater detail: It is the responsibility of the church to support its teachers. Paul dedicates the entire ninth chapter of 1 Corinthians to establishing his right to earn a living from his labor as a teacher and evangelist.

While the Law of Moses commanded the Israelites to give part of their income to support the work of the priests in the Temple, the New Covenant determines no specific amount or percentage by which to support the people that labor in the church.

What, then, should motivate a believer in Jesus today to give for the work of God and the support of his teachers?

This giving depends entirely on the believer's generosity, love, and spiritual maturity.

7 *"Do not be deceived, God is not mocked!"* — Paul warns that whereas we may be able to deceive people, we cannot deceive God. If we invest and give just a little, we cannot expect to receive a lot. Even common sense tells us that:

"Whatever a man sows, that he will also reap." — Whoever invests mainly in and for himself will get back exactly what he invested: temporary gain (**2 Cor. 9:6-7**).

8 *"For he who sows to his flesh will of the flesh reap corruption."* — Whoever depends on his ability to keep the ordinances of the Law, whoever dedicates himself to keeping obsolete commandments — that is, things God no longer requires — will in the future reap corruption. He rejects the grace of Christ and therefore cannot benefit from the influence of the Holy Spirit in his life. All he can reap is the fruit of the flesh, which cannot save or take away the sting of death (**1 Cor. 15**).

"But he who sows to the Spirit will of the Spirit reap everlasting life." — Whoever dedicates himself to the things Paul means by "sowing to the Spirit" — the study of the Word of God, spreading the gospel, and helping others — whoever does so out of faith in Jesus and while leaning on the grace of God, is sowing in the field of God.

Unlike the fruit of the flesh, the fruit of God promises to supply all the needs of today (**Mt. 6:30-33**), and will be plentiful for eternity: The believers who sow to the Spirit will live forever in the Kingdom of God.

"Will of the Spirit reap everlasting life." — There is an additional meaning here: *"He who sows to the Spirit"* by spreading the gospel — whether he preaches himself or supports others to do so — will see the salvation of souls. They will inherit everlasting life together with him.

Do Good — To *all* Men!

"And let us not grow weary while doing good, for in due season we shall reap if we do not lose heart." — Do not give up! — We want to see immediate results after sowing seeds, but that is not how nature works. Growth takes months or even years. If we have sown according to the principles of God's Word, we have no reason to give up or lose patience. God will cause the seed to multiply, and the fruit will eventually show, bringing glory to Christ. We must keep in mind that we will see some of the fruit only when we stand before the Lord. (**See also James 5:7.**)

"Let us not grow weary while doing good" includes — among other things — helping the needy in the church. They have nothing to give back to us, and there are some who will, as far as we can tell, stay needy for a very long time. But nevertheless, the Word of God says: *"Let us not grow weary while doing good!"*

We must always remember that our giving, our works, must bring glory to the name of Christ. Whatever is done for personal gain, self-satisfaction, or self-honor is "sowing to the flesh," and will end in destruction.

Note!

Why does the apostle encourage the believers to give? Not in order to grow rich by their property, as is clear from **1 Corinthians 9:18**. He wants them to receive God's blessings. The same principle is found in the Old Testament also, in **Proverbs 3:9-10**:

> *Honor the Lord with your possessions, and with the firstfruits of all your increase; so your barns will be filled with plenty, and your vats will overflow with new wine.*

From here it follows that Galatians 6:6-10 establishes what should be the believer's relationship to money and property, and how he should use them:

1. **The Relationship:**

    The believer's main effort should be in living by the will of God. Heaven help us if the purpose of our lives should be to acquire possessions. Property is a tool for service, not the purpose of our life **(Prov. 23:4)**.

2. **The Use:**

    a. investment in the teaching of God's Word in the church — taking part in the material support of the teachers;

    b. investment in the mission field — furthering the proclamation of the gospel to all men;

    c. helping brothers in need.

    Ideally, those are the three main areas in which a church should invest its money.

10 *"Therefore, as we have opportunity, let us do good to all."* — Here is another important principle: Believers in Jesus have a measure of responsibility to do good *"to all."* When Jesus Christ performed the miracle of the five loaves and two fish, He gave food to all the 5,000 present, whether they believed in Him or not. In the same way the generosity of believers should include helping unbelievers. If only we had the same unconditional love that was in our Savior **(Rom. 12:17-21; 1 Tim. 6:17-19)**.

"Especially to those who are of the household of faith." — The principle is to *"do good to all,"* but first priority has to be given to our brothers in faith. After all, this is true also in our natural relations: the needs of my family come before the needs of my neighbors.

So then, as a church of believers in Jesus we are called first of all to look after the weak and needy within our own ranks, but we must also never forget the needy of our city or nation. The church is called to help the unbelievers around her, as she is able. By so doing the disciples of Jesus will show the same love Jesus demonstrated when He was among us.

Intermediate Summary — Putting the Law of Christ Into Effect

In the verses we have studied so far in Galatians 6, the apostle explains the "law of Christ" in detail (v. 2):

- It is practically expressed through our cooperation with and help to others,
- in love,
- using the tools God has given us,
- and all for His glory.

Keeping the law of Christ perfectly will create a perfect church. We will not arrive at perfection before Christ's return, but we should certainly aim for it.

- If a believer has received guidance and support within the church, and now his life evidences spiritual growth and success — then his success is not a personal achievement, it is an achievement of the church — *and all for the glory of Christ!*

- On the other hand, if there is a hungry believer in the church (through no fault of his own), or a homeless person, or someone with torn clothing — then the failure is shared by all.

Spiritual life, so we have learned, is characterized by efforts and investments that bring the body of Christ to health, maturity, and service to the Lord (Eph. 4). Where success is measured by the level of giving and investing in others, there is no place for pride or competition on a personal level.

The teaching of God's Word, evangelism, and help to the needy are areas that bring eternal gain. More than that, they build up a healthy church that brings glory to the name of Christ.

Jesus said: *"A new commandment I give to you, that you love one another; as I have loved you, that you also love one another. By this all will know that you are My disciples, if you have love for one another"* (Jn. 13:34-35). This is the Mk. of the church of Christ, and such achievement is possible only in the strength of God.

Conclusion of the Epistle

In the last verses of Galatians 6, the apostle Paul points out the vast difference between him and the false teachers:

- They put emphasis on outward things — circumcision and other commandments, the fulfillment of which can be measured by the naked eye. — Thus they can take pride in their powerful influence on people. They have also fabricated for themselves a "law" that spares them suffering for the name of Jesus (**v. 12**).

- The faithful apostle of Christ, on the other hand, writes:

Galatians 6:11-18:

> ¹¹ See with what large letters I have written to you with my own hand! ¹² As many as desire to make a good showing in the flesh, these would compel you to be circumcised, only that they may not suffer persecution for the cross of Christ. ¹³ For not even those who are circumcised keep the law, but they desire to have you circumcised that they may boast in your flesh. ¹⁴ But God forbid that I should boast except in the cross of our Lord Jesus Christ, by whom the world has been crucified to me, and I to the world. ¹⁵ For in Christ Jesus neither circumcision nor uncircumcision avails anything, but a new creation.
>
> ¹⁶ And as many as walk according to this rule, peace and mercy be upon them, and upon the Israel of God.
>
> ¹⁷ From now on let no one trouble me, for I bear in my body the marks of the Lord Jesus.
>
> ¹⁸ Brethren, the grace of our Lord Jesus Christ be with your spirit. Amen.

11 *"See with what large letters I have written to you with my own hand!"* — Why does Paul make a point of mentioning that he has written large letters with his own hand?

1. In order to underline the seriousness of what the false teachers are doing, and the urgency and importance of corrective teaching.

2. It could be that the apostle suffered from impaired vision. The fact that he writes with large letters emphasizes the problem with his eyes (**see 4:13-15**), and the fact that he is writing with his own hand — the urgency to deal with the problems in Galatia. That goes with what is related in **Acts 23:1-5**: Paul stands before the Sanhedrin. Ananias the high priest commands the men standing by Paul to strike his mouth, and the apostle responds with the reprimand: *"God will strike you, you whitewashed wall!"* When rebuked how he dared to chide the high

priest, Paul apologizes immediately and says he did not know he was the high priest. This mistake came, perhaps, from Paul's inability to see clearly the special clothing and other identifying marks of the high priest. This would back up the interpretation which takes Galatians 6:11 to mean that Paul suffered from impaired sight.

We may assume that reading an epistle personally penned by the apostle with large letters shocked the hearts of the members of the church and brought home to them the seriousness of their spiritual condition.

Some Seek Honor

12—13 *"As many as desire to make a good showing in the flesh, these would compel you to be circumcised, only that they may not suffer persecution for the cross of Christ."* — Throughout the epistle, Paul exposes the motives of the false teachers in Galatia, who forced the believers to be circumcised and to keep the ordinances of the Law:

1. They were trying to please men (1:10). On the outside they seemed religious, honorable, honest and sincere, but that was just because they wished *"to make a good showing in the flesh."*

2. They feared and avoided the persecution and suffering that could result from identifying with Jesus Christ.

3. *"But they desire to have you circumcised that they may boast in your flesh."* — In other words, they are interested in boasting over the number of Gentiles they managed to convert to Judaism.

It is worthwhile mentioning that by that time even the Roman authorities understood the difference between Christians and Jews. The Jews were given permission to worship God in their way (a status that was called *religio licita*: "legal/authorized religion"). This same permission was not given to Christians. They were accused of the crime of establishing a new religion, and whoever was called "Christian" could be put to death for his faith.

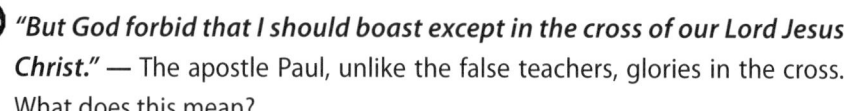 *"But God forbid that I should boast except in the cross of our Lord Jesus Christ."* — The apostle Paul, unlike the false teachers, glories in the cross. What does this mean?

 ### How does one boast in the cross of Christ?

In the beginning of his path, Paul was like the false teachers, boasting in the flesh, in the observance of commandments and in belonging to the Chosen People **(Phil. 3:1-11)**. But he learned that all these advantages of the flesh are worthless compared to the change Jesus brought about in him by the atonement on the cross.

1. Paul glories in the inner change, the change God has wrought in each one who has received Jesus Christ as Lord and Savior.

2. He glories in bearing the cross of Jesus, that is, in perfect obedience to the Word of Christ even at the cost of suffering — if need be at the cost of his life.

Paul is not trying to hide the cross, he is not ashamed to live his Christian life openly and is not afraid of identifying with Jesus Christ at any opportunity **(Rom. 8:1-3; 1 Cor. 2:2-3; 2 Tim. 3:12; 1 Pet. 2:20-25)**.

"By whom the world has been crucified to me, and I to the world." — This sentence is parallel to what Paul said in **Galatians 2:20:** *"I have been crucified with Christ; it is no longer I who live, but Christ lives in me; and the life which I now live in the flesh I live by faith in the Son of God, who loved me and gave Himself for me."*

The atonement he received through the death of Jesus on the cross changed Paul's life and purpose. As a result of salvation he received a new life, a life dedicated to doing the will of God. He is no longer drawn to anything belonging to this world **(Rom. 12:1-2)**. Now his only ambition is to do the will of God and to promote the Kingdom of Christ **(Mt. 6:33)**, even if this should cost him his life. This life, after all, is not his personal property, but belongs to the Lord. This is the full meaning of the expression *"Christ has redeemed [bought] us"* (**Gal. 3:13; 4:5**).

A New Creation

"For in Christ Jesus neither circumcision nor uncircumcision avails anything, but a new creation." — Paul knew firsthand that observing the commandments would not bring him salvation (**Phil. 3:1-11**). He understood that the greatest gift man can aspire to in his life is the atonement for sins and salvation from the wrath of God.

The new identity given to the believer in Jesus, whether Jew or Gentile, is far more important than any national, earthly identity.

"A new creation" means being born again through the Holy Spirit (**Jn. 3:3; 2 Cor. 5:17**). Only by the help of the Holy Spirit can the believer:

- understand and take in the Word of God (**Jn. 14-16; 1 Cor. 2:10-15**);
- put God's will into practice;
- become more like Christ, exhibiting divine character traits;
- recognize the hand of God at work in creation and in people's individual lives (**Jn. 3; 1 Cor. 2:10-15**);
- call God with perfect confidence "Abba, my Father" (**Rom. 8:17; Gal. 4:6**);
- be delivered from the wrath of God, which is to come upon the world before Jesus Christ returns to establish His thousand-year Kingdom on Earth, centered in Jerusalem (**1 Th. 5:1-11**);
- trust in the promise that he will enjoy eternity with God, serving Him in truth, righteousness, purity, and holiness (**Rev. 22:5**).

Religion and works that are done by man's strength cannot give us these wonderful promises which fill the heart of the believer with divine peace.

Just Obey — And the Blessing is Yours!

16 *"And as many as walk according to this rule, peace and mercy be upon them, and upon the Israel of God."* — All who agree with the apostle — that is, who are saved by faith in Jesus Christ and are filled with the Holy Spirit — are blessed with the peace of God and His mercy.

Paul lists two groups of people in verse 16:

1. *"as many as walk according to this rule"*;
2. *"the Israel of God."*

Group 1 is made up of all Gentiles who trust in Jesus as their Lord and Savior. God's peace and mercy are given to Gentile believers in Jesus in the same measure as to believers of the house of Israel.

Group 2 are *"the Israel of God."* — Not all of Israel is blessed, experiencing the peace and mercy of God. Jewish identity and belonging to the physical seed of Abraham do not guarantee salvation and God's eternal blessing. **The Israel of God** are those of the people of Israel, descendants of Abraham, Isaac, and Jacob, who believe in Jesus as their Lord and Savior. **(See also Romans 2:29; 4:12; 9:6.)**

God Has Not Rejected His People

Some understand the phrase **the Israel of God** to mean that the church, which is made up of believing Jews and Gentiles, has taken the place of the people of Israel. That is wrong! If Paul believed that the church has replaced the Chosen People and is now the Israel of God, he would certainly not have written chapters 9—11 of the epistle to the Romans.

Today, the people of Israel reject Jesus Christ. Therefore they cannot fulfill their role as a royal priesthood leading the Gentiles to their Savior. As long as Israel as a whole rejects Jesus Christ, the people cannot receive all of God's blessings. At this point the church **temporarily** fulfills the role of a *"royal priesthood and a holy nation"* (1 Pet. 2:9-10) and labors to bring the word of salvation to all men.

But God has not forgotten the people of Israel, and they will not reject Jesus forever (Rom. 9—11). When Christ returns to reign over the world (following the *time of Jacob's trouble* — the Great Tribulation) the entire remnant of Israel, descendants of Abraham, Isaac, and Jacob, will be saved (Rom. 11:26). Then the people of Israel will serve the Messiah for a 1,000 years as a royal priesthood on Earth (Ezek. 36:22-38; 48; Zech. 8:23; Rev. 7:4-8; 20:1-6).

17 *"From now on let no one trouble me, for I bear in my body the marks of the Lord Jesus."* — Paul concludes his epistle to the Galatians with a clear request: "Stop all this fighting and squabbling among yourselves. Return to the pure gospel. Forsake those who divert you from the truth you have heard from me, and have nothing to do with them! Do not give me more sorrow then I already have."

Paul can prove his faithfulness as a witness of Christ by the scars in his body. He received all of them because of his faithfulness to Christ **(1 Cor. 4:11; 2 Cor. 4:10-11; 6:5, 9; 11:24-25)**. The scars prove that his life does not belong to him, but to the Lord Jesus, whom he serves sacrificially.

Just as slaves in the ancient world bore the marks of their masters on their body, so Paul uses the same language to say: "I bear in my body the marks of the Master I serve — Jesus."

18 *"Brethren, the grace of our Lord Jesus Christ be with your spirit. Amen."* — The end of the epistle is like its opening (1:3). Paul hopes that the Galatians will drive out the false teachers, so that the congregations may continue to enjoy the grace of the Messiah.

The fact that Paul calls the Galatians brethren, shows that many of them were indeed saved. His hope is that they will learn to differentiate between truth and lie, and will exhibit spiritual growth.

And in Conclusion

Let us remember the two key passages of the epistle to the Galatians, which summarize it all:

1. Galatians 3:10-11:

> *For as many as are of the works of the law are under the curse; for it is written, "Cursed is everyone who does not continue in all things which are written in the book of the law, to do them." ¹¹But that no one is justified by the law in the sight of God is evident, for "the just shall live by faith."*

- The commandments never saved anyone! People have only been saved by faith in Jesus as Lord and Savior, with no difference between Jew or Gentile.

2. Galatians 5:1:

> *Stand fast therefore in the liberty by which Christ has made us free, and do not be entangled again with a yoke of bondage.*

- The atoning sacrifice of Christ redeemed us from the slavery to obsolete commandments. The believer is required only to fulfill the law of Christ. This is a monumental task, but we do not face it alone. The Holy Spirit, who dwells within us, helps us to live by the will of God. In His strength we can fulfill the commandments of God — not because of written laws, but because of the love of Jesus Christ **(Rom. 7:6; 2 Cor. 3)**.

God expressed His love and mercy to us by accepting the life of His only Son as an atoning sacrifice for our sins. Please, do not let anyone defile such grace! We are a new creation, a creation in which God dwells and which He desires to use for His glory.

Let us pray that we will fulfill this holy calling: to bring glory and honor to **God.**

Appendices

Now that we have studied the epistle of Paul to the Galatians, it would be worth our while to stop and look a bit deeper, even if only briefly,

A. at the purpose for which God created and chose the people of Israel. We will discuss this under the title *"The Original Plan."*

B. at the development of the Oral Law, up to the point where it has been given authority above and beyond that of the Scriptures, the written Word of God. This final chapter is entitled *"When a Jew Says 'Torah' (Law), What Does He Mean?"*

And for the sake of those readers who do not have the patience to read through a whole book but immediately turn to the last pages to see how the story ends, we have added a shortcut, one last appendix entitled:

C. *Frequently Asked Questions*

A. The Original Plan

Why Did God Choose the People of Israel, and For What Purpose?

In **Deuteronomy 7:7-8** God lists three reasons why He chose the people of Israel:

> ⁷ *The* LORD *did not set His love on you nor choose you because you were more in number than any other people, for you were the least of all peoples;* ⁸ *but because the* LORD *loves you, and because He would keep the oath which He swore to your fathers, the* LORD *has brought you out with a mighty hand, and redeemed you from the house of bondage, from the hand of Pharaoh king of Egypt.*

1. Israel was chosen because it was *"the least of all peoples"* — that is, any success of the people, which was weaker and smaller than the other nations, would be evidence of God at work within the nation.

2. *"Because the LORD loves you."* — God chose the people of Israel out of love.

3. *"He would keep the oath which He swore to your fathers."* — God acted and continues to act on behalf of the people of Israel because He is faithful to the promises of the covenant He made with the fathers of the nation — Abraham, Isaac, and Jacob. God never goes back on His decisions, and we are assured that He will perform what He has promised (**Rom. 11:29; see also Dt. 10:15**).

Note:

God's choice of the people of Israel is entirely of His sovereignty and mercy, not because the people are especially good, smart, strong, or successful (**Dt. 9:1-6; Ezek. 36:22**).

God's Purpose For the People of Israel

is described in the following Scriptures:

Isaiah 43:21:

> *This people I have formed for Myself; they shall declare My praise.*

God intended Israel to be His tool. By observing His work in their lives, they should have understood the extent of God's love and grace. Furthermore, they should have lived by His commandments, becoming an example to the other nations. In this way Israel was to declare the praises of God, both by words and by the fact of its existence, demonstrating God's majesty.

Deuteronomy 7:6:

> *For you are a holy people to the LORD your God; the LORD your God has chosen you to be a people for Himself, a special treasure above all the peoples on the face of the earth.*

The nation of Israel was intended to be holy (separate and different) from the pagan nations. They were precious in the eyes of God (a chosen nation) because God had chosen to reveal Himself and His work through them to the rest of mankind (**Dt. 14:2; 26:18-19**).

Exodus 19:5-6:

> *Now therefore if you will indeed obey My voice and keep My covenant, then you shall be a special treasure to Me above all people; for all the earth is Mine. And you shall be to Me a kingdom of priests and a holy nation.*

God chose the people of Israel to be a tool through whom He would prove to all mankind — Jews and Gentiles,

- His existence,
- His sovereignty (**Dt. 28:37, 46**),

and reveal to them

- His Word (the Scriptures — **Dt. 4:5-6; Ps. 147:19-20; Rom. 3:2**),
- His character and His will (**Ex. 19—20; Dt. 28:15, 20, 48, 64-66**),
- His salvation (**Gen. 3:15; 49:10; Isa. 7:14; 9:6-7; 52:13—53:12; Dan. 7:13-14; Mic. 5:2; Zech. 14; Ps. 2; 22:1-18; Rom. 9:4-5**),
- His righteousness (**Ezek. 36:18-38; Rom. 9—11**).

God calls the nation of Israel *"My firstborn"* (**Ex. 4:22**). As a father, God wants His firstborn son to be an example to others and a model of how the other nations should relate to their Creator. (**See also Isaiah 43.**)

The Privileges

God accorded the people of Israel a special status that came with special prerogatives:

- The people received the status of adopted sons of God (**Ex. 4:22-23; Rom. 9:4**).
- They heard the voice of God speaking to them (**Dt. 4:10, 12, 22-33**).
- God dwelt among them (**Ex. 24:16-17; 40:34-38; Dt. 4:36; 1 Ki. 8:1; Rom. 9:4**).
- God made a covenant with the nation of Israel, a privilege that no other nation has ever had (**Rom. 9:4**).
- God gave them the Law (**Dt. 4:5-6, 8, 13; Ps. 147:19-20; Rom. 9:4**).
- God established His earthly abode at the Temple in the land of Israel, and the people were called to serve Him as priests (**Ex. 25:8-9; 29:43-46; 1 Ki. 6:11-14; Rom. 9:4; Heb. 9:1-10**).
- God gave promises to Israel that were not given to any other nation (**Dt. 1:11; 6:3; 12:20; 15:6; 19:8; 26:18; 28; Rom. 9:4**).
- The people of Israel have a special, close relationship with God (**Dt. 4:7**).
- God intervened on their behalf, delivering them from Egypt *"by a mighty hand and an outstretched arm."* He did not do this for any other nation (**Dt. 4:32, 34**).
- Israel received possession of the land of Canaan directly from God (**Gen. 12:7; 13:14-15; 15:18-21; 17:8; Dt. 9:1-6**).
- God determined the land of Israel to be holy and Jerusalem to be the holy city. They are unique because God Himself dwells there (**Ezek. 48; Zech. 2:10-12; Neh. 11:1; Rev. 11:2**).

Remember:

God has declared that His special relationship with Israel would last forever (**2 Sam. 7:23-24; Rom. 11:1, 29**).

Leaving the Way

In reality, Israel abandoned the Law of God and turned to all the ways of the idolatrous Gentiles. Because it was the majority of the nation who chose to walk in sin, Scripture describes **all** of the people as unfaithful to God (**Dt. 9; Isa. 1; Jer. 2:12-13; Ezek. 36:21-23, 31-32**).

For long periods throughout history many of God's people treated God as if He were an idol. They covered themselves with a cloak of religion, but their hearts were hardened against their Creator and estranged from Him.

God reminds His people again and again that He hates sin, exhorting them to confess their sin and repent. God demands the "circumcision of the heart." He is not satisfied by outward observance and by sacrifices of lambs and bulls on the altar (**Dt. 10:12-22; Isa. 1:10-20; 59:1-8; Mic. 6:6-8**).

Has God r e j e c t e d His "firstborn son" — Israel — because of his estrangement from Him?

No! God has not rejected His people and will never change His mind. The people have failed, but God will keep all His promises in order to bring glory to His name (**Isa. 43:21; 44:23; Jer. 29:11-14; Ezek. 36:22-38; Rom. 11:1, 29**).

We must remember that God chose Israel of His own will. He is Lord over the whole universe, and nothing can limit Him. So then, nothing Israel can do will ever cause God to change His sovereign plan.

The Days of Isaiah

Isaiah prophesied in the kingdom of Judah at about 800 B.C., and his was a very hard message throughout. In the first chapter of his book, the prophet expresses God's sorrow in the face of the rebellion and spiritual unfaithfulness of the chosen nation. Isaiah says that even the ox and the donkey submit to their masters and obey those who give them food and shelter, but the people of Israel are not thankful to God for all He has done for them. They even go so far as to curse the Holy One of Israel, and turn their back on Him.

As the first chapter continues, Isaiah — as God's spokesman — describes his own nation as *"rulers of Sodom"* and *"people of Gomorrah"* (**Isa. 1:10**).

The rich among the people abused their position and power to buy off justice with money. The priests and the spiritual establishment were corrupt and biased. The poor people, the widows, the orphans, and the foreigners — the weak elements of society — were taken advantage of. The love of God was far from the hearts of the Chosen People (**Isa. 1; Mic. 3**).

Isaiah's message was not unusual. All the prophets, with no exception, warned the people of Israel against abandoning the way of God's Law. Not one of the prophets came to the people with a message such as, "You did it! Great job!"

"The Commandment of Men"

During the centuries in which the citizens of Judah were sinning and defying the will of God, most of them kept up religious appearances. The hearts of the spiritual leaders, the judges, and those in authority were empty of the Spirit of God, but outwardly they gave the impression of being truly devout. They observed strictly all rituals and religious rites — those ordinances of the Law that could be measured outwardly.

God, on His part, continued to remind the Chosen People that He finds pleasure in a heart that submits to Him in love and that He desires a personal relationship with His children. He is not interested in the mechanical observance of the Law, done out of a sense of duty. That kind of observance is empty. It does not express a personal relationship with the Creator, and it does not come from a heart that truly repents over its sins (**Dt. 10:12-22; Hos. 6:6; Mic. 6:6-8**).

In **Isaiah 29:13-14** God tells the prophet:

> *Inasmuch as these people draw near with their mouths and honor Me with their lips, but have removed their hearts far from*

> *Me, and their fear toward Me is taught by the commandment of men, ¹⁴ therefore, behold, I will again do a marvelous work among this people, a marvelous work and a wonder; for the wisdom of their wise men shall perish, and the understanding of their prudent men shall be hidden.*

Even in the days of the prophets, men were seeking for easy ways of serving God:

- Instead of studying and learning the Word of God for themselves;
- instead of sticking as closely as possible to the literal, direct teaching of the Law;
- instead of praying to God for wisdom, understanding, and the strength to obey;
- instead of developing a close, personal relationship with the Creator;

the people chose to learn of God only through their learned men, to learn of God secondhand in a way that was not always faithful to the original.

> *Over time the teaching of the scholars — "the commandment of men" — took the place of God's Word.*

God has indeed commanded His people to heed those who teach His Law, but at the same time He expects them to examine what they are taught, to make sure that it is faithful to God's written Word.

In Deuteronomy 13 and at the end of chapter 18, God warns the people of false prophets. The principle of these chapters is clear: "Check everything you hear or learn against the Word of God." A wonderful example of obedience to this command is in **Acts 17:11**: The Jews in the synagogue of Berea were called "fair-minded" because they tested the words of the apostle Paul by the written Scriptures.

Moreover, **Deuteronomy 6:4-9** places the responsibility of studying and learning the Word of God on the head of every household in Israel.

In short: What is it that God condemns in Isaiah 29:13-14?

- ***Israel honors the teaching of its sages as if they were God, even when they contradict the clear Word of God.***

- ***The reverence in which they hold their sages is considered to be as the reverence of God Himself.***

Repeated Warnings

The righteous and holy God sent many prophets to correct the ways of His people. These prophets brought a message of admonition and correction and a warning of punishment to come if the people continued in the way of sin (**Mt. 21-22**; see particularly Jesus' parables in these two chapters).

The kingdom of Israel (the 10 tribes) continued in their wicked ways. In the year 722 B.C. God brought **Tiglath-Pileser [the 3rd] king of Assyria (2 Ki. 15:29)** against them, who carried them away captive to Assyria.

The sons of Judah and the inhabitants of Jerusalem failed to learn from the fate of the northern kingdom and continued to live in sin. The prophet Jeremiah warned them of the destruction that would come upon them because of their empty religion and lack of faith:

Jeremiah 6:16-21:

> [16] *Thus says the* LORD*: "Stand in the ways and see, and ask for the old paths, where the good way is, and walk in it; then you will find rest for your souls. But they said, 'We will not walk in it.'*
>
> [17] *Also, I set watchmen over you, saying, 'Listen to the sound of the trumpet!' But they said, 'We will not listen.'* [18] *Therefore hear, you nations, and know, O congregation, what is among them.* [19] *Hear, O earth! Behold, I will certainly bring calamity on this people — the fruit of their thoughts, because they have not heeded My words nor My law, but rejected it.* [20] *For what*

> *purpose to Me comes frankincense from Sheba, and sweet cane from a far country? Your burnt offerings are not acceptable, nor your sacrifices sweet to Me."*
>
> *[21] Therefore thus says the Lord: "Behold, I will lay stumbling blocks before this people, and the fathers and the sons together shall fall on them. The neighbor and his friend shall perish."*

The Calamity — The Babylonian Exile

Jeremiah prophesied that the king of Babylon (Nebuchadnezzar) would come against Judah and carry off its inhabitants into exile. This happened in the year 586 B.C. (the third and final conquest). The people of Judah were exiled for 70 years because of their sins (**Jer. 25:1-11; 2 Chr. 36:21**).

The trek into exile and life under the oppressive hand of the Gentiles were extremely hard. During this terrible time hundreds of thousands of Jews lost their lives, and countless families were completely wiped out (**compare Ps. 137**).

Only those who believed the promises of God had comfort under those gruelling conditions: they knew that the exile would not last beyond 70 years (**Jer. 29:10; Dan. 9:2**).

The exile left a deep scar in the hearts of those who did eventually return to the land of Israel.

The Return to Zion

After 70 years of captivity, the Jews began to return to their country. The numbers were not great, and many chose to remain in exile, since conditions there had improved. The description of the return to the land of Israel and the names of the families are recorded mainly in Ezra, Nehemiah, and Zechariah.

The land they returned to was no garden of roses. It goes without saying that the cities and towns needed to be rebuilt and the fields had to be prepared for cultivation. The task of restoration undertaken by a handful of Jews was a heavy enough burden, but that was not all! From without, they suffered under constant pressure from their enemies, who used every possible opportunity to harass and harm those who had returned from exile. From within — as today, so it was then — there was no lack of internal conflict.

This dismal setting provided the background for a spiritual reawakening among the returnees from exile. The Temple was rebuilt and the priests returned to fulfilling their appointed duties. With Ezra and Nehemiah the remnant of Israel had God-fearing leaders. They instituted public readings of the Law, so that all the people would be able to hear and obey the will of God as laid down in His written Word. (See for example **Nehemiah 8:1-11**).

B. When a Jew Says "Torah" — What Does He Mean?

The Oral Law (Rabbinical Judaism)

In the days of Ezra and Nehemiah, the elders (sages) of the people began to interpret, clarify, and simplify the written Law. The original intention was great: to make the clear message of the Torah available to everyone in Israel, so that each individual would understand it, take it to heart and follow its commandments consistently and correctly.

In addition to the written Law given by Moses on Mt. Sinai, there developed a collection of interpretations and commentaries that kept growing in the course of time. New laws, injunctions, and traditions were added and passed on from father to son and from one generation to the next. Some of these were intended to answer in detail questions and needs that the Law did not refer to specifically. Others came from the need to simplify the written Law and to create a kind of "safety fence" around it. This "fence" involved detailed precepts of what was forbidden and what was permitted, and was intended to prevent anyone from even coming close to inadvertently breaking the actual Laws of Torah.

It was only from 250 B.C. and through the first century — the period of the *zugot** — that these oral commentaries and interpretations were actually written down.

The writing continued all through the days of the Tannaim,** and this is how the Mishnah was compiled and codified (up to the year A.D. 220).

As is true regarding any people, the Jewish nation is made up of many strata, ensuring differences of opinion and schisms. A number of factions formed from the days of the Hasmoneans through to the second century B.C., the two main ones being the Pharisees and the Sadducees.

- The **Pharisees** fully adopted the Oral Law and lived their lives according to it. For them, the commentaries of the sages were the ultimate authority in understanding the Law and applying it to their lives. In the opinion of the Pharisees, God gave the sages the wisdom to understand His written Law, and so it was incumbent on the people to obey them as if their commands were the Word of God Himself.

- The **Sadducees** (most of whom belonged to the Temple priesthood and the aristocracy) did not reject the Oral Law (*"the tradition of the elders"* — **Mt. 15:2**) but dissented in several points regarding the resurrection from the dead, the belief in angels, the dates determined for the holy days, and more (**Mt. 22:23-46; Lk. 20:27; Acts 23:7-8**).

---

* *Zugot* refers to the period during the time of the second Temple (515 B.C. — A.D. 70), in which the spiritual leadership of the Jewish people was in the hands of five successive generations of pairs (Hebrew *zugot*) of religious teachers.
From Wikipedia http://en.wikipedia.org/wiki/Zugot

** *Tannaim* is the title of the rabbinic sages whose views are recorded in the Mishnah. The Tannaim, as teachers of the Oral Law, were direct transmitters of an oral tradition passed from teacher to student, that was written and codified as the basis for the Mishnah, Tosefta, and tannaitic teachings of the Talmud. According to tradition, the Tannaim were the last generation in a long sequence of oral teachers that began with Moses.
From Wikipedia http://en.wikipedia.org/wiki/Tannaim

Jesus Christ's Public Ministry

In the days Jesus Christ lived on Earth, the traditions of the sages were deeply rooted in the people. The religious observance of a Jew and his devotion to God were measured by his adherence to the tradition of the elders, that is, to the Oral Law **(Mk. 7:1-23)**.

Note:

During the earthly life of Jesus, He showed all those around Him how God desires every Jew to live by the Law given by Moses at Mt. Sinai. Until His death on the cross, that Law of ordinances and commandments was still valid. Thus even Jesus Himself was obliged to observe every jot and tittle of the Law **(Mt. 5:18)**. Throughout His life Jesus Christ was the perfect example of how to live by the Law. He did not come to destroy or transgress so much as one commandment, but He fulfilled them all. (**Mt. 5:17:** *"Do not think that I came to destroy the Law or the Prophets. I did not come to destroy but to fulfill."*)

The Gospels record many occasions when the Pharisees accused Jesus of breaking the Law and the traditions. However, Jesus never broke a single commandment of God's actual Law. Every time the Pharisees criticized something in Jesus or in His actions, it in fact proved a wrong understanding of the Law on **their** part, putting their own behavior at fault.

The Law of God and the Tradition of the Sages — They Are **Not** the Same

Following are 13 instances where Jesus reproves the Pharisees for straying from the Law of God in favor of tradition, the Oral Law, which relies on man's wisdom. The purpose of these examples is to show to what extent the people of Israel had strayed from the spiritual meaning of the commandments of God's Law as early as in the days of the second Temple. The people had abandoned the literal, straightforward understanding of the written Law and depended exclusively on the teaching and interpretation of the Pharisees and scribes.

Since rabbinical Judaism today continues in the way of the Pharisees, these examples demonstrate how far it has strayed from the Law of God and why believers in Jesus should distance themselves from rabbinical influence, teaching, and authority. Jesus warned for a good reason: "Unless your righteousness exceeds the righteousness of the scribes and Pharisees, you will by no means enter the kingdom of heaven" (Mt. 5:20).

1. **Lk. 14:1-6:**

> ¹*Now it happened, as He [Jesus] went into the house of one of the rulers of the Pharisees to eat bread on the Sabbath, that they watched Him closely.* ²*And behold, there was a certain man before Him who had dropsy.* ³*And Jesus, answering, spoke to the lawyers and Pharisees, saying, "Is it lawful to heal on the Sabbath?"*
>
> ⁴*But they kept silent.*
>
> *And He took him and healed him, and let him go.* ⁵*Then He answered them, saying, "Which of you, having a donkey or an ox that has fallen into a pit, will not immediately pull him out on the Sabbath day?"* ⁶*And they could not answer Him regarding these things.*

All along, Jesus proved His great love for people. This is why the Pharisees present at the meal remain silent, waiting for Him to give them reason to accuse Him — in this instance, by healing a sick man on the Sabbath. Jesus does perform the healing and thus demonstrates what is permitted to do on the Sabbath.

2. **Mk. 3:1-6:**

> ¹*And He entered the synagogue again, and a man was there who had a withered hand.* ²*So they watched Him closely, whether He would heal him on the Sabbath, so that*

> they might accuse Him. ³And He said to the man who had the withered hand, "Step forward." ⁴Then He said to them, "Is it lawful on the Sabbath to do good or to do evil, to save life or to kill?"
>
> But they kept silent.
>
> ⁵And when He had looked around at them with anger, being grieved by the hardness of their hearts, He said to the man, "Stretch out your hand." And he stretched it out, and his hand was restored as whole as the other. ⁶Then the Pharisees went out and immediately plotted with the Herodians against Him, how they might destroy Him.

Once again, Jesus heals on the Sabbath. He does it intentionally on this day, in order to show the Pharisees how far they are from understanding the Law. Instead of submitting to Him after He has proved His authority to them with innumerable signs and miracles, there is only one thing they can think of: *killing Him*.

Since half of the examples brought here have to do with the Sabbath, we must emphasize: Jesus Christ never desecrated the Sabbath! All through His life on Earth He remained perfectly sinless, and He is the only person who ever fulfilled all the requirements of the Law perfectly. — Therefore:

*If there is a "law" that forbids doing what Jesus does or pronounces legal in these examples, then it is **man's** law, not the Law of God.*

3. Lk. 13:10-17:

> ¹⁰Now He was teaching in one of the synagogues on the Sabbath. ¹¹And behold, there was a woman who had a spirit of infirmity eighteen years, and was bent over and could in no way raise herself up. ¹²But when Jesus saw her, He called her to Him and said to her, "Woman, you are loosed

> from your infirmity." **¹³ And He laid His hands on her, and immediately she was made straight, and glorified God.**
>
> **¹⁴ But the ruler of the synagogue answered with indignation, because Jesus had healed on the Sabbath; and he said to the crowd, "There are six days on which men ought to work; therefore come and be healed on them, and not on the Sabbath day."**
>
> **¹⁵ The Lord then answered him and said, "Hypocrite! Does not each one of you on the Sabbath loose his ox or donkey from the stall, and lead it away to water it? ¹⁶ So ought not this woman, being a daughter of Abraham, whom Satan has bound — think of it — for eighteen years, be loosed from this bond on the Sabbath?" ¹⁷ And when He said these things, all His adversaries were put to shame; and all the multitude rejoiced for all the glorious things that were done by Him.**

Here too Jesus was criticized for healing on the Sabbath, this time by the ruler of the synagogue. Jesus called him and his supporters **"hypocrites."** He reminds these religious men of the work they themselves do on the Sabbath by caring for their domestic animals, to prevent financial loss. Jesus demonstrates that those who come to the synagogue, the weak and poor, should receive at the very least the same level of love and care given to one's animals on the Sabbath.

4. John 5:8-10, 17-18:

> **⁸ Jesus said to him, "Rise, take up your bed and walk." ⁹ And immediately the man was made well, took up his bed, and walked.**
>
> **And that day was the Sabbath. ¹⁰ The Jews therefore said to him who was cured, "It is the Sabbath; it is not lawful for you to carry your bed."**

> ¹⁷ But Jesus answered them, "My Father has been working until now, and I have been working."
>
> ¹⁸ Therefore the Jews sought all the more to kill Him, because He not only broke the Sabbath, but also said that God was His Father, making Himself equal with God.

On the Sabbath, Jesus heals a man who has been severely handicapped for four decades. Jesus commands him to walk and carry his stretcher. He thereby once again does what the Pharisees see as a violation of the Law. Because Jesus never disobeyed even **one** of God's commandments, we have here further proof of how far the Pharisees and Sadducees were from the Law of God. We must not accept the interpretation of the Pharisees and those who continue in their ways, rabbinical Judaism, of any law pertaining to the Sabbath, since already 2,000 years ago they failed to comprehend the meaning of the Law of the Sabbath and its purpose. (**See Hebrews 4**).

5. John 9 (read the entire chapter):

This chapter gives an additional example concerning healing on the Sabbath, this time of a man who was blind from birth. As part of the process of healing, Jesus prepared a paste from dust and spittle. This act triggered a sharp reaction from the Pharisees and led to the excommunication of the man healed from blindness, because he sided with Jesus.

6. Luke 6:1-5:

> ¹ Now it happened on the second Sabbath after the first that He went through the grainfields. And His disciples plucked the heads of grain and ate them, rubbing them in their hands. ² And some of the Pharisees said to them, "Why are you doing what is not lawful to do on the Sabbath?"
>
> ³ But Jesus answering them said, "Have you not even read this, what David did when he was hungry, he and those who were with him: ⁴ how he went into the house of God,

> took and ate the showbread, and also gave some to those with him, which is not lawful for any but the priests to eat?" ⁵And He said to them, "The Son of Man is also Lord of the Sabbath."

The disciples picked ears of grain, separated the grains from the chaff and ate. Everything was done in Jesus' presence, and therefore with His consent. Since the Pharisees considered this to be a violation of the law of Sabbath, Jesus brought them an example from the Bible that showed them where they were wrong. Once again Jesus contradicted the Pharisees' understanding of the Law and taught them what **God's intention** had been in giving these commandments.

7. Mark 7:1-8; see also Luke 11:37-54:

> ¹Then the Pharisees and some of the scribes came together to Him, having come from Jerusalem. ²Now when they saw some of His disciples eat bread with defiled, that is, with unwashed hands, they found fault. ³For the Pharisees and all the Jews do not eat unless they wash their hands in a special way, holding the tradition of the elders. ⁴When they come from the marketplace, they do not eat unless they wash. And there are many other things which they have received and hold, like the washing of cups, pitchers, copper vessels, and couches.
>
> ⁵Then the Pharisees and scribes asked Him, "Why do Your disciples not walk according to the tradition of the elders, but eat bread with unwashed hands?"
>
> ⁶He answered and said to them, "Well did Isaiah prophesy of you hypocrites, as it is written: 'This people honors Me with their lips, but their heart is far from Me. ⁷And in vain they worship Me, teaching as doctrines the commandments of men.' ⁸For laying aside the commandment of God, you hold the tradition of men."

In the parallel passage in Lk. **(11:37-54)**, we are told that Jesus **Himself** was chided by the Pharisees for failing to wash His hands in the customary way before the meal. Here, in the Gospel of Mark, the accusation is indirect, holding Him responsible for His disciples' actions. There is, of course, nothing wrong with washing hands before a meal or after doing dirty work, but on the other hand there is no commandment in the Law to do so.

In both passages Jesus speaks very sharply. He condemns the Pharisees for placing more importance on the commandments of men than on the commandments of God: *"For laying aside the commandment of God, you hold the tradition of men."*

Jesus here quotes from **Isaiah 29:13-14** and says: *"Isaiah was prophesying of you!"* He applies these verses to the behavior of the Pharisees and scribes in His days, who in turn are the religious and ideological foundation of today's rabbinical Judaism.

8. Mark 7:9-13:

> *⁹He said to them, "All too well you reject the commandment of God, that you may keep your tradition. ¹⁰For Moses said, 'Honor your father and your mother'; and, 'He who curses father or mother, let him be put to death.' ¹¹But you say, 'If a man says to his father or mother, "Whatever profit you might have received from me is Corban"—' (that is, a gift to God), ¹²then you no longer let him do anything for his father or his mother, ¹³making the word of God of no effect through your tradition which you have handed down. And many such things you do."*

Jesus accuses the Pharisees and scribes of causing people to violate the fifth commandment by one of their traditions. This is the important commandment to honor one's father and mother. Here too, as in the previous example, we see a trend that continues today: the commandments of men (the Oral Law) are given more authority than the commandments of God.

9. Mark 7:14-15, 21-23:

> [14] When He had called all the multitude to Himself, He said to them, "Hear Me, everyone, and understand: [15] There is nothing that enters a man from outside which can defile him; but the things which come out of him, those are the things that defile a man.
>
> [21] For from within, out of the heart of men, proceed evil thoughts, adulteries, fornications, murders, [22] thefts, covetousness, wickedness, deceit, lewdness, an evil eye, blasphemy, pride, foolishness. [23] All these evil things come from within and defile a man."

Jesus turns to the crowd, and in a few summary sentences pronounces the Pharisees and scribes blind.

After all, if our impurity comes from our thoughts, then it is not going to go away by washing our hands, dishes, or even our whole body! (Mk. 7:1-8) — And what is the value of sacrificing to God while blatantly ignoring His words? (Mk. 7:9-13).

10. John 4 (read the whole chapter):

During one of His journeys, Jesus Christ

- intentionally chooses a route through the region of Samaria,
- initiates a conversation with a Samaritan woman,
- asks her to give Him water to drink from her own jar,
- sends His disciples to buy food in a Samaritan village,
- finally takes up lodging with the Samaritans for two days.

Every one of these actions was a violation of the Law in the eyes of the Pharisees, because the Samaritans were considered unclean. By socializing with the Samaritans without any reservations, Jesus demonstrates that even as early as 2,000 years ago the Pharisees were following an entire set of commandments that were foreign to the ways of God's Law. Jesus kept the Law, but not as the Pharisees understood it. I have no doubt that Jesus Christ understood the Law better than the Pharisees and the scribes.

The Word of God encourages us to preach the gospel to everyone, including the Samaritan. That was also the purpose of the people of Israel — Pharisees included — and thus they would have fulfilled their task as a priestly nation and a light to the world. Proclaiming the gospel is an expression of love, because without faith in the gospel of life there is no atonement for sin and no salvation. The Pharisees did not have a gospel of life and salvation. That is why they behaved the way they did.

11. Matthew 19:3-9:

> ³ *The Pharisees also came to Him, testing Him, and saying to Him, "Is it lawful for a man to divorce his wife for just any reason?"*
>
> ⁴ *And He answered and said to them, "Have you not read that He who made them at the beginning 'made them male and female,'* ⁵ *and said, 'For this reason a man shall leave his father and mother and be joined to his wife, and the two shall become one flesh'?* ⁶ *So then, they are no longer two but one flesh. Therefore what God has joined together, let not man separate."*
>
> ⁷ *They said to Him, "Why then did Moses command to give a certificate of divorce, and to put her away?"*
>
> ⁸ *He said to them, "Moses, because of the hardness of your hearts, permitted you to divorce your wives, but from the beginning it was not so.* ⁹ *And I say to you, whoever divorces his wife, except for sexual immorality, and marries*

> another, commits adultery; and whoever marries her who is divorced commits adultery."

The law of the Pharisees and scribes made it easy for anyone who wished to get a divorce. Jesus explains that this policy contradicts the Law of God and opens the way to adultery and fornication in the nation of Israel.

12. Matthew 23 (read the whole chapter):

In this chapter Jesus describes bluntly but clearly how God sees the Pharisees and scribes. The spiritual leadership of the people holds authority but abuses it. Jesus tells His listeners to heed the words of the Pharisees and scribes as long as these are based on the Law of God — but to beware of their personal example. In other words: "Examine well whether their teaching is according to the Word of God, and live by God's Word alone!" This is another one of the various Scriptures warning us not to live under the authority of the Pharisees or their commands.

In verse 33 Jesus asks the Pharisees: *"How can you escape the condemnation of hell?"* — What He means is that every man following their ways and their teaching is actually on the way to eternal hell, even though he is constantly occupied with an impressive display of external religious observance. No one wants to end up in eternal damnation, therefore let us follow the words of the Lord Jesus and distance ourselves from *"the leaven of the Pharisees and the Sadducees"* (Mt. 5:20; 16:6).

13. Matthew 5—7 (the Sermon on the Mount):

Jesus Christ stands before a large crowd and teaches the commandments of God. All His listeners understand that there is an enormous difference between the original intention of the commandments and the guidance and instruction they have received from their spiritual leaders. Jesus needs to affirm over and over again: *"You have heard that it was said ... (but) I say to you,"* and every time He clarifies what God meant when He gave the commandments in the first place.

Intermediate Summary —

The Law of God Versus the Traditions of the Elders

In light of the examples given above we can draw several important conclusions:

1. Rabbinical Judaism — which is the direct continuation of the way of the Pharisees — has strayed from God's Law and submitted to traditions of men that contradict the way of God. Whoever walks in them finds himself fighting against God. He is walking in the same path as the enemies of Christ (Jn. 8:19, 42).

2. The fact that the Pharisees hated Jesus and worked against Him should warn all fearers of God — all those who know Jesus as Lord and Savior — not to submit to the authority of rabbinical Judaism and its laws.

3. Jesus called the teaching of the Pharisees "leaven" — that is, something that negatively affects everything it comes in contact with. This means that believers should be wary of mixing Bible truth with the laws and traditions of the Pharisees (Mt. 23).

4. Jesus fulfilled the commandments of the Law exactly the way God had always intended them to be obeyed. The spiritual leaders in His day proved their spiritual blindness and the chasm between them and the truth of God when

    a. they did not recognize the Messiah, whose coming was foretold by the prophets in the Bible;

    b. they accused Him of breaking commandments, blaspheming God, and being worthy of death.

Had they understood the Law of Moses, they would have recognized Jesus to be their Messiah, their Lord, and their Savior from sin (see Lk. 16:29-31; Jn. 8:19, 42; 14:6-9; Gal. 3:23-25).

In Matthew 15:13 Jesus says: *"Every plant which My heavenly Father has not planted will be uprooted."* **By the word "plant" He means the traditions grown out of man's wisdom. The Pharisees made themselves out to be the defenders of the Law and lovers of Moses, but Jesus said of them:** *"If they had known Moses [the Law] they would have known Me; if they had known My Father they would have known Me also."* **The Pharisees did not know God, so they could not lead anyone to salvation** (Mt. 5:20; 13:14; Lk. 16:31; Jn. 8:19, 39-47).

There is no getting around what Jeremiah already declared two and a half millennia ago: Whoever leaves the source of living water will find himself splashing in the muddy residue of a leaking cistern (Jer. 2:11-13).

"Jewishness" in Light of What We Have Studied so Far

Almost everything considered "Jewish" today, is a fruit of the tradition of the Pharisees and those who continue in their ways. From what Jesus Christ said in the examples given above, we have no reason to believe that God ever affirmed those traditions that add to His Word and in some cases even contradict it. Therefore, whoever adopts these traditions in order to please God — will fail. Jewishness should be expressed by performing the spirit and letter of God's Word, which will lead to faith in Jesus Christ.

 Jesus Christ showed the way — let us follow Him! People — Jews and Gentiles alike — were designed to strive for **Christ-likeness.**

We were all meant to imitate the way of Jesus and to obey His Word in faith and in love. True and complete fulfillment can only be found in Jesus, and once that has happened, there is no need to take on any characteristics based on the wisdom of men and traditions. Any such man-made identity is temporary, earthly, and does not bring glory to God.

We must remember, however, that the freedom of a believer in Jesus includes the right to observe traditions such as keeping kosher, wearing certain clothing, and so on, as long as this is done on the understanding that these things are optional, they are not a condition for salvation. Also, there is no room for demanding that other believers do likewise. (See more on this subject in chapter 5, "Freedom in Christ," page 188 ff.).

On to the Next Tragedy: Ignoring the Prophecies of the Bible

- The religious leadership had the Scriptures and knew to answer correctly when asked: *"Where is the King of the Jews to be born?"* (Mt. 2:4-5). But they did not submit to this King nor serve Him in love.

- Zechariah prophesied that the Messiah would enter Jerusalem riding on the foal of a donkey (Zech. 9:9), a prophecy Jesus fulfilled in detail (Mt. 21).

- The prophet Daniel noted the exact time the Messiah would enter Jerusalem and be *"cut off"* there (Dan. 9:24-27).

All this information was right before their eyes, but the spiritual leaders chose to stick to the traditions of the elders rather than submit to the Messiah promised in the Scriptures.

- Jesus was a practical example of one who kept the Law of God perfectly.

- He intentionally followed the definitions and prophecies in the Bible that were recognized by His people as descriptions of the Messiah.

- When Jesus was born (before the destruction of the second Temple, when genealogical records had not yet been destroyed) it was not difficult to confirm that He was indeed a son of David, and therefore His contemporaries never questioned this claim.

- He proved His divinity by signs and wonders that only God Himself is able to perform.

Despite all this the leaders of the people chose to be the driving force in rejecting Him.

Note:

The people of Israel were not punished for crucifying Christ, because He came in order to die on the cross as an atoning sacrifice for sin. His crucifixion is God's **victory** over sin, over death, and over Satan! — The people of Israel and the rest of mankind are punished for rejecting Him and refusing to submit to Him.

Another Warning: Jesus Prophesies the Destruction of the Second Temple

Luke 19:28-44 describes Jesus' *going up to Jerusalem* for the Passover feast at which He is going to be crucified. He is surrounded by disciples and a crowd of pilgrims cheering Him: *"Blessed is the King who comes in the name of the Lord! Peace in heaven and glory in the highest!"*

As Jesus draws near to the city He weeps over her, saying (**Lk. 19:42-44**):

> *"If you had known, even you, especially in this your day, the things that make for your peace! But now they are hidden from your eyes. 43 For days will come upon you when your enemies will build an embankment around you, surround you and close you in on every side, 44 and level you, and your children within you, to the ground; and they will not leave in you one stone upon another, because you did not know the time of your visitation."*

In the few days that passed between this emotional reception on the way up to Jerusalem for the Feast of Passover, through to the death of Jesus on the cross, the leaders of the people were given another chance to acknowledge Him as the Messiah of Israel. While representatives of the Pharisees asked Him hypocritically, *"Tell us, by what authority are You doing these things? Or who is he who gave You this authority?"* **(Lk. 20:2)**, there were those among them who knew the answer. Nicodemus, who was part of the leadership, had confessed already three years earlier: *"Rabbi, **we know** that You are a teacher come from God; for no one can do these signs that You do unless God is with him"* **(Jn. 3:2)**.

The New Covenant — Alive and Well

After the death and resurrection of Jesus Christ in A.D. 32, the Christian faith began to spread throughout the land of Israel and beyond. At the Feast of Pentecost seven weeks after the resurrection of Jesus, 3,000 people came to faith, most of them Jews. Shortly after that, the believers in Jesus in Jerusalem already numbered 5,000 souls **(Acts 2:41; 4:4)**. The proclamation of the gospel was accompanied by signs and wonders done by God through Christ's apostles.

But even then the spiritual leaders of the people of Israel had not yet understood that the death of Christ was the time appointed by God for the inauguration of the New Covenant that had been promised to His people through the prophet Jeremiah:

Jeremiah 31:31-34:

> [31] *Behold, the days are coming, says the LORD, when I will make a new covenant with the house of Israel and with the house of Judah —* [32] *not according to the covenant that I made with their fathers in the day that I took them by the hand to lead them out of the land of Egypt, My covenant which they broke, though I was a husband to them, says the LORD.* [33] *But this is the covenant that I will make with the house of Israel after those days, says the LORD: I will put My law in their minds, and write it on their*

> *hearts; and I will be their God, and they shall be My people.* ³⁴ *No more shall every man teach his neighbor, and every man his brother, saying, "Know the LORD" for they all shall know Me, from the least of them to the greatest of them, says the LORD. For I will forgive their iniquity, and their sin I will remember no more.*

Also at this stage the Jewish leadership was unable to see the writing on the wall. They preferred to rely on the interpretations of their sages, rather than accept at face value the literal written Word of God. Instead of submitting to the promised Jewish Messiah, they rejected Him in disgust and took upon themselves commandments that proffered no blessings, that had fulfilled their purpose, and were now obsolete.

God Creates a New Reality: The Destruction of the Second Temple

This stubborn preference of the traditions of men over the truth of God led to catastrophe for the people and the land — to the destruction of the second Temple in A.D. 70 and to exile. In contrast to the Babylonian exile, biblical prophecy did not set a limit to how long this exile was to last. It brought on indescribable suffering — for almost 2,000 years.

Another fact should have caught the attention of the spiritual leadership. During the horrors of the destruction of Jerusalem and the Temple, a treasured national possession was forever lost: All of the genealogical records of the tribes of Israel went up in flames. Now — even if Israel were to build a third Temple — it would not be possible to reinstate the priesthood in accordance with God's Law. (For instructions governing the reinstatement of priests and the crucial role of the genealogical records see **Ezra 2:61-62; Nehemiah 7:61-65.**)

> *From that day on until today, no one claiming to be the Messiah is able to prove that he is indeed a son of David.*

The Days of Yavne: Determining Alternatives

The destruction of the second Temple, the devastation of the land and the bloody decimation of the people of Israel presented the leadership with a difficult dilemma:

On the one hand

- God has given Israel His Law, and its commandments cannot be challenged — even in a time of crisis.
- The requirements of the Law make it clear to every Jew (in fact, to every man) that he is a sinner and is unable to meet the standard of holiness God has set.
- The Law determines that there is only one correct response to the disease of sin: honest repentance, the shedding of blood of a sacrificial animal and its offering up on the altar — and as a result of that atonement, forgiveness of sin.
- The Law determines that this process can only be followed at the Tabernacle and later at the Temple, which is on Mount Moriah in Jerusalem.
- The Law is very specific about who can and who cannot serve as a priest in this process.

On the other hand, God has now permitted

- the destruction of the Temple;
- the loss of the conditions necessary for the proper functioning of the priesthood.
- In that way He has cut the people of Israel off from the only means given by the Law to receive atonement and forgiveness for sin.

All this time, as the leadership of the people was grappling with the question "Why has all this happened?" the body of believers in Jesus

Galatians bibliography:

1. Clarke, Adam. *Clarke's Commentary*. New York, NY: Abingdon Press, 1810.
2. Gaebelein, Frank E. *The Expositor's Bible Commentary*. Grand Rapids, MI: Regency-Zondervan, 1976.
3. Ironside, H. A. *Ironside Expository Commentary:* Romans and Galatians. Grand Rapids, MI: Kregel, reprint, 2006.
4. Levy, David M. *Guarding the Gospel of Grace*. Bellmawr, NJ: The Friends of Israel Gospel Ministry, Inc., 1997.
5. MacArthur, John. *The MacArthur New Testament Commentary*. Chicago, IL: Moody, 1987.
6. _____. *The MacArthur Study Bible*. Nashville, TN: Moody Publishers, 2006.
7. Showers, Renald E. *Five Facts You Should Know About Israel*. Bellmawr, NJ: The Friends of Israel Gospel Ministry, Inc.
8. Walvoord, John F. and Roy B Zuck, eds. *The Bible Knowledge Commentary*. Wheaton, IL: Victor Books, 1984.
9. Wiersbe, Warren W. *The Bible Exposition Commentary*. Wheaton, IL: Victor Books, 1994.

God established commandments for a certain era, and at the end of that era, these commandments are no longer obligatory, their authority is over.

And one last question, specifically about our book:

 Why do we need a verse-by-verse study of the epistle to the Galatians, out of all the New Testament books?

 Did you think the questions raised throughout the chapters and in this Q&A section trouble only modern day believers? — No! Already the believers in Galatia struggled with them, less than 20 years after the birth of the church at Pentecost.

This is why Paul needed to give answers, solutions, and clear guidelines to define

- the identity of the Christian believer — whether he be Jewish or not;
- what each Christian believer should do regarding the Mosaic Law and man's traditions.

 *In short — the epistle to the Galatians gives answers to questions we have, as believers in Jesus Christ **today**. It is not an expression of the apostle Paul's personal opinion, which can be interpreted any way we wish. This epistle is the Word of God! That is why it is so important to*

study it!

out the work of the Holy Spirit in the saved person, he would not be able to take in what he reads and live by it in faith (**Jn. 3; 1 Cor. 2:10-16**).

QUESTION Is a believer in Jesus permitted to keep commandments which are no longer required, like the Jewish dietary laws (i.e., commandments which were symbols foreshadowing the Messiah and His work)?

ANSWER Yes! — Everyone has the freedom to keep these commandments, as long as he knows there is no obligation to keep them and that he will not gain atonement for his sins through them. In the same way, the one who chooses to keep such commandments must not criticize others who choose not to.

QUESTION What about those commandments in the Law God commanded to be kept "forever"?

About the Day of Atonement, for example, it is written: *"It shall be a statute **forever** throughout your generations in all your dwellings"* (**Lev. 23:31**). There are similar examples in **Exodus 12:24** (Passover); **Exodus 28:43**, **Deuteronomy 18:5** (the Aaronic priesthood); **Exodus 31:16-17** (the Sabbath). What should we do regarding these commandments?

ANSWER Since we will not slaughter sheep and bulls as sacrifices in God's eternal Kingdom, it cannot be that the Day of Atonement is required to be observed for all eternity. In view of this, the word *forever* refers — at least in the instances mentioned — to a dispensation, a certain period of time, an era — to the time for which that same covenant is valid.

See also **Exodus 21:6**, regarding the slave who desires to stay with his master: *"Then his master shall bring him to the judges. He shall also bring him to the door, or to the doorpost, and his master shall pierce his ear with an awl; and he shall serve him **forever**."* It is clear here that "forever" means to the end of his life, not for eternity.

 When Jesus inaugurated the New Covenant, **all** the commandments of the Mosaic Covenant became obsolete. Jesus Christ fulfilled them when He came to live on Earth, kept them perfectly and fulfilled their purpose (Mt. 5:17-18).

All the commandments of the Mosaic Covenant are part of the package deal. Removing one of them causes the removal of all the rest of the commandments in the same covenant. These commandments no longer have any authority over us or over anyone.

The condition for salvation has always been faith in Jesus Christ — faith in God who came to Earth in the form of man in order to be an atoning sacrifice for man's sin (Isa. 53:6; Rom. 10:9-10).

 *The believer in Jesus keeps all commandments that reflect the eternal characteristics of God.*

That is not because he is subject to the authority of the written letter (Mt. 5—7; Rom. 7:6; 2 Cor. 3), but because he desires to keep all that the author of the written Word intended. He obeys out of love to God and because the Holy Spirit of God dwells within him and guides him to act and to live in a manner worthy of a child of God. (See **John 14—16:** the role of the Holy Spirit in the body of the believer; also p. 139 ff., "The Role of the Holy Spirit.")

He certainly does not observe the commandments in order to receive atonement for his sins, to achieve salvation, or to earn anything from God. Some of the commandments of the Mosaic Covenant are also part of the New Covenant that was sealed by the blood of Christ, and of course they are binding on the disciples of Christ.

 How can the believer in Jesus know what God likes and how He wants him to live?

 This information is learned by reading and studying the Scriptures — the Old and New Testaments. The Holy Spirit helps the believer to understand what is written and how to apply it in his life. With-

The aim of the commandments of the Law was to educate and preserve the people of Israel, so that they would recognize and accept Jesus the Messiah when He came to establish the New Covenant, as God promised by Jeremiah the prophet.

Atonement for sin and the salvation of man are the fruit of our faith in God, who atoned for our sin by sacrificing — in Christ — His own life. Keeping all the other commandments is a side-effect of the love of God in the life of the believer.

The apostle Paul, as well as the author of the epistle to the Hebrews, make it crystal clear that the commandments of the Mosaic Covenant were symbols and patterns that foreshadowed the Messiah and His work (**Isa. 53:5-6; Gal. 3:8-11, 23-25; Col. 2:16-23; Heb. 8:1-6; 9:23-26; 10:1-4**).

 Does the New Covenant established by Jesus Christ through His atoning death replace the covenant God made with Moses at Mount Sinai?

 The Scriptures answer this question very clearly too:

    a. Jeremiah 31:27-34;

    b. Hebrews 7:11-13; 8:7-13;

    c. Galatians 3:23-25;

    d. 2 Corinthians 3:6-17.

In His atoning death, Jesus Christ established the New Covenant. At the same time He brought an end to the Mosaic Covenant, which was intended to prepare the people of Israel for the New Covenant with their Savior.

 Have the commands: "Do not kill," "Do not commit adultery," "Do not steal," and all the other commandments of the Mosaic Covenant lost their validity since the New Covenant has come into effect? Do these commandments not have any more authority over us? Are we no longer required to keep them?

C. Frequently Asked Questions

 Were the commandments of the Mosaic Covenant intended to save man and atone for his sins?

 The Scriptures answer this question very clearly. The commandments of the Mosaic Covenant were not intended to save or to deliver sinful man from the curse of sin. Salvation of man has always been through faith in God as Lord and personal Savior. Even before the giving of the Law we are told of believers such as Noah and Abraham, whom God counted as righteous.

Also after the giving of the Law, man was saved by faith in God. This is the meaning of the verse *"the just shall live by his faith"* **(Hab. 2:4)**. The believer in God was required to keep the commandments because thus it was written in the Law. If he was a genuine believer, he had an additional motivation for keeping the commandments: his love for God. However, observance was never a means of earning salvation. Salvation was always received as a gift of grace from God, on the basis of faith in Him as the atoner of our sins.

 If so, what was the purpose of the ordinances in the Mosaic Covenant?

 The ordinances of the Law were intended to teach the people of Israel (and through them the rest of the world)

- about God;
- about sin;
- about purity and holiness;
- about the identity and work of the Savior;
- about the desperate need of every man for atonement for his sin, which is given by the sacrifice of the Savior.

> one mourns for his only son, and grieve for Him as one grieves for a firstborn.

The remnant of Israel will yet cheer and exalt Jesus in the streets of Jerusalem out of believing hearts that overflow with thankfulness: *"Blessed is He who comes in the name of the LORD!"* (Ps. 118:26; Mt. 21:9). This hope will definitely be fulfilled — all Israel will be saved:

Zechariah 13:9: *"I will bring the one-third through the fire, will refine them as silver is refined, and test them as gold is tested. They will call on My name, and I will answer them. I will say, 'This is My people'; and each one will say, 'The LORD is my God.'"*

Romans 11:26-27: *"And so all Israel will be saved, as it is written: 'The Deliverer will come out of Zion, and He will turn away ungodliness from Jacob; For this is My covenant with them, when I take away their sins.'"*

The Body of Christ — The Church

Over the past 2,000 years nothing has changed regarding rabbinical Judaism's attitude towards Jesus and His disciples.

The spiritual struggle of believers in Jesus has not changed either. The struggle of the apostle Paul and the Galatian churches, as described in the epistle we have studied, is the same believers in Jesus face today.

Also the believers themselves have not changed. Now, as then, they

- study and teach the Scriptures (the Old and New Testaments);
- pray for the salvation of Israel and of all mankind;
- proclaim the gospel of salvation to all who will hear;
- serve their people and their country faithfully in order to be a worthy testimony of Jesus Christ.

From the moment the people of Israel strayed from the Word of God and took upon themselves the traditions of the sages, the Oral Law, they adopted a religious, ceremonial, and national character that God never required. Since then, every Jewish person's obedience to God is measured by his degree of faithfulness to the Oral Law.

Rabbinical Judaism — The Judaism of Today

So then, today's Judaism is not the same one the prophets of the Bible knew and lived by. It is therefore rightly called "rabbinical Judaism." Since almost all Jews adopt its ways — or at least consider them authoritative — it follows that the terms *Judaism* and *Jew* refer to followers of this stream of Judaism, unless specified otherwise.

Jews who believe in Jesus as their Lord and Savior are considered by our people's religious leadership as belonging to another religion. Despite the fact that they are part of the people of Israel, fear God, are faithful to His law, pray for the salvation of Israel, and serve their people faithfully, they are called disgraceful names by the rabbinical leadership — *minim* ("heretics"), *meshumadim* ("apostates"), and so on. Furthermore, the *Amidah*, which is said every weekday in the synagogues, includes a prayer that God would destroy apostates, including Jewish believers in Jesus.

The Judaism of the Future

Rabbinical Judaism, which denies the Messiahship of Jesus, is destined to change. The day will come when God will open the eyes of the remnant of Israel. They will realize their millennia-old mistake and confess their sins:

Zechariah 12:10:

> And I will pour on the house of David and on the inhabitants of Jerusalem the Spirit of grace and supplication; then they will look on Me whom they pierced. Yes, they will mourn for Him as

> *righteousness, has not attained to the law of righteousness.* ³²*Why? Because they did not seek it by faith, but as it were, by the works of the law. For they stumbled at that stumbling stone.* ³³*As it is written:*
>
>> *"Behold, I lay in Zion a stumbling stone and rock of offense,*
>> *And whoever believes on Him will not be put to shame."*
>
> ¹*Brethren, my heart's desire and prayer to God for Israel is that they may be saved.* ²*For I bear them witness that they have a zeal for God, but not according to knowledge.* ³*For they being ignorant of God's righteousness, and seeking to establish their own righteousness, have not submitted to the righteousness of God.* ⁴*For Christ is the end of the law for righteousness to everyone who believes.*

Since

- the Messiah is the end of the Law (**Rom. 10:4**);
- and only faith in Him as our Savior and atonement for sin can give us eternal life (**Acts 4:12; Rom. 10:9-10**);

then any "law" that teaches anyone to reject Jesus

- is contrary to the will of God;
- is "a different gospel," that is, a gospel that has no power to save (see commentary to Gal. 1:6-7, pp. 35-42);
- cannot be authoritative for a believer in Jesus Christ.

Although rabbinical Judaism boasts impressive religious ceremony as well as wonderful exegesis and commentary on the Old Testament Scriptures, it has no salvation. Since it denies the Messiahship of Jesus and His Divinity, it cannot save its followers from everlasting contempt (Dan. 12:2).

A Fatal Claim:
"Our Words Are the Law of God"

According to the tradition of the Jewish sages, the Oral Law was given in its entirety to Moses at Mt. Sinai. They claim that God gives wisdom to the elders of the people in each generation, who add commentary, interpretations, and new regulations to the Law — all of which were actually received at Mt. Sinai, but only now are revealed to us.

Maimonides (Rabbi Moses Ben-Maimon, 1138-1204) composed Judaism's Thirteen Principles of Faith. The eighth principle states that "The Torah is from heaven [God]. We believe that all of this Torah that was given by Moses, that it is all from the mouth of God.... And similarly the explanation of the Torah (the Oral Law) was also received from God."*

So then, the Oral Law is accorded the authority of the Torah of Mt. Sinai — **the Word of God**.

"Their Own Righteousness" (Rom. 10:3)

If the Oral Law had only dealt with minor issues, so be it. But that is not the case. The Oral Law instructs the people of Israel in every area of life. It even presents a way to obtain righteousness and atonement that is different from that which God has prescribed in the Bible. The Oral Law rejects Jesus as the Messiah of Israel and ostracizes any Jew who believes in Him.

The apostle Paul mentions this in the letter he wrote to the believers in Rome (**Rom. 9:30—10:4**):

> ³⁰ What shall we say then? That Gentiles, who did not pursue righteousness, have attained to righteousness, even the righteousness of faith; ³¹ but Israel, pursuing the law of

---

* From http://www.mesora.org/13principles.html, translated by Marc Mermelstein.

1. ***Zera'im*** ("Seeds" — subjects related to agriculture)
2. ***Mo'ed*** ("Appointed time" — all about the Sabbath, holidays, and fasts)
3. ***Nashim*** ("Women" / "Wives" — laws related to women and family life)
4. ***Nezikin*** ("Damages" — regulations regarding property, compensation, civil and criminal law)
5. ***Kodashim*** ("Holy things" deals largely with the various sacrifices and the religious service within the Temple)
6. ***Toharot*** ("Purities" — deals with the distinction of clean/unclean, with ritual purity and family purity)

The six orders — called **Mishnah** — were not the final word on the interpretations and rulings that were added to the Law. Over the next 300 years the sages and their disciples, both in the exile and in the land of Israel (the *Amoraim*) continued to analyze and interpret what was written in the *Mishnah* and add further rulings.

Around the sixth century the collection of post-Mishnaic writings was edited. These writings are called — **Gemarah**.

The *Gemarah* written by the sages of the people was added to the original *Mishnah*, and this compilation became known as the **Talmud**.

There is the Babylonian Talmud, where the Mishnah is accompanied by the Gemarah written by the sages of the exile, and the Palestinian Talmud (or Jerusalem Talmud), which comes with the Gemarah written in the land of Israel. Until today, the Babylonian Talmud is the main volume of study in the Yeshivah (rabbinical seminary) and the Beit Midrash (house of Torah study).

The sages who wrote *halacha* (Jewish law) are called by various titles: *Savora'im* (A.D. 500-590), *Ge'onim* (A.D. 590-1050), *Rishonim* (1050-1492, the expulsion from Spain) and *Acharonim* (from 1492 on).

- Rabbinical Judaism interprets *"righteousness"* (Heb. *tsdaka*) as doing good deeds to others, **giving** — in order that our good deeds be counted in our favor on God's Day of Judgment. In today's language our people mean only one thing when they say *tsdaka*: money. **"Redeem your sins with righteousness (tsdaka)"** is interpreted to mean: "Donate an amount of money — and you will be forgiven."

Did God ever confirm these solutions?

No! — The efforts of the sages to establish alternatives and to adapt the Law to the new painful reality of the day distanced them ever farther from the true Messiah of Israel. Thus the way was paved for the next tragedy:

The Bar-Kochba Revolt

In A.D. 132-136 another rebellion against the Romans broke out. During this uprising Rabbi Akiva proclaimed Shimon Bar-Kochba, leader of the rebels, to be the Messiah. After the rebellion was quelled, the land devastated and hundreds of thousands of Jews killed, Rabbi Akiva realized that Bar-Kochba was not the Messiah.

Did the spiritual leadership now understand that it had made a mistake and that Jesus, who was born in Bethlehem Ephrathah and raised in Nazareth, really was the true Messiah? — No! And not only that — it continued to glorify the name of Rabbi Akiva even though he had proclaimed a false messiah. His influence on the Mishnah and rabbinical Judaism is still evident today.

The Time of the Mishnah and the Talmud

In A.D. 220, fearing that the Oral Law would be forgotten and in order to ensure consistent teaching of the people, Rabbi Yehuda HaNasi (Judah the Prince) took on himself to edit the laws and compile them in six orders that cover all areas of life:

graciously, that we may present the fruit of our lips.'" The verse is interpreted as permission to bring words to God instead of sacrifices, since the term here translated *"fruit of our lips"* can also be rendered *"oxen (sacrifices) of our lips."* (See NKJV.)

- The Temple in Jerusalem has been replaced by the "little sanctuary" — the synagogue (based on **Ezek. 11:16**, even though that verse is not about buildings, but is a promise that God Himself will be a sanctuary for His people in exile).

- The priesthood has been replaced by the rabbinate.

The rabbinical response to the problem of sin is found in the *"Mussaf"* prayer for the first day of the Jewish New Year, *Rosh Hashanah*: "Repentance, prayer, and righteousness remove the evil decree." The following Scripture portions are cited in support:

- **Repentance:** *"For I have no pleasure in the death of one who dies," says the Lord GOD. "Therefore turn and live"* (**Ezek. 18:32**).

- **Prayer:** *"For we will offer the sacrifice of our lips"* (**Hos. 14:2** — see explanation above).

- **Righteousness:** *"Therefore, O King, let my advice be acceptable to you; break off your sins by being righteous, and your iniquities by showing mercy to the poor"* (**Dan. 4:27**).

These words sound very pious, but we must remember that prayer and repentance without a personal knowledge of the One who atones for our sin — Jesus Christ — counts for nothing in God's eyes (**Jn. 8:19, 42; 14:6-7; Acts 4:12**).

Moreover, there is a marked difference between the interpretation of the word *righteousness* in rabbinical Judaism and its meaning in the Word of God:

- The Scriptures teach us that righteousness is doing the will of God, which springs from a saving faith, that is, from a personal knowledge of the true Savior Jesus Christ.

Christ was growing and developing among them. The latter's doctrine did in fact offer a solution to the dilemma facing the rabbis:

- There is no further need of sacrifices, because: *"Christ also suffered once for sins, the just for the unjust, that He might bring us to God"* **(1 Pet. 3:18)**.

- There is no longer a need for a temple: *"Do you not know that **you** are the temple of God and that the Spirit of God dwells in you?"* **(1 Cor. 3:16)**.

- There is no longer a need for the Aaronic priesthood, because: *"Christ came as High Priest of the good things to come, with the greater and more perfect tabernacle not made with hands, that is, not of this creation. Not with the blood of goats and calves, but with His own blood He entered the Most Holy Place once for all, having obtained eternal redemption"* **(Heb. 9:11-12)**.

- There is no longer any need for the symbolic commandments of the Mosaic Covenant that pointed us to Christ. He fulfilled them: *"In that He [God] says 'A new covenant'* **[Jer. 31:31]**, *He has made the first obsolete. Now what is becoming obsolete and growing old is ready to vanish away"* **(Heb. 8:13)**.

The explanations of the believers for the tragedy of the Jewish people were rejected out of hand. Even though the history of Israel had proved that destruction of the land and exile are a result of leaving the way of God's truth and righteousness, the religious leadership chose to cling yet tighter to the traditions of the sages — the Oral Law. Before long they had established alternatives to what had been lost:

- Prayers replaced sacrifices as a means to obtain atonement and forgiveness for sin. Two Scriptures are cited as a basis for this regulation: **Psalm 119:108**, which reads, *"Accept, I pray, the freewill offerings of my mouth, O Lord"* (offerings = sacrifices; my mouth = prayers); and **Hos. 14:2** (NASB): *"Take words with you and return to the Lord. Say to Him, 'Take away all iniquity and receive us*